Additional praise for *Religious Conversion: Religion Scholars Thinking Together*

In this path-breaking and immensely valuable work, divergent voices decipher the issue of conversions – an issue which has long remained a persistent and provocative presence at the tables of inter-religious dialogue. The strength and success of this project lies in the inter-religious nature of its authorship. Distinctive voices, each deeply rooted within their own religious tradition, draw the threads of their experience and expertise to weave together a rich tapestry of thought which can foster dialogue on a potentially divisive theme. Premawardhana should be commended for envisioning this creative work of critical importance and courageously bringing it to fruition!

Peniel Jesudason Rufus Rajkumar
World Council of Churches, Geneva

Religious Conversion

Religion Scholars Thinking Together

Edited by

Shanta Premawardhana

WILEY Blackwell

Library of Congress Cataloging-in-Publication data applied for

Hardback ISBN: 9781118972380
Paperback ISBN: 9781118972373

A catalogue record for this book is available from the British Library.

Set in 10.5/12.5pt Palatino by SPi Global, Pondicherry, India
Printed and bound in Malaysia by Vivar Printing Sdn Bhd

1   2015

Contents

Contents

Notes on Contributors

S. Wesley Ariarajah is Professor of Ecumenical Theology at Drew University School of Theology. Before Joining Drew he served at the World Council of Churches in Geneva for 16 years as the Director of its Interfaith Dialogue Program and as its Deputy General Secretary. He has given lectures and seminars on Ecumenism and Interfaith Dialogue in many parts of the world. His publications include *The Bible and People of Other Faiths* (1985, translated into German, Spanish, Swedish, Dutch, Arabic, Swahili, Malayalam, Sinhalese, Indonesian, Korean, and Japanese), *Hindus and Christians: A Century of Protestant Ecumenical Thought* (1991), *Not Without My Neighbour: Issues in Inter-religious Relations* (1999), *Axis of Peace: Christian Faith in Times of Violence and War* (2005), and *We Live by His Gifts – D.T. Niles: Preacher, Teacher and Ecumenist* (2009).

Mahinda Deegalle, a Buddhist monk from Sri Lanka, is a Senior Lecturer in the School of Humanities and Cultural Industries at Bath Spa University, United Kingdom. He serves on the Steering Committee of the Buddhism Section of the American Academy of Religion and on the managing committee of Spalding Symposium on Indian Religions. He is the editor of the journal *Buddhist–Christian Studies*. His publications include *Popularizing Buddhism* (2006), *Dharma to the UK* (2008), *Buddhism, Conflict and Violence in Modern Sri Lanka* (2006), and *Pāli Buddhism* (1996).

Amy Eilberg is the first woman ordained as a Conservative rabbi by the Jewish Theological Seminary of America. After many years of work in pastoral care, hospice, and spiritual direction, Rabbi Eilberg now directs interfaith dialogue programs in Minneapolis/St. Paul, Minnesota, including at the Jay Phillips Center for Interfaith Learning and the St. Paul Interfaith Network. She teaches the art of compassionate listening in venues throughout the United States, and is deeply engaged in peace and reconciliation efforts in connection with the Israeli–Palestinian conflict, as well as with issues of conflict within the Jewish community. She lectures and writes on issues of Jewish healing, spiritual direction, interfaith dialogue, and peace making.

Rita M. Gross is a Buddhist scholar-practitioner who has made significant contributions to scholarship on Buddhism and gender and to interfaith interchanges as a Buddhist. She is professor emerita of Comparative Studies in Religion at the University of Wisconsin–Eau Claire and a past president of the Society for Buddhist–Christian Studies. Her best known book is *Buddhism After Patriarchy: A Feminist History, Analysis, and Reconstruction of Buddhism* (1992), and she has many other significant publications. She also functions as a Buddhist dharma teacher at Lotus Garden, the North American center of the Mindrolling lineage of Tibetan Buddhism and in that capacity she teaches Buddhist meditation throughout North America.

Rabia Terri Harris, an essayist, activist, and theologian, is founder and director of the Muslim Peace Fellowship. Established in 1994, MPF is the only organization specifically dedicated to the theory and practice of Islamic non-violence. Harris, an Elder of the Community of Living Traditions at Stony Point, NY (an Abrahamic residential peace community), has spent two decades engaged in interreligious peace and justice work. She is a practicing community chaplain and concurrently teaches in the Intellectual Heritage program at Temple University in Philadelphia, PA. Harris holds a BA in Religion from Princeton University, an MA in Middle Eastern Languages and Cultures from Columbia University, and a Graduate Certificate in Islamic Chaplaincy from Hartford Seminary. She is a senior member of the Jerrahi Order of America, the Western branch of a 300-year-old Sufi order headquartered in Istanbul.

A. Rashied Omar is a Research Scholar of Islamic Studies and Peacebuilding at the Joan B. Kroc Institute for International Peace Studies, University of Notre Dame, USA. He completed an MA and a PhD in Religious Studies from the University of Cape Town.

He also holds a Master's degree in International Peace Studies from the Kroc Institute, University of Notre Dame. Omar's research and teaching are focused in the area of Religion, Violence, and Peacebuilding with a twin focus on the Islamic Ethics of War and Peace and Interreligious Dialogue. In addition to being a university-based researcher and teacher, Omar puts theory to practice. He serves as the coordinating Imam at the Claremont Main Road Mosque in South Africa, international trustee of the Council for a Parliament of the World's Religions in Chicago, and international advisor to the Dutch-based Knowledge Forum on Religion and Development.

Shanta Premawardhana is the president of the Seminary Consortium for Urban Pastoral Education in Chicago. Previously he was the director of the program Interreligious Dialogue and Cooperation at the World Council of Churches. Prior to that, he was the Associate General Secretary for Interfaith Relations at the National Council of Churches, USA. A native of Sri Lanka, he is a Baptist minister with long pastoral, interreligious dialogue and community organizing experience. He received his PhD from Northwestern University in Evanston in the History and Literature of Religions with specialization in Buddhism and Hinduism. He is the author of numerous articles and lectures widely on subjects pertaining to interreligious dialogue.

Anantanand Rambachan is Chair and Professor of Religion, Philosophy, and Asian Studies at Saint Olaf College, Minnesota, USA, where he has been teaching since 1985. Professor Rambachan is the author of several books, book chapters, and articles in scholarly journals. Among his books are *Accomplishing the Accomplished* (1991), *The Limits of Scripture* (1994), *The Advaita Worldview: God, World and Humanity* (2012), *The Hindu Vision and Gitamrtam: The Essential Teachings of the Bhagavadgita* (1992). His writings include a series of commentaries on the Ramayana. The British Broadcasting Corporation transmitted a series of 25 lectures by Professor Rambachan around the world.

Ravin Ramdass is an admitted advocate of the High Court of the Republic of South Africa. He is also a specialist family physician and a qualified teacher. He obtained a Master's degree from the University of KwaZulu-Natal for his dissertation entitled

"Hinduism and Abortion, a Traditional View." He was a student activist in the anti-apartheid struggle and has been involved in interfaith dialogue for the past 30 years. He is Chairperson of the Greytown Hindu Forum.

Jay T. Rock has served, since 2003, as the Coordinator for Interfaith Relations for the Presbyterian Church (USA). From 1987 to 2003 he directed the Interfaith Relations Office of the National Council of the Churches of Christ in the USA. He holds a PhD in History and Phenomenology of Religions from the Graduate Theological Union, and is an ordained minister in the Presbyterian Church (USA). His experience of interreligious relations, and perspective on the issues, rooted in North America, has been enlarged by short-term visits, engagements, and dialogues in the Southern Caribbean, Israel/Palestine, Africa, and Europe, and by many conversations sponsored by the World Council of Churches, especially the Thinking Together project.

M. Thomas Thangaraj retired as the D.W. & Ruth Brooks Associate Professor of World Christianity at the Candler School of Theology, Emory University, Atlanta, GA, USA in 2008. He has published widely both in English and in Tamil, and his most recent publications are *The Crucified Guru: An Experiment in Cross-Cultural Christology* (1994), *Relating to People of Other Religions: What Every Christian Needs to Know* (1997), and *The Common Task: A Theology of Christian Mission* (1999). Currently, Professor Thangaraj is teaching at Oklahoma City University's Wimberly School of Religion during spring semesters, and is associated with the work of the Bishop Stephen Neill Research and Study Centre, Tirunelveli, India.

Hans Ucko is an ordained minister of the Church of Sweden and has throughout his ministry been involved in Jewish–Christian and interreligious dialogue with research at the Institut Eglise et Monde Juif in Paris, the Swedish Theological Institute and at the David Hartman Institute, both in Jerusalem. He received his doctorate in theology at the Senate of Serampore College, Calcutta, India, where he wrote his thesis on the concepts of "people" and "people of God" as integral to the Jewish tradition and to Asian contextual theologies. He was, from 1981 to 1989, the Executive Secretary of the Church of Sweden for Jewish–Christian Relations, interreligious dialogue, and East Asian Relations, and from 1989 to 2008 was

Program Executive for the Office of Interreligious Relations and Dialogue of the World Council of Churches in Geneva, Switzerland. He is now the President of Religions for Peace Europe and an interfaith advisor to the Arigatou Foundation.

Deborah Weissman, a resident of Jerusalem since 1972, is an Orthodox Jewish educator with extensive professional experience in Israel and in 17 other countries. Her PhD in Jewish Education was earned at the Hebrew University in Jerusalem for work on the social history of Jewish women's education. She is Co-Chair of the Inter-Religious Coordinating Council in Israel and is heavily involved in interfaith dialogue and teaching on both the local and international levels. She is a practicing Orthodox Jew, active in the religious feminist movement and the religious peace movement. Weissman has lectured and written widely, both in Hebrew and in English.

Introduction

Shanta Premawardhana

When I was growing up in Sri Lanka, there was a saying, "When you convert to Christianity you get a British accent." Today they say, "When you convert you develop a taste for Coca Cola!" These comments succinctly describe the subtext in the new controversies raging in many countries on the question of conversion today: identity and power.

The anxiety that Sri Lankan Buddhists feel about the question of conversion cannot be divorced from the political domination they experienced for five centuries under the colonial powers. The oppressions that Buddhist monks, temples, and communities had to undergo as well as the aggressive evangelistic methods used to convert people during that period are well documented.[1] Colonial governments that originally disdained the missionary movement later supported the missionaries, when they discovered that conversion to Christianity also shifted the political allegiances of many in favor of the colonial government, or that it at least subdued the potential for political agitation.

While it is indeed true that some converted to Christianity seeking privileges such as education and employment, others clearly converted out of spiritual conviction. While some also attempted to be more like the colonial masters and did acquire British accents, others sought to maintain loyalty to their ethnic and national identities

Religious Conversion: Religion Scholars Thinking Together, First Edition.
Edited by Shanta Premawardhana.
© 2015 World Council of Churches Publications. Published 2015 by John Wiley & Sons, Ltd.

despite the change in their religious identity. Their compatriots, however, generally considered the converts as traitors; not because of the change of religion, but because conversion implied that now they were politically allied with the colonial masters. The struggle for independence therefore included not only a desire for political and social self-determination, but also for a particular kind of religious freedom: the freedom from conversion.

In the post-independence era, the iconic American evangelist Billy Graham, who traveled the world preaching to packed stadiums with his strong theological emphasis on each person making a "decision" to receive Jesus Christ as his or her "own personal savior," had a significant impact on some parts of the Christian world. This particular American brand, different from the more church-oriented message of the previous generation of missionaries, appealed to large numbers of people, many of whom, following their conversion, were effectively trained to be evangelists themselves, giving new life to the worldwide Evangelical movement. The gathering of its leaders from across the world, in Lausanne, Switzerland in 1974 for the International Congress on World Evangelization was a critical organizing moment for this movement. A key sentence from the Lausanne Covenant describes one of the movement's primary motivations: "World evangelization requires the whole Church to take the whole gospel to the whole world."[2]

Expressed in such grand terms, this goal is not without its antecedents. It stands in the tradition of the so-called Great Commission (Matthew 28:18–20) which calls Christians to "make disciples of all nations." In one of the most significant ecumenical councils of the twentieth century the International Missionary Council, which met in Edinburgh in 1910, called Christians to engage in evangelizing the world in this generation.[3] While such key phrases in these texts as "take the whole gospel," "make disciples," or "evangelize the world" can make for interesting missiological debate, these statements are perceived by many Christians as calls to make the whole world Christian. Whether it is theologically legitimate or desirable to attempt to do so is a question that requires serious consideration but is not within the scope of this book. The more serious problem with such a goal, though, is that other religious communities can and sometimes do perceive it as an existential threat.[4]

Energized by the Lausanne Covenant of 1974 and subsequent congresses that further refined and amplified the theme, largely US,

European, and South Korean Evangelical Christians began to arrive in various Asian, African, and Latin American countries for the express purpose of evangelization. The liberalization of travel and trade provided the necessary access for these evangelists. I have met, and know that many – perhaps most – such evangelists engage in this activity with sincere intentions and use ethical practices in their evangelism. However, there are others who use aggressive evangelistic methods and unethical practices that create serious problems not only for the religious communities in the host country, but also for the churches that have been there for centuries. For example, the use of aid as an instrument of evangelization by numerous Western Evangelical groups following the disastrous South Asian tsunami of 2004 was an egregious example of unethical evangelism. In several affected countries, this resulted in significantly heightened tensions between religious communities and violence against many churches and their clergy regardless of denominational affiliation.

This new missionary movement, coinciding as it did with spreading economic globalization, was seen by the religious communities at the receiving end as ominous. If the missionary movement of the previous era effectively softened the ground for political oppression, the argument goes, the present movement would soften the ground for economic globalization – which is worse, because it is more subtle. Therefore it must be vigorously opposed.

A few years ago in Sri Lanka, a parliamentary bill banning conversions, in which both the converter and the converted get a fine of Rs. 500,000 (approx. US $5000) and a five year jail sentence almost became law. Similar laws have already been enacted in several states of India, as in Pakistan. The public discussion in many of these countries includes the sentiment that conversion to Christianity means that converts would cast their sympathies politically with the West and therefore with its hegemonic tendencies.

The World Council of Churches (WCC), which arose from the ecumenical strand within the colonial missionary movement, began struggling with these questions a century ago. When its precursor, the International Missionary Conference, met in Edinburgh in 1910, it was at least partly to consider a new realization that had arisen among the missionaries that among people of other religions there are those who have a genuine and devout spirituality. Even though the Edinburgh conference ended with a call to evangelize the world, in the ensuing conferences, the question persisted. The

3

Asian theologians who participated in the conference at Tambaram, South India in 1938, for example, forcefully argued that interreligious dialogue should be the way Christians relate to other religious persons, rather than seeking their conversion. The Asian theologians did not win the day, but over the following decades significant progress was made leading to the establishment of a Sub-unit on Dialogue with People of Living Faiths and Ideologies in 1971. Yet, questions of mission, evangelism, and conversion and their relation to interreligious dialogue have continued to be in the forefront of the ecumenical movement's agenda. While most have accepted the value of dialogue as the preferred method of relating to people of other faiths, other churches remain unconvinced.

In 2005, the WCC convened 130 leaders of many religions to a conference entitled "Critical Moment in Interreligious Dialogue." One of the urgent questions for the ecumenical movement, as well as for those who engage in interreligious dialogue, was brought to the floor by the Ven. Bhiksuni Chueh Men of Taiwan. When she and others spoke forcefully about how in many Asian countries Evangelical Christians were using unethical methods to seek conversions, it was necessary to take note. In response the WCC initiated two actions. The first resulted in an historic agreement between the three largest global Christian bodies: the Vatican, the World Evangelial Alliance and the World Council of Churches. The result, "Christian Witness in a Multi-Religious World: Recommendations for Conduct" was released in June 2011. The second is the present project on Thinking Together on conversion.[5]

Thinking Together, an experiment in cutting-edge research in interreligious dialogue, brought together religious scholars from five major religious traditions as a think-tank to work on subjects of common concern. The articles they wrote from the point of view of their own religious tradition were subject to critique by their colleagues from other religions. In their review, these colleagues sought as much as possible to view the document from the writer's own religious perspective while remaining faithful to their own religious commitments. The final product, therefore, while being authentic to each religious tradition, has emerged from the sharpening and refining that result from this endeavor.

The story of the Thinking Together group and the uniqueness of the methodologies that were used in engaging this question are outlined in the essay by Thomas Thangaraj entitled "Thinking Together: a Story

4

and a Method." This is immediately followed by a second essay, also by him, in which, engaging the thinking of several religious traditions, Thangaraj points the reader to the complexities of defining religious conversion. Rita Gross's essay, "Models of Religious Belonging," invites us to explore the variety of ways in which religions understand themselves, and draws our attention to how these differences impact the different ways in which religions view the question of conversion. Hans Ucko, who coordinated the Thinking Together group for most of its 10-year history, points in his essay "Conversion Sought and Feared" to several interesting questions. Himself a convert, Ucko points to the ways in which a convert's view of conversion is different from the ways in which those who attempt to convert view the same.

In the second section of the book, a member from each religion – Mahinda Deegalle on Buddhism, Jay Rock on Christianity, Anantanand Rambachan on Hinduism, A. Rashied Omar and Rabia Terri Harris on Islam, and Amy Eilberg on Judaism – offers a perspective of how that particular religion views conversion. Their essays come to us following a rigorous process of peer review by colleagues from other religions and include ways in which this unique reflection has helped each of them to broaden his or her own understanding of conversion.

The question of conversion is never far removed from the questions around religious freedom, about which the book includes two essays. The first, by Wesley Ariarajah, gives a more general introduction to the question, and is followed by Ravin Ramdass's essay, which gives more detailed legal analysis of the issues including, specifically, how these are spelled out in the South African context. In the final chapter the group reflects together on what it has learned through this entire process and offers several encouragements to religious communities. This is followed by a study guide to help religious communities to engage in their own reflections.

I want to express my deep gratitude to all the members of the Thinking Together group for their sustained commitment to the process of Thinking Together, for their willingness to subject their own deep faith commitments to the rigorous scrutiny of members of other religious communities, and for the high level of trust with which each treated the other. I am particularly grateful to my teacher and colleague Thomas Thangaraj, whose help in the initial editing of the material was of immense value; to Hans Ucko, my predecessor at the WCC who coordinated the work of this group for many years; and to Yvette Milosevic, who assisted in the organizing of the

5

meetings and in the final processes of getting the book ready for print. Finally, I am grateful to the World Council of Churches for being willing to take the bold step of experimenting with an interreligious group, for providing it with the funding it needed, and for allowing the group the freedom to work at its own pace.

At one point in the group process, I expressed to the group my gratitude for addressing what has mostly been a problem created by Christians. This sentiment was quickly disowned by the group. It's a problem for all of us, they said. All our traditions in one way or another have to deal with the question of how people move in and out of our religious communities. Despite those sentiments, I still believe that this is a question that has particular salience for Christians. Our churches are still struggling with the difficult questions that arise in the intersection of mission, evangelism, and interreligious dialogue. Even though the Ecumenical movement has a century of thinking behind these questions, they don't easily translate in the day-to-day functioning of our churches. It is my fervent hope that this volume and the process it represents will provide a valuable opportunity for churches, and indeed mosques, synagogues, temples, and other religious institutions, to engage with these questions.

Notes

1 For a recent analysis of this question, see Elizabeth J. Harris, *Theravada Buddhism and the British Encounter: Religious, Missionary and Colonial Experience in Nineteenth Century Sri Lanka* (London and New York: Routledge, 2006).

2 Lausanne Covenant: http://www.lausanne.org/covenant.

3 *World Missionary Conference 1910: The History and Records of the Conference Together with Addresses Delivered at the Evening Meetings* (Edinburgh: Oliphant, Anderson & Ferrier; New York: F.H. Revell).

4 The 2009 *Report of the Commission to Examine Unethical Conversions of Sri Lankan Buddhists of the All Ceylon Buddhist Congress* (Colombo: All Ceylon Buddhist Congress, 2009), (in Sinhala) identifies Christian literature that points to such an interpretation. That such a perception is an existential threat to Buddhism in Sri Lanka is clear from the report; see especially pp. 11–32.

5 Christian Witness in a Multi-Religious World: Recommendations for Conduct: https://www.oikoumene.org/en/resources/documents/wcc-programmes/interreligious-dialogue-and-cooperation/christian-identity-in-pluralistic-societies/christian-witness-in-a-multi-religious-world

Part I

Preliminary Considerations

1

Thinking Together
A Story and a Method

M. Thomas Thangaraj

What is the next stage in our journey of interreligious dialogue and cooperation? In other words, while we have been engaged in constructing and articulating a theology *of* and *for* interreligious dialogue, what would our own theologies look like if our experiences of dialogue were brought right into the very process of theologizing?[1] This is what many who were participating in the programs of the Office of Interreligious Relations at the World Council of Churches (WCC) or in events and ventures in their own local settings were asking. In the early years of WCC's involvement in interreligious dialogue, the focus was on discovering a biblical or theological warrant for such interreligious engagement. This was rightly called a theology *for* dialogue. The next stage was viewing dialogue as a theological issue in order to reflect on it and to articulate a theology *of* dialogue. So the question now was to reconstruct one's own theology in light of and in the process of engaging in active interreligious dialogue. Could this be the next stage in our journey of interfaith relations?

Interestingly, this initiative by the WCC coincided with the challenges faced by theologians and thinkers in various religious traditions in different parts of the world who themselves were actively involved in interreligious conversations. They were asking themselves more and more the following question: Why is it that my own

Religious Conversion: Religion Scholars Thinking Together, First Edition.
Edited by Shanta Premawardhana.
© 2015 World Council of Churches Publications. Published 2015 by John Wiley & Sons, Ltd.

theological thinking is always done in my solitude, in the privacy of my study, or in consultation with theologians of my own religious community, and without the physical presence of all my interreligious conversation partners, while my life is lived out in lively interfaith relations and dialogical engagements? The Christian theologians in the academy began to address this question with utmost seriousness. The emergence of a discipline, called Comparative Theology, is a result of this ferment. Francis Clooney is one of the pioneers in the development of this discipline.[2] Several others have also worked along these lines in constructing their theologies in conversation with other religious traditions. As John Thattamanil, a comparative theologian, writes:

> Comparative theology is conversational theology. Such theology goes beyond taking an inventory of other people's convictions for the sake of specifically Western intellectual projects like comparative religion or ethnography. Comparative theology takes the content of other people's ideas seriously, seriously enough to be changed by those ideas. Comparative theology, as a work of Christian faith, strives mightily to avoid bearing false witness against our neighbors. We do this by entering into dialogue with them in a common inquiry about ultimate matters.[3]

Comparative theology is by no means peculiar to Christian theological enterprise alone. For example, some members of the Thinking Together group have been involved in such comparative thinking for some time. Rita Gross has been involved in comparative "theological" thinking for years, Rambachan's writings clearly exhibit a comparative character, and so do Rashied Omar's.

Thinking Together: Our Story

Once this ferment was discovered, it became clear to Dr. Hans Ucko, the Director of the Office of Interreligious Relations, that such a move involved constructing one's own religious or theological thinking in the presence or in the company of thinkers and theologians belonging to religious traditions other than one's own. With this in mind, a group was invited to *think together*, and, as the group began to meet yearly, it took "Thinking Together" as its name. The mandate for this group of 12–15 theologians/thinkers from five different religious traditions, such as Buddhism, Christianity, Hinduism, Islam, and Judaism, was to engage in thinking and articulating their own religious tradition in the presence of others. The group met for the first time in Bossey, Switzerland to address the question: What difference does religious plurality make for my thinking and my theology?

Over the years the composition of the group changed because some of the invitees left the group due to personal and professional reasons. While some found this method of *thinking together* unsuitable for their own theological/religious thinking, others were unable to devote the amount of time and the kind of energy this process demanded. New members were invited to take their places. The group was saddened to lose Professor Tikva Frymer-Kensky, who taught Hebrew Bible and the History of Judaism at University of Chicago Divinity School. She passed away in 2006 after a four-year battle against breast cancer. She made a lasting impression on the members of the group through her insightful contribution toward our thinking together.

The current group, which has been responsible for this volume on religious conversion, consists of Vinu, a medical doctor who works among the poor in South India; Mahinda, a Buddhist monk from Sri Lanka, and Parichart, a Buddhist lay woman from Thailand, both of whom are professors in universities in England and Thailand respectively; Rita, a Buddhist teacher and professor from Wisconsin, USA; Debbie, an Orthodox Jewish educator in Israel; Amy, a rabbi from Minnesota, USA; Anant, a Hindu from Trinidad who teaches religion in St. Olaf's College in Minnesota, USA; Thomas, a Christian theologian from India who taught World Christianity in Atlanta, USA; Rashied, an imam and professor from South Africa; Rabia, a Muslim educator from the USA; Jay, a Presbyterian church leader in the USA; Hans, the former Director of the Office of Interreligious Relations, WCC, Geneva; Ravin, a Hindu who is a specialist in medicine and an advocate in South Africa; Wesley, a veteran in interfaith dialogue who had served as the Director of the Office of Interreligious Relations of the WCC for many years and currently teaches theology at Drew University School of Theology in the USA; and Shanta, a Christian theologian from Sri Lanka and the USA, who succeeded Hans Ucko as the Director of the program.

The tragedy of September 11, 2001 brought a sense of urgency and seriousness to the group as it met in St. Petersburg, Florida in

11

January 2002. Engaging the theme of religion and violence, the group moved to think together on how each religious tradition viewed the "other" or the "outsider," during the years 2003 and 2004.[4] The discussion on "the other," was crystallized in a book, entitled *Faces of the Other: A Contribution by the Group – Thinking Together*.[5] Two conferences that took place in Geneva in 2005 – Critical Moment in Interfaith Dialogue and Interfaith Youth Event – brought to the forefront the issue of religious conversion as the next agenda for Thinking Together. That interest coincided with what was happening in India and Sri Lanka with regard to the legitimacy and the legality of religious activities that aim at converting the other.[6] The group met in 2006 at Shanti Ashram in Coimbatore, India to begin its thinking on religious conversion, and it continued its wrestling with the issue through 2007 and 2008. What is found in this book is the result of three years of thinking together as Buddhists, Christians, Hindus, Jews, and Muslims on religious conversion.

There has been a great sense of excitement about this process of thinking together among the members of the group. We always looked forward to every meeting with great expectation and enthusiasm. There were several factors that helped the success of this group to think together, as I discuss below.

Freedom from constraints

The group is indebted to WCC whose generous funding made this process possible. Without this, theologians and thinkers from different parts of the world representing five different religions could not have met year after year like this. Therefore, the group experienced great freedom from financial restraints. Further, under the leadership of Hans Ucko, the WCC gave us utmost freedom to shape the direction and dynamics of this process. We were never compelled or constrained to come up with a particular product or result. WCC took the risk of letting the process discover and gain its own direction. The participants experienced a safe space and a holding environment within which one could think *boldly* together. This was possible because we met for several years and came to know each other as fellow travelers on the path of religious life. Another source of freedom was that none of us in the group were chosen as "official representatives" of our religious traditions. Our accountability was to one another, even though we were quite conscious of our commitment and responsibility to our own religious communities. Therefore, religions were not in conversation; but practitioners and thinkers of various traditions were. It was not a dialogue among systems and institutions, but rather an encounter of minds, a dialogue of hearts, and a conversation of souls with an experience of true religious freedom.

Celebration of diversity

Even though most of the participants held jobs in the United States of America during this period, the group did represent significant geographical diversity – hailing from India, Sri Lanka, Trinidad, South Africa, Thailand, Israel, Sweden, and the USA. The group was intentionally inclusive with regard to gender, unlike many interreligious dialogue activities that tend to be dominated by men. Our meetings were held in English even though for most of us English is our second language and not our mother tongue. This meant that we spoke English each in our own peculiar ways. Vocationally, we had differences too, even though most of us were educators of one kind or another. Some were ordained leaders in their religious traditions such as Amy, a rabbi, Rashied, an imam, Wesley, a Christian minister, and Rita, a recognized Buddhist mentor. The coming together of lay and ordained made our diversity richer and more valuable it than otherwise would have been. Diversity was not simply something we brought to the group but something we discovered in the very process of thinking together. The national and political backgrounds from which we came were diverse as well: India, the largest democracy, America the most powerful nation, South Africa, a community in transformation with a history of religious and political persecution, Israel with all its political and religious challenges, Sri Lanka with its ethnic conflicts, and so on. As a policy we made sure that there were at least two persons from each religious tradition so that we could appreciate the intra-religious diversity. The recognition of similarities in our commitments and intentions often led to the epiphany of our differences. We stood amazed at how much *together* we could be in the midst of this rich variety of religions commitments!

13

Exploring common concerns

One of the strengths of our thinking together was that the agenda was not set by someone outside the group; the agenda grew out of our recognizing common concerns that affect each and every one of us in the group and our religious communities. Of course, the first two sessions did have themes that were suggested by Hans Ucko. It was not just a particular religion's problem that we were going to think about; rather we were focusing on matters that affected all of us, though in various forms and at various times. Violence attributed to religion was indeed one such issue that gripped us all following the horrific event of September 11, 2001. In addressing this issue, we discovered another common concern. We together recognized that our perception of the other often led to violence and so we focused on how each of our religious traditions viewed the outsider. The interreligious conflicts in India, Sri Lanka, and elsewhere triggered by the issue religious conversion became our common concern after 2007. Since the concerns were commonly and corporately discovered, our thinking truly became thinking *together*.

Risks of self-disclosure and self-criticism

Our ability to engage in self-critical thinking did not come easily to us. It was our regular, repeated, and sustained meetings year after year that helped the development of a true and genuine friendship among us. We became a community of friends. This was strengthened by what we did apart from meeting around tables for discussion. We ate together, took walks together, climbed a small hill together, prayed together, shared family news with each other, and literally lived together whenever we met. It was this experience of intimate friendship that enabled us to take the risk of self-disclosure – sharing the joys and sorrows, ecstasies and agonies, successes and failures, and the beauty and the ugliness of each of our religious traditions. We were willing, as well, to expose our ignorance of the other's religious tradition. When we took a walk over a hill which had lovely trees with beautiful flowers, I just recited a text from the New Testament: "Consider the lilies of the field, how they grow; they neither toil nor spin; yet I tell you, even Solomon in all his glory was not clothed like one of these."[7] Amy, a rabbi among us, said: "Thomas! That is beautiful. Did you make that up right now?"

"Well," I told her, "these are the words of Rabbi Jesus!!" Amy was so pleasantly surprised that she shared the story with her Jewish congregation in Minnesota when she returned home!

One major element in the area of self-criticism is that all of us in the group have been impacted and shaped by what one would call historical consciousness. When one is historically conscious, one knows that all our religious traditions have been shaped in and by the processes of history. No religion has come out of the blue like a thunderbolt; each has been nurtured in the sociopolitical and economic realities of its history. Once we recognize the historicist character of our religious traditions, it becomes easier to acknowledge the dark aspects or the underside of our religious traditions. Such historical consciousness has instilled in all of us a critical approach to our own traditions and a genuine hesitancy to uncritically privilege our tradition over others. Further, it does not allow us to rush into absolutist claims about our own religion and its history. We feel compelled to ask, when we read and interpret our sacred texts, questions such as: What did this text mean at the time it was written? What could it mean today? Are there things in our sacred texts that need to be questioned and rejected? Such historical and critical questions were accepted by the group as important questions to ask while interpreting our religious traditions.

Experience of self-discovery and growth

Thinking together truly enabled us to discover ourselves anew and grow in our own religious belonging. Debbie, during our meetings in India, and through her conversations with Anant and others, was able to discover her Jewish faith to be not so distant nor disconnected from the Hindu tradition; rather there were significant points of contact and continuity between these two traditions. Our self-discovery included acknowledging the darker side of each of our religions and their histories. Mahinda, the Buddhist monk, discovering stories within the Buddhist religious tradition that might promote violence, was one such experience. Christians in the group were ready to acknowledge with sadness the violence against and the destruction of peoples in the name of Christian missionary expansion. We all experienced growth in and enhancement of our own individual religious faith. We felt strengthened in our commitment to our own religious traditions. We became better religious persons in the process and thus better human beings.

Journeying in religious freedom

The journey we took was indeed a journey in religious freedom. If religious freedom included the freedom to embrace a religion, to remain in that religion, and to share that faith with others, we accomplished all those three in our thinking together. We did not have to be apologetic about being Buddhists, Hindus, Christians, Jews, or Muslims in this group. We were each grounded in and committed to our faith. The intimate friendship we had with one another prevented us from seeing the other as one who is attempting to displace me and remove me from my tradition. One had the freedom to stay in one's religion with a sense of pride and ownership. Yet we never took that freedom to be indifferent to the other; but rather shared one's faith with the other in utter humility and candor.

Moreover, some in the group were themselves converts. Rita converted to Buddhism from a particular form of Christianity, Hans to the Christian faith from Judaism, and Jay saw himself as a convert from the North American secular tradition to the Christian faith. Wesley and Thomas had a memory of their ancestors converting to Christianity from Hinduism. Therefore, the issue of religious conversion was not something we could analyze with cold objectivity; it was close to home for some of us. It meant that we had to learn to offer religious freedom to one another in discussing the issue of religious conversion.

From conversation to trust

From 1970 onward, the WCC and other international religious bodies have been involved in creating and sustaining communities of interreligious conversation. Especially after 2001, there has been a significant increase in interfaith organizations that promote conversation and collaboration. Very often those who participate in programs of interreligious dialogue feel frustrated that conversations do not always lead to mutual trust and friendship. The beauty of the Thinking Together process was that even though we began as a community of conversation, we became a community of trust. The sense of humor with which we approached our religious traditions and shared our insights went a long way to build trust among us. Rabbi Irving Greenburg once said, "I do not care which religion you belong to as long as you are ashamed of it." We were willing to be "ashamed" of our traditions in the presence of each other. We were able to "laugh" at each other's traditions as well, without feeling hurt or diminished.

The way John Thattamanil describes Comparative theology was true of us too. He writes:

> In the course of such conversation, our initial and somewhat minimal motivation to avoid misrepresenting our religious neighbors is caught up in a deeper movement of the Spirit. In the space between my neighbor and me, something like affection, respect, admiration begins to grow. We will find it difficult to bypass the central experiences, practices, and insights that animate and sustain persons of other faiths. Should we embrace the calling to love our neighbors, we will find ourselves vulnerable to what is healing and life-giving in their traditions ... It is risky work, a labor of mind and heart that will require us to rethink our own convictions.[8]

These words aptly capture what our story was all about and what it continues to be.

Thinking Together: A Method

Thinking Together is not only a story about thinkers from five different religious traditions who met, conversed, and constructed their own religious thinking in the presence of others; the process revealed or helped emerge a particular way of engaging in theology or religious thinking. In other words, out of this history, a *method* of thinking has evolved. How would one describe that method? Let me approach this question with the idea of foci in theological or religious thinking. Being a Christian theologian, I will be mainly using illustrative material from Christian theology. There is a theological method or religious thought that operates in a unifocal manner. The word *unifocal* means "arising from or occurring in a single focus or location," according to Merriam-Webster's Dictionary on the Internet.[9] Such theologies operate with a singular concern of teaching their constituencies the correct beliefs of their particular religion. In Christian theological circles, this would be seen as thinking through the various doctrines and articulating them in ways that are intelligible and understandable to the faithful. There is no apologetic motive or desire behind this unifocal activity. Most often, commentaries on religious texts in various religions operate in this didactic mode.

In modern and postmodern times, there has been a dissatisfaction with such a unifocal approach to theology or religious thinking and a desire to relate one's religious thought or theology to contemporary demands and challenges and thus reconstruct one's theological tradition. One may call this the bifocal method. This is true of all religious traditions today, even though the degree and extent of such involvement may vary from religion to religion. For example, Mahatma Gandhi's commentary on the Bhagavadgita was an attempt to make sense of that religious text in the context of the struggle for political independence in India. Paul Tillich, one of the leading American Christian theologians in the twentieth century, spoke of this approach as the method of "correlation." He wrote: "In using the method of correlation, systematic theology proceeds in the following way: it makes an analysis of the human situation out of which the existential questions arise, and it demonstrates that the symbols used in the Christian message are the answers to these questions."[10] Such thinking takes the context seriously and attempts to address the issues and problems of the contemporary situation; but it often limits itself to one's own religious tradition only. It sees other religions and other religionists as part of the contemporary situation and deals with them in appropriate ways – appropriate to its own theological viewpoint.

Thinking Together is not satisfied with such a bifocal approach to religious thinking or theology. Tillich himself was dissatisfied with his method as he began to engage in dialogue with Buddhist philosophers and thinkers. In discussing Christian–Jewish relations, he noted that "a community of conversation which has changed both sides of the dialogue" had come into being[11] and that one should hope that such a community would also happen in relation to the Muslim community. He wrote, "Not conversion, but dialogue. It would be a tremendous step forward if Christianity were to accept this."[12] Thinking Together is neither unifocal nor bifocal; rather, it is multifocal. It means that when we think about any aspect of our religious tradition, we ask the question regarding not only the context and its demands but also the challenges and learnings from traditions other than our own religion. As Anantanand Rambachan noted in one of our sessions, thinking together had transformed his writings to those that listen to and register other voices and responses, not being limited to the Hindu tradition alone.

The method is simply this: Every time one theologizes or engages in religious thinking, one makes it a methodological requirement to ask what my brothers and sisters in other religious traditions have to offer that may challenge, enlighten, or even transform my perspective. Since one is surrounded by several religious traditions in one's setting, our thinking has to be multifocal. Others do not become objects of our theological reflection; rather they become partners in our thinking and companions on our journey. One thing is clear: if one wants to adopt this method in constructing one's theology, one needs to be participating in a process such as Thinking Together. Without the development of friendship with one another, without a trust in one another's commitment to common good, and without experiencing sheer delight in the presence of the other, one cannot engage in the kind of multifocal method we are referring to here. We were fortunate to be part of this story and engage in this method.

This multifocal method of doing theology or religious thinking is gaining ground within academia in many parts of the world. Conversation, dialogue, learning, and thinking together are being recognized as the most helpful way of engaging in theological thinking. As Gordon Kaufman, a leading American theologian, writes:

> In conversation every voice knows that it is not complete in itself, that its contribution is in response to, and therefore depends upon, the voice(s) that came before, and that other voices coming after will develop further ... Free flowing conversation presupposes a consciousness of being but one participant in a larger developing yet open-ended pattern of many voices, each having its own integrity, none being reducible to any of the others; and it presuppose a willingness to be but one voice in this developing texture of words and ideas, with no desire to control the entire movement ... When theological or religious truth is conceived in these pluralistic and dialogical terms, no single voice can lay on it, for each understands that only in the ongoing conversation as a whole is truth brought into being.[13]

Ours was such an experience of conversation that offered us glimpses into truth as it was brought into being right in front of our eyes.

Notes

1   I am aware that the word *theology* is not common to all the religious traditions, and especially it does not make any sense in the Buddhist context. Yet, in our group our Buddhist and Hindu friends were willing to work with this term, and we as a group meant by it "intense and intentional reflection on and articulation of one's own religious tradition."

2   See Francis X. *Clooney's books on comparative theology: Theology after Vedanta: An Experiment in Comparative Theology* (Albany: State University of New York Press, 1993), *Divine Mother, Blessed Mother: Hindu Goddesess and the Virgin Mary* (New York: Oxford University Press, 2004), and *Hindu God, Christian God: How Reason Helps Break Down the Boundaries between Religions* (New York: Oxford University Press, 2001). Clooney offers a good survey of comparative theological writings in "Comparative Theology: A Review of Recent Books (1989–1995)," *Theological Studies* 56.3 (1995), 521–550.

3   John J. Thattamanil, *The Immanent Divine: God, Creation, and the Human Predicament* (Minneapolis: Fortress Press, 2006), p. xii.

4   For a longer narrative on the history of the group, including the meeting in Florida in 2002, see M. Thomas Thangaraj, "Thinking Together: A Narrative," *Current Dialogue*: http://wcc-coe.org/wcc/what/interreligious/cd39-09.html.

5   Hans Ucko (ed.), *Faces of the Other: A Contribution by the Group – Thinking Together* (Geneva: WCC, 2005).

6   Several states within India passed legislation banning religious conversion by coercion, specifically aiming at the Christian evangelistic programs in India, especially those that are run by para-church and fundamentalist Christian groups.

7   Matthew 6:28, 29 (New Revised Standard Version).

8   Thattamanil, *Immanent Divine*, pp. xiif.

9   http://www.merriam-webster.com/medical/unifocal.

10 Paul Tillich, *Systematic Theology*, Vol. 1 (Chicago: University of Chicago Press, 1951), p. 62.

11 Paul Tillich, *Christianity and the Encounter of the World Religions* (New York: Columbia University Press, 1963), p. 95.

12 Ibid.

13 Gordon D. Kaufman, *In Face of Mystery: A Constructive Theology* (Cambridge, MA: Harvard University Press, 1993), pp. 66–67.

2

Defining Religious Conversion

M. Thomas Thangaraj

The word "conversion" is not a religious term as such, though it is widely used in religious discourse. A quick look at the various meanings of "conversion" in any standard dictionary will show us that this term is used in a variety of fields such as finance, religion, language, industry, and currency. Even Microsoft Word "converts" documents from one format to another. Webster's Third New International Dictionary gives, among many, the following meanings for conversion: "change from one belief, view, course, party, or principle to another," "the act of interchanging the forms of a proposition," "the exchange of outstanding currency," and "the act of converting an insurance policy."[1] The verb "convert" has even more diverse meanings. What is common in all these multiple meanings is the idea of change. Therefore, in a basic sense, religious conversion is about change that is brought about in one's religiosity or religious belonging. Of course, change as such is only a formal category and the material content of it may vary. The material content of the term "change" will require asking questions, such as change from what and change to what. Moreover, the kind of religious belonging one is moving from or moving into brings its own variety. Different religions do see the phenomenon of religious belonging in diverse ways. It is sufficient at this point to say that religious conversion has a plurality of meanings.

Religious Conversion: Religion Scholars Thinking Together, First Edition.
Edited by Shanta Premawardhana.
© 2015 World Council of Churches Publications. Published 2015 by John Wiley & Sons, Ltd.

William James, a keen observer and scholar of religious experience, defines conversion as "the process, gradual or sudden, by which a self, hitherto divided, consciously wrong, inferior and unhappy, becomes unified and consciously right, superior and happy in consequence of its firmer hold upon religious realities."[2] James uses phrases such as, "to be regenerated, to receive grace, to experience religion, to gain assurance,"[3] as being synonymous with the word "conversion" as well. If we look more closely at this definition of conversion, we can detect several interesting features. This definition is highly influenced by a Christian understanding of the phenomenon of conversion. For example, phrases such as "regeneration" and "gaining assurance" are clearly Christian categories for this religious experience, whereas a Buddhist might talk of this as "enlightenment," a Jew as "turning to God," and a Hindu as "realization." No Hindu or Buddhist will name that experience as conversion.

While acknowledging its Christian bias, James's definition accommodates within itself a variety of descriptions of this phenomenon. Yet, if we attempt to define conversion in a setting of religious plurality, we need to take note of a wider variety of descriptions and work through them to arrive at a more robust definition of religious conversion. Moreover, James's definition views conversion as something that happens in an individual, whereas the history of religion shows that religious conversion can be a group activity, a social transformation, and/or a political shift. For example, in 1804, the people in my hometown in South India converted to Christianity as a village and changed the name of the village to Nazareth. Such conversions are generally referred to as mass conversions. In the middle of the twentieth century, a large group of Dalits (those who belong to the lowest rung in the caste ladder in India) turned away from the Hindu religion and converted to Buddhism under the leadership of Dr. Ambedkhar as a mark of religious and sociopolitical protest. One can cite several more historical events in which groups and communities shifted their allegiance from one religion to another.

Furthermore, James portrays the life of the self prior to conversion in the most negative fashion using phrases such as "divided," "wrong," "inferior," and "unhappy." This likewise needs to be deconstructed, because a careful study of the phenomenon of conversion in a multi-religious setting will show that not all converts see their condition prior to conversion in such negative terms. Conversion can engender different attitudes to the religious situation prior to conversion. For example, there have been Christian theologians and leaders in India who did not view their prior Hindu faith as "wrong" or "inferior" after they converted to Christianity. For example, Brahmabandhab Upadhyaya, an Indian theologian of the twentieth century, saw himself as both Hindu and Christian at the same time, even after his becoming a Christian through baptism.[4] The next chapter deals in detail with this interesting question of multiple religious belonging. It should also be noted that any view of conversion is to a large extent dependent on the type of belonging a particular religion operates with. I offer in the following pages a descriptive definition of religious conversion, and indicate which definition is most dominant in the discussion of religious conversion in today's context.

Religious conversion may be understood at least in four different ways. Each has its own peculiar character, purpose, process, and consequences. Let us look at each of them in turn.

Religious Conversion as Rediscovery

There are persons who are not committed to any particular religious tradition as such and others who are members of a particular religious community only in a nominal way. When any of them turn to religion and commit themselves to any one of the religions of the world, some would name that change as conversion. For example, if a person brought up in a totally secular family and setting at some point in life embraces a religion such as Christianity or Islam, she or he is supposed to have gone through a religious conversion. This could happen either through familiarizing oneself with the teachings of a particular religion or through the impact a religious person has on one. On the other hand, there are persons who belong to religious communities only in a nominal or superficial way who, in situations of crisis such as illness, bereavement, or personal tragedy may turn to religion and experience conversion or change in their religious belonging.

The kind of conversion we are referring to here can express itself two different ways. When conversion happens, one may take up clear and identifiable membership in a religious community or tradition. Here someone may, for example, claim that he or she had no faith earlier but now has a particular faith – Christian, Hindu, Buddhist, Jewish, or Islamic. Another expression of conversion as rediscovery happens when people who did not earlier appreciate any form of religiosity now find themselves interested in and committed to what is often called "spirituality." Such people most often wish to claim that they are not religious but spiritual. They have awakened to such a new sense of spiritual awareness that their experience can be named as conversion. This kind of conversion does not require – and at times deliberately avoids membership in – the institutional/associational aspect of a religious tradition. Such conversions may aptly be called rediscovery.

As one can see, conversion as rediscovery is a highly individual matter. Individuals lay claim on religious beliefs and practices and they may or may not choose to belong to any organized religious community. Generally, neighbors and friends are pleased with such a conversion and celebrate the newly found religion or spirituality of the convert. When so-called non-believers convert to religion or spirituality, one does not see any negative ripples in the community around. Similarly when a nominal Christian or a cultural Jew or Hindu takes his or her religion seriously and recommits himself or herself to it, it does not any way upset the balance and equilibrium of the surrounding community. Moreover, there is no need to portray the pre-conversion status as wrong or inferior so as to defend one's new identity; nor does such negative description of the past affect interreligious relationships.

Religious Conversion as Preference

This is a type of conversion in which someone converts from one sub-tradition to another within the same religious tradition. This is purely an intra-religious activity. For example, in the Hindu tradition one may choose a God of one's own liking (*ishtadeva*), moving away from earlier held attachment. For example, a Saivite (one who names Ultimate Reality as Shiva) may choose to become a Vaishnavite (one who names Ultimate Reality as Vishnu) by shifting his or her attachment from the iconic form of Shiva to that of Vishnu. In such a setting one may even choose Jesus as one's *ishtadeva* while remaining a Hindu for all practical purposes. Since many Hindus believe in multiple incarnations of God in the history of the world, adoring Jesus as one of the incarnations does not remove oneself from the Hindu religious tradition. This kind of conversion is a shift that happens in an *individual* and within a single religious community, and therefore it does not have any serious implications for or impact on interreligious relations as such.

Moreover, this form of conversion does not generally make any judgments regarding the rightness or wrongness of the various traditions, but only expresses one's preference. James's definition of conversion as a move from "wrong" to "right" is not applicable here. Therefore, it is quite appropriate to name this conversion as preference. Such conversion is not found in the Hindu tradition alone; it is prevalent in other traditions too. For example, a Roman Catholic Christian may choose to become a Baptist or a Methodist or a Presbyterian, and such change is conversion too, expressed primarily as a personal preference. A conservative Jew may choose to join the Reform tradition and the Jewish tradition may not name that shift as "conversion." Such intra-conversions can happen in any religious tradition and those do happen quite often in highly individualized societies. Even though these "conversions" take place *within* a religious tradition, they are not always readily accepted, or widely recommended. Some Protestant groups view conversion to Roman Catholicism as a fall into idolatry and papal domination and therefore vehemently oppose such conversions. Similarly an Orthodox Jew may not appreciate a move to the Reform tradition since such a change results in a dramatic shift in the lifestyle of the "convert."

At times, the cultural unity between two religious groups is such that moving from one to another does not question or threaten the other. Such conversions may not have the kind of dramatic change that James talks about. The Eastern Orthodox Christians in India, for example, were accommodated within the Hindu cultural ethos in such a way that their conversion can perhaps be termed as a change in preference.[5]

Religious Conversion as Extension

Swami Yogeshananda is a monk of the Ramakrishna Mission and a teacher of Vedanta, who "converted" from Christianity to the Vedanta tradition of Hinduism. Since he is a white American born to

25

parents who were Christian missionaries to China, one is quick to see his becoming a Hindu monk as conversion. But when asked, "Did you convert to Hinduism?" Swami Yogeshananda would say, "No, I have not converted; I have only extended myself!" What has happened here is that he was attracted to a tradition other than his own and added that new tradition to his already held beliefs. In other words, one "extends" one's religious belonging to include other religious practices and beliefs. For example, a Christian may choose to regularly attend Buddhist meditations or Sufi rituals as a way of extending and enriching their spirituality. A Hindu may attend Christian worship without becoming a member of any particular church. Mahatma Gandhi, who was opposed to the idea of religious conversion, did practice conversion as extension. He was very open to incorporating the beliefs and practices of other religious traditions while remaining a committed Hindu. His attachment to and reverence for the Sermon of the Mount of Jesus illustrates such extension clearly. All these may sound easy and simple, but they are not. Such extensions are complicated and complex, as we will see.

We live at a time when this sort of conversion is increasingly popular, especially in Western countries, where newly found religious diversity leads to such extensions. This is certainly possible when the tradition that is added does not require an exclusive membership. For example, a Christian who practices Zen meditative practices does not renounce membership in the Christian community; nor does he or she understand the new religiosity as double membership. Here again this process of extension is individual oriented and it does not lead to any major shifts in the way one's society is organized. One does not renounce or reject the religious tradition one belongs to but only adds on to it another tradition and its practices. Of course, in doing so one is transformed by such an extension. In that sense there is conversion.

Swami Yogeshananda's claim that he had not "converted" but only "extended" is more complex than what appears on the surface. By joining the Ramakrishna Order, he relinquished his membership in the Christian church. He did not simply add a few Hindu/ Vedanta practices to his earlier held Christian beliefs and practices; he joined a different religious order. Therefore, in some cases, the phenomenon of extension is more than a simple addition, but rather a shifting of one's membership from one to another religious community. Interestingly, many of those who attend Swami's weekly worship and meditation sessions are Christians who have extended themselves to include Vedanta without relinquishing their membership in local Christian congregations. As far as they are concerned, this conversion is simply an extension. However, in the case of certain religions and their view of religious belonging, such extension is simply not possible. For example, one cannot be a Jew and a Christian at the same time. For a Jew to say that she has extended herself to include Christianity in her religiosity is a contradiction in terms as far as Jewish faith is concerned. To include Christian faith is to deny Jewish faith, because to claim Jesus of Nazareth as Messiah is to give up one's membership in the Jewish community. This is intensified by the fact that both these religions understand religious belonging in particular ways that does not allow such extension to happen. On the other hand, a Jew may extend himself to selectively include Hindu or Buddhist meditative practice; that does not result in a shift in membership due to the open-ended nature of the organizational and institutional structure, or the lack thereof, among Buddhists and Hindus.

Before we move to examine the fourth option for defining and describing religious conversion, we need to register one important observation. The first three descriptions are not always named as conversions. If the child of a Jewish mother, previously non-religious, becomes engaged in Jewish religious life, that is not considered "conversion." The tradition calls such a person a "ba'al teshuva" – literally, a "master of return," meaning "one who returns – in the transcendent sense – to God, to self, to the right path." An uncommitted Hindu becoming a devoted and practicing Hindu is not described as converting, even though such a change in a Christian would be called conversion by many in the Christian community. An Orthodox Jew becoming a Reform Jew would not be named as conversion; neither would a Protestant Christian's embrace of Roman Catholicism nor a Muslim's shift from either Sunni or Shi'a tradition to Sufi mysticism. It would rightly be seen as personal or individual preference. The idea of extension is also something that is not always signified by the term conversion. It would be viewed as one's broadening of one's spirituality rather than religious conversion. We also noted that in certain cases, claiming that the religious change was simply an extension is not viable either. All these three phenomena – rediscovery, preference, and extension – of course will be seen as religious change or change in one's religiosity. Yet these may not be called religious *conversions*. In Judaism, however, "religious conversion" does not describe a change in attitude or life practice, but a specific ritual performed for the purpose of becoming a Jew.

The fourth option that we examine now is definitely referred to as religious conversion by almost all religious and secular folk.

Religious Conversion as Replacement

Here is the most dramatic and public form of conversion. One rejects one's current religious tradition and "converts" to a different religious tradition. A Hindu becomes a Christian; a Christian converts and becomes a Buddhist; a Muslim chooses to become a Jew, and so on. In general, people think of this type of conversion when they hear the phrase "religious conversion." In this type of conversion, two things change: the religious identity of the individual and the character of religious belonging or religious membership. A clear definition of one's new religious identity emerges, and a demarcation of new and specific religious and communal boundaries takes place. For example, when a Jew converts to the Christian faith, she has a new religious identity as a Christian and belongs thereafter to a different community, called the church. When a Hindu becomes a Muslim, he has left the Hindu community and has joined the community of Muslims all over the world. Because of this double-sidedness – identity and community – conversion is not simply an individual matter; it has serious implications for the way the surrounding community is organized and maintained. This is especially true for a person who converts from Hinduism to Christianity, because such conversion demands a move from one's community, which is often defined in terms of caste, to take membership in a voluntary association, called the church. One is aware that in such conversions the converts do not give up their caste membership, even though they have taken a new identity and new membership in the church. The impact of conversion is greatest on the community when mass conversions take place.

I am using the word "replacement" because in most cases this type of conversion demands that one rejects one's earlier religion and replaces it with the new religion. One leaves a certain community and joins another community. James is right in defining conversion the way he does because he is operating with the view of conversion as replacement. That is why he is able to describe the process of conversion in such dramatic terms and as a movement from inferior to superior, wrong to right, and unhappy to happy. The replacement idea is dominant in Christian, Jewish, and Islamic traditions. Hinduism and Buddhism do not see conversion in these terms because of their view of the nature of truth claims and because their understandings of religious belonging are different from those traditions.

When conversion functions as replacement, it gains a much more public character, especially in the case of mass conversions. There is a clear renouncing of the earlier held religion and a public acknowledgment of the embracing of the new religion. Most often religious communities tend to celebrate the arrival of a new "convert" and take pride in publicly announcing the event. In a similar fashion, communities that lose a member to another religion through such conversion may publicly condemn it (some traditions see such conversion as apostasy). Due to its public character, even an individual's converting to another religion is not simply an individual matter. It does have a communal impact. The event of conversion impacts the surrounding community in more significant ways than do the models of preference or extension that were discussed earlier.

Another important aspect of the replacement model is that not only individuals convert. There have been, throughout human history, groups, communities, tribes, and villages who convert to a new or different religion. For example, in South India during the nineteenth century there were particular caste groups and villages who renounced Hinduism and embraced Christianity. There are "Christian" villages taking on biblical names such as Nazareth, Jerusalem, and Samaria, and they illustrate such mass conversions that replace the earlier religio-cultural ethos with a newly found religion. The high percentage of Christians in the population of Nagaland, Mizoram, Meghalaya, and other such northeastern states within India is due to such mass conversions in the nineteenth century.[6] This type of conversion tends to have a serious impact on the equilibrium of a particular society and is often seen as "destabilizing" current social arrangements. Such destabilization of

29

community is seen in various ways. The converted group may claim their conversion as an event of liberation and the gaining of dignity and honor. For example, the conversion of the so-called barbarian tribes in Europe may be seen as gaining their dignity and thus securing new power and privilege. In the same manner, Dalits who converted to Buddhism in twentieth-century India claim their conversion as coming to new selfhood. Others in the society may see the whole phenomenon as upsetting the peaceful balance of power and sharing of resources within that society. They would also view it as something that happened due to "unethical" means of coercion, promise of material well-being, and so on. Dalits, on the other hand, would see their conversion as challenging the apparent peace and balance of power that maintained the unjust conditions under which they lived.

There is one more aspect to consider before we conclude, namely, the verb-form of conversion. The verb "to convert" has been used in two specific ways. In the first, the person who converted to another religion may say that he converted to such and such religion. In the second, a person says that he or she wants to convert others into their religion. In the former, the convert is the subject of the action and as a free individual he or she has the right to do so. In the latter, the convert becomes the object of someone else's attempt to convert him or her. This objectification of the convert problematizes the right of a religious person to convert others. The question of religious freedom and religious human rights are matters that shape our understanding of religious conversion, and they are picked up and discussed in detail later in the volume.

To conclude, the four descriptions of religious conversion are offered primarily to bring adequate clarity to the phrase *religious conversion*. When people oppose or support religious conversion, it is important to know what view of conversion they subscribe to, because the conflict may be triggered by their very definition of conversion. For example, those who view religious conversion in terms of a replacement tend to vehemently oppose the extension or preference models. Likewise, those who support the extension or preference model find the replacement model unacceptable. Therefore, we need to be conscious of what definition of conversion we are operating with when we think and make judgments about religious conversion.

Notes

1   *Webster's Third New International Dictionary of the English Language Unabridged*, Vol. I (Chicago: Encyclopaedia Britannica, Inc., 1976), p. 499.
2   As quoted by E. Stanley Jones in his book, *Conversion* (Nashville, TN, 1959), pp. 46–47.
3   Ibid.
4   Robin Boyd, *An Introduction to Indian Christian Theology* (Delhi, India: ISPCK, 1975), p. 68.
5   See Corinne G. Dempsey, *Kerala Christian Sainthood: Collisions of Culture and Worldview in South India* (Oxford, Oxford University Press, 2001), pp. 5ff.
6   See Frederick F. Downs, *History of Christianity in India*, Volume V, Part 5: *North East India in the Nineteenth and Twentieth Centuries* (Bangalore, India: The Church History Association of India, 1992).

3

Models of Religious Belonging

Rita M. Gross

Once, a reporter who was interviewing me declared that religious people necessarily think that their own religion is the best and should be adhered to universally. Another way of saying the same thing is to claim that all religions necessarily make exclusive truth claims. This assumption is indeed widespread in many parts of the world. However, there is a very persuasive counter-argument – that it simply is not true, if one investigates religious communities globally rather than relying only on culturally familiar information. To make exclusive truth claims about one's own religion is not the only position regarding religious diversity, or even the most common position. One of the great liberating and sobering effects of the cross-cultural, comparative study of religion, including our work in the Thinking Together group, is the discovery that human beings do not always do things in the ways that are most familiar to us, and that others may even have some more adequate and compassionate ways of proceeding. We can learn about and adopt those customs and practices and we can critique our own common assumptions, such as the assumption that everyone makes universal truth claims, on the basis of those alternate practices and understandings.

As part of our discussions of the ethics of religious conversion, in this chapter we will consider one of the more useful ways of classifying the world's religions, a sociological rather than a doctrinal

Religious Conversion: Religion Scholars Thinking Together, First Edition.
Edited by Shanta Premawardhana.
© 2015 World Council of Churches Publications. Published 2015 by John Wiley & Sons, Ltd.

classification. After discussing these major types of religion, we will discuss the various models or styles of religious belonging practiced in these different kinds of religions. We will find that only one model of religious belonging involves exclusive truth claims or views the ideal situation as one in which everyone would belong to the same religion.

Classifying religions broadly into two categories, "ethno-religions" and "universalizing religions," is helpful for gaining insights into why some religions think it is important to seek converts and others do not. Ethno-religions are very closely tied to their culture, whereas universalizing religions are portable wanderers that can be practiced in any cultural context.[1] This classification is useful, in part, because it does not follow the superficial but usual classification of religions as "Eastern" and "Western." There are "Eastern" and "Western" religions in each category.

An ethno-religion is truly a way of life in which it is almost impossible to separate religion from culture. Customs and behaviors are far more important than beliefs, which can be quite flexible. Typically, matters that are considered "secular" in the context of many universalizing religions, such as diet, dress, marriage and divorce, and laws regulating society and politics, are far more important than doctrines, beliefs, and creeds. The only way to "convert" to an ethno-religion is to join the society and be adopted by its members. Ethno-religions are usually quite localized and usually have no dreams of empire or universal relevance.

Universalizing religions, by contrast, are based on a set of ideas that transcend culture. These must be "portable," abstract and general enough to attract followers from a wide variety of cultures, and to attract followers away from their culture of origin. A very detailed code for daily living is usually not as important to a universalizing religion as its core beliefs and doctrines, but it must believe that its message is universally relevant, that all people would benefit from hearing and absorbing that message. Almost by definition, a universalizing religion has spread widely from its point of origin. A portable religion, of course, must have porters – usually men – who have good reasons to travel extensively and little to tie them to any specific location. Merchants, monks, and soldiers are the best candidates and they have had a lot to do with the spread of the universalizing religions.

There are three major universalizing religions: Buddhism, Christianity, and Islam. Each claims to have a message that would be relevant and useful to everyone, no matter what their culture or daily lifestyle might be. Though difficult issues often arise, each religion tries not to disrupt the daily lifestyle of their new converts too much. However, Islam does impose a fairly strict code of daily living, Buddhism prohibits certain occupations, such as butchering, hunting, soldiering, and Christianity usually insists on monogamy and other aspects of its code of sexual behavior. Christianity and Islam both have vigorous missionary movements and have often spread through conquest. In many parts of the world, one of them holds almost a monopoly on religious affiliation. They also both claim to be the religion that God has given to humanity, thus making exclusive truth claims for themselves. Both have justifiable reputations for engaging in wars of religion, though there have always been significant voices arguing against religious use of violence in each tradition.

Buddhism has also spread widely and its current transmission to the West is arousing both concern and interest. Buddhism makes universal claims but, though exclusive truth claims have occurred in some Buddhist sects, they are not characteristic. To explain, Buddhists say that their description of the human condition and how to work with it applies to all people. But usually they have have not insisted that solving the riddle of human existence, finding peace or salvation, can only be done through Buddhist methods or that all people would need to express their realization in Buddhist words and concepts. Buddhism has typically been quite accommodating to indigenous religious traditions, and in many of the places to which it spread it did not become the dominant religion. Typically, it has not engaged in the large-scale imperial conquests, whether economic or military, accompanied by mass conversions in which religions sometimes participate. The Chinese adoption of Buddhism is the only instance in which the religion of one major culture area (South Asia) has been adopted in another major culture area (East Asia). Most of this adoption came from Chinese rather than Indian initiative. Tibet's adoption of Buddhism is actually a reverse missionary movement! Tibetans traveled to India to find teachers and texts and to take the religion back to Tibet. So this case of a universalizing religion seems to be rather different from those of Christianity and Islam. To discover that a religion could make universal claims without also making exclusive claims adds a great deal to the discussion of religious diversity and theologies of religion.

The division between ethno-religions and universalizing religions is not always so sharp. A universalizing religion can take on many local features when it has been established for a long time in any particular culture and has lost touch with other forms of that religion in other parts of the world. This happened to Buddhism, to such an extent that some suggest that Buddhism is not a single religion,[2] and that if we regard Buddhism as a single religion, we could also regard Judaism, Christianity, and Islam as different sects of an overarching monotheistic religion – a claim I find quite cogent. A religion that was once a universalizing religion can become an ethno-religion due to historical circumstances and hardship, as happened to Judaism. A religion that has not become universalizing because it has not spread widely could become so in different circumstances. There is no reason why Confucian or Daoist ideas could not appeal widely. They have as much general relevance as Buddhist, Christian, or Muslim ideas, but they have not had the historical fortune to spread widely. Even a stereotypical ethno- religion can have widespread appeal. Indigenous Native American religions are very reluctant to open their practices to outsiders, but a few teachers do. As I watched blonde Germans who traveled to South Dakota every year to dance in the annual Sundance, I watched the categories "ethno-religion" and "universalizing religion" collapse before my eyes. Nevertheless, they are useful generalizations.

Among the world's religions, we can isolate at least four distinct ways of negotiating religious diversity, four ways that individuals who belong to one of the religions are encouraged to think about the diversity of the world's religions. Some religions tend to discourage others from joining their ranks. Other religions permit multiple religious belonging, while still others demonstrate great internal diversity and approve of multiple paths to salvation. Finally, some religions proclaim that they alone possess religious truth and that the world would be a better place if everyone belonged to their religion. Thus we can see that only a minority of the world's religions make exclusive truth claims.

In the first model of religious belonging, among ethno-religious contexts, and in some other situations, believers may erect barriers against outsiders, rather than trying to lure them into religious participation. They clearly do not believe that it is necessary for the salvation of outsiders that they begin to think and act like the insiders of any particular religious context. As already noted, ethno-religions are characterized by a close intertwining of religion and culture, which helps explain their attitudes toward religious others. To practice the religion, an outsider would have to join the culture completely, and there is little reason to promote or accept such a conversion. While members of an ethno-religion obviously prefer their own religion and culture to any other, they do not regard it as categorically superior in the same way that those who make exclusive truth claims proclaim superiority for their religions.

Ethno-religions and some others present another interesting counter-example to the expectation that everyone should practice the same religion. Even within a single ethno-religion, people may not know the details of each other's religious experiences or the specifics of their beliefs and practices. This secrecy is simply accepted and no one feels deprived because they are not privy to the religious practices of others. People feel that it is simply inappropriate to share one's own religious experiences with anyone except one's teacher or closest companions. Though, as a Buddhist, I belong to a universalizing religion, many aspects of my particular path as a practitioner of Tibetan Vajrayana Buddhism predispose me to be very sympathetic to this ethno-religious approach. There is a great deal of secrecy in Vajrayana Buddhism. The view is that too much information too soon could be destructive rather than helpful because the path of spiritual development is long and complex. Profound secrets disclosed too soon are usually either dangerous or easily trivialized. For Vajrayana Buddhists, the preferred practice is to introduce basics to those who request such instruction and gradually introduce other aspects of the tradition when appropriate.

Such reticence to share one's beliefs and practices may well be a useful counter-position to those who feel that it is their supreme duty to share their religious beliefs and practices as widely as possible, and in that process to wipe out alternative visions of the real, the good, and the beautiful. Instead, in some contexts, such as North American Indigenous religions, extreme reluctance to share religion with outsiders has developed and those who teach outsiders some of the more esoteric and important aspects of religious belief and practice are accused of "selling the religion." This attitude is the exact opposite of the notion than one should send missionaries to the ends of the earth to bring all people into our correct belief system.

Multiple religious belonging is a second possibility not explored or imagined by those who assume that all religious people make exclusive truth claims. In East Asia, people typically "belong" to several religious traditions, using each one to meet specific needs. Or one could say that ordinary people belong to no specific religious tradition because they utilize them all, either simultaneously or sequentially. Only religious specialists belong to a specific tradition. Usually such specialists acknowledge and promote the multi-religious context in which they operate, though examples of sectarian rivalry and exclusive loyalty, both among laity and religious specialists, are not unknown. The most striking demonstration of the reality of East Asian multiple religious belonging is that Japanese census figures routinely turn up nearly twice as many religious affiliations as the population of Japan.[3] Most people participate in at least Shinto and Buddhist activities and it would not occur to them to choose one over the other. Instead, Shinto specializes in religious events pertaining to birth and fertility, while most people turn to Buddhism to deal with death and the afterlife. Thus, New Year celebrations occur in a largely Shinto context, but death anniversaries are memorialized at Buddhist temples. The same person who would be taken to a Shinto shrine soon after birth will probably have a Buddhist funeral. Though the practice is dying out, traditional homes would have both a Shinto shrine for the *kami* (Shinto divine beings) and a Buddhist altar, where the family ancestors are remembered, and both would be used regularly.

Much the same situation prevailed in traditional China regarding the Three Traditions – Buddhism, Confucianism, and Daoism. Where early Western scholars had seen competing distinct traditions, the Chinese saw cooperating traditions. Confucianism governed public life, etiquette, and the state, while Daoism inspired poetry, the arts, and private contemplation. Buddhism was often the favorite religion of women, who played little part in public life, while Confucianism was the preferred outlook for upper-class men. As in Japan, most people participated in more than one religion during their lifetimes.[4] The plurality of religious perspectives was built into the architecture of pilgrimage sites. One observer of Chinese culture narrated her growing understanding of the plurality of Chinese religious perspectives as she participated in a pilgrimage up a mountain. The lower reaches of the mountain were dedicated to temples for various deities of Daoist folk religion and other aspects of popular folk religion, including vivid portrayals of the many tales of popular religion. As the pilgrimage route wound further up the mountain, the imagery changed from Daoist and folk religions to Buddhist imagery.[5] One should not think that the three traditions did not compete with each other – they did; and Buddhism especially often faced disapproval because of its foreign origins. But the competition resulted in ensuring that no one tradition ever became too dominant, rather than the elimination of one or more tradition. To reduce religions to one which would be adhered to by everyone does not seem ever to have been a goal, and competition for power rather than doctrinal conflict seems to have motivated much interreligious rivalry.

Things changed, however, with the introduction of Christianity. Martin C. Yang's classic account, *A Chinese Village: Taitou, Shantung Province*, narrates not only how Chinese Christians separated themselves from the rest of village, regarding everyone else as sinners and themselves as the "chosen people," but also how Catholics and Protestants mutually regarded the others as sinners while regarding themselves as the chosen people. Neither group celebrated the overarching practices of Chinese religion, such as ancestor veneration and veneration of the Kitchen God and the Earth God, which all other Chinese would observe even if they personally were more devoted to the Buddhist, Daoist, or Confucian perspectives.[6]

Negotiating religious diversity through allowing or encouraging multiple religious belonging clearly promotes a cultural situation in which different religions will flourish side by side, often in healthy competition with one another, but without the rancor generated when one religion really regards itself as the One True Faith and its competitors as misguided. Such a solution also allows individuals to tailor-make their religious paths to fit their own needs, at least to some extent.

A third way of negotiating religious belonging is common in "Hinduism," which is actually an umbrella term that covers a multitude of religious options – many deities, many paths, many practices, many religious groups. The abundant plurality of what is called "Hinduism" defies neat classification. But Hinduism does not solve the issue of religious belonging by advocating exclusive loyalty to one religious path which is then regarded as the most appropriate path for everyone. One introduction to Hinduism tried to orient students to this diversity by suggesting that, no matter what facet of Indian society one observed, one would see diverse, ever-shifting patterns. For example, regarding a typical family:

> The mother, a widow, is a devout worshipper of Shiva; her sister-in-law, equally devout, follows the teachings of Ramakrishna; the eldest son is an engineer trained in England, a worshipper of Shiva, but not as knowledgeable or dedicated ... as his mother and younger brother; his wife's father worships Krishna, as does all her family.
>
> ...
>
> The family worships Shiva in the home; they go to a temple of the Goddess ... for special occasions; they visit a temple and teaching center dedicated to Vishnu; they sing devotional songs to Krishna.[7]

Because Hinduism is so diverse, it is hard to make generalizations. Certainly in some ways, Hindus make sharp divisions between themselves and others, especially in the dictum – not always enforced and somewhat controversial – that it is difficult or impossible to convert to Hinduism. Nor, except for a few modern forms of Hinduism, has there been any attempt to spread Hinduism outside of Indian ethnic populations. In this regard, Hinduism contrasts strongly with its Indian cousin – Buddhism.

But regarding religious beliefs and practices, the dominant motif in Hinduism is unquestionably pluralistic. Many versions of Hinduism would claim that salvation is available to all, no matter what path they follow, what deity they worship, or what their station in life may be. Hinduism is the one religion that traditionally has advocated the "pluralist" position, which claims that there are many true paths to the same goal, regarding religious diversity. However, this theological pluralism should not be mistaken for a lack of vigorous theological and philosophical debate, both among Hindu schools of thought and with competing religions. Thus, a pluralistic theology regarding the existence of many religious options does not mean that no normative claims are made or that the validity of these various claims is not debated and discussed.

The confusing pluralism of Hinduism is perhaps best illustrated by looking at a typical Hindu temple. A temple will be dedicated to a main deity but there will also be icons of most other major deities of the Hindu pantheon in the same temple. For example, one prominent temple in Delhi displays icons of Krishna and Radha in its center, an icon of Shiva to the right and an icon of the goddess Durga to the left. These are the three major contenders for loyalty in the vast Hindu pantheon, but they are only rarely pitted against each other. In this temple, as in many others, a devotee can approach any one of them or all three of them. Hindu literature includes many instances of particular individuals who are intensely devoted to one of the deities, but there are also stories of deities rejecting the offerings of a devotee who wants only to acknowledge one of the deities.

This Hindu model is not like the East Asian model of multiple religious belonging. Instead, it presents a model of shifting centers, with no teaching and no deity holding or claiming ultimate authority and loyalty. Unlike the East Asian situation, in which indigenous participants identify with multiple religions, Hindus do not regard devotees of the various deities or various teachings as members of different religions. Yet Hindus also did and do differentiate themselves from other religions, such as Buddhism and Islam. In most cases, Hindus would agree that members of those religions may gain salvation, whatever that might be, but they also recognize them to be different religions, or, alternatively, distinct sects within Hinduism. I have been told many times that, because I am Buddhist, I am really Hindu.

This model of religious belonging presents yet another option. It is possible for religious believers to recognize sharp divisions among themselves and others, either within their own broad umbrella or among those clearly recognized as outsiders, and still not consider those outsiders to be in need of conversion. This model of diversity is not like the East Asian model, in which indigenous participants participate in several different religious traditions and report multiple belongings. In this Hindu case, people can have very specific loyalties and yet not claim exclusive relevance for their particular "chosen path." They also recognize a difference between their own internally diverse tradition and other "outside" traditions. Buddhism and Islam are definitely recognized as separate traditions, but they too are recognized as valid spiritual paths, contemporary Hindu–Muslim tension not withstanding.

All of these models contrast with the position of the reporter, cited at the beginning of this chapter, who was sure that all religious people think that their own religion is the best religion for everyone and that any one person can only have one religious affiliation at a time. They also present alternatives to the tendency of some religions to engage in deliberate missionary activity and to seek converts. Thus, we see that most of the world's religious traditions do very well without claiming exclusive truth for themselves and seeking to bring all of humanity into their fold. In all cases, these are old, well-established religious traditions that have served their followers well for millennia. This fact undercuts the claim of some advocates of exclusive truth claims that anyone who really takes his religion seriously and is accomplished in it would naturally and inevitably desire to spread it, not only universally, which is unproblematic, but also exclusively, which creates many problems and great suffering.

This fourth model for negotiating religious diversity – making exclusive truth claims for one's own religion – is found only in universalizing religions and is especially prevalent in some but not all monotheisms. A universalizing, monotheistic religion almost faces double jeopardy for making exclusive truth claims. Any universalizing religion will see its claims as relevant for everyone, no matter their cultural background. It is also understandable that monotheists would, in addition, claim exclusive relevance for their religions because of their belief that the sole, universal deity communicated its recommendations for religious belief and behavior in revealed texts. If such claims could be verified, the cogency of exclusive truth claims would be very high indeed. The difficulty of taking exclusive truth claims seriously, however, is the fact that several monotheistic religions make identical exclusive truth claims about several different scriptures and theologies.

In exploring these questions further, it is important to look at two other pieces of information – the historical reluctance of the earliest monotheists to seek converts, and the fact that only those monotheisms that are successful in creating empires and attaining great political domination continue to claim exclusive and universal relevance for themselves.

The early history of Jewish monotheism is quite instructive in this regard. Early Israelite monotheism was essentially an ethno-religion which emphasized that Israelites should worship only Yahweh, their specific deity, but none of the deities worshipped by other people. (The existence of these deities was not denied in early times. They simply should not be venerated by Israelites.) The Hebrew scriptures record that, for Israelites, learning to worship Yahweh alone with singular commitment was a gradual process that took place over a long period of time. The breakthrough seems to have occurred after the destruction of the first temple, when Israelites chose to remain loyal to Yahweh, despite their own defeat and exile. They could do

41

this because of a theological revolution: their deity, they determined, was actually the universal ruler of history, and the defeat and exile experienced by the Israelites was due not to the weakness of Yahweh, but to his universal rulership. He had chosen to allow defeat and exile to the Israelites and victory to their conquerors because of Israelite apostasy, but he was still in charge. Israelites in captivity proclaimed Yahweh to be the universal deity in charge of everything. This is probably the first time such a claim was made.

When Israelites returned to Palestine and rebuilt their temple, they became players in the kaleidoscopic competition for religious adherents that prevailed in the Roman Empire. They proclaimed the reign of a universal deity and many outsiders sought entrance. After all, a universal deity who accepted only a very small segment of humanity was an oxymoron. But for some Israelites, Yahweh was their deity and outsiders were not welcome, despite his universal rule. This debate was won by those who accepted converts, and this battle over whether or not to accept converts is usually said to be the lesson of the Book of Ruth in the Hebrew Bible. After that point, Judaism became a religion that readily accepted converts. It was quite successful in gaining converts well into the late Roman Empire, until a newly ascendant Christianity made it illegal for Jews, among others, to accept converts. At that point, Jews reverted to a more ethno-religious perspective; though they worshipped a deity who was the universal sovereign, that deity had established multiple covenants with the peoples of the earth which ensured that the "righteous of all nations" would inherit "the Kingdom of God." Judaism was for Jews; others did not need to join, but they were not damned because of their different perspectives.

Thus we see that even a monotheism, which is theologically pre-disposed to claim both exclusive and universal truth, can cope with a situation in which it becomes improbable to assert that all people would be better off if they only would join up. Christians and Muslims usually have not come to that conclusion, mainly for one reason: they have been too successful politically. Both religions became the favored religions of large empires, very early in their histories in both cases. From that favored political position, both religions have been able to use their influence to undercut and destroy competing religions and to enforce an orthodoxy of belief within their own ranks.

The problems inherent in situations in which large religions also hold great political power are not limited to monotheisms, of course.

They would occur in any situation in which powerful religions cooperate with powerful empires and could probably be documented in many East Asian and South Asian contexts, in addition to European and Middle Eastern contexts. For example, such cooperation between Japanese Buddhist organizations and the Japanese government in pre-World War II Japan has been well documented.[8] The only remaining question is whether non-monotheistic religions also use political power to enforce religious orthodoxy internally.

Making exclusive truth claims for one's own religion is only one among four main ways of negotiating religious diversity. Such a way of dealing with religious diversity, if successful, would eventually eliminate religious diversity. Thus, anyone who values religious diversity should find this way of negotiating religious diversity to be extremely problematic. It has none of the virtues of the other ways of negotiating religious diversity discussed in this chapter. The world's many ethno-religions demonstrate that one can value one's own religious tradition but not wish to share it with outsiders. The possibility of multiple religious belonging allows believers to participate in all the religious options found in their culture, whether simultaneously or sequentially. Hindu pluralism demonstrates the possibility of the coexistence of many strongly argued theological and philosophical positions, with a pluralistic acceptance of this variety as normative.

Even though making exclusive truth claims may not be an appropriate response to religious diversity, it is also important to remember several other points. Although it is inappropriate to make exclusive truth claims, this does not mean that people are disallowed from proclaiming their faith or seeking converts to it. They are only asked to proclaim and promote their religion without claiming that it alone among all religions is exclusively true and deserves universal adherence. Separating claims of *universal relevance* from claims of *exclusive relevance* is not difficult and should be expected of all participants in our pluralistic universe. Finally, though historically monotheism has been more prone to make exclusive truth claims than other types of religion, the problems are with the exclusive truth claims, not with monotheism as a religious system. Monotheism certainly has adequate theological resources to free itself from entanglement with exclusive truth claims. Throughout the history of monotheism, many thinkers within Christianity, from Justin Martyr to Marjorie Suchocki, have done so.

Rita M. Gross

Notes

1 See Milton C. Sernett, "Religion and Group Identity: Believers as Behavers," in T. William Hall (ed.), *Introduction to the Study of Religion* (San Francisco: Harper and Row, 1978), pp. 217–230 for the article that first introduced me to this classification.
2 This argument is made in the fifth edition of a classic textbook on Buddhism. Richard H. Robinson, Willard L. Johnson, and Thanissaro Bhikkhu, *Buddhist Religions: A Historical Introduction* (Belmont, CA: Thomson/Wadsworth, 2005), pp. xix–xxiii.
3 Judith Berling cites it in her provocative book *A Pilgrim in Chinese Culture: Negotiating Religious Diversity* (Maryknoll, NY: Orbis Books, 1997), p. 43 and traces its ancestry in her footnote.
4 Berling, *Pilgrim in Chinese Culture*, p. 43.
5 Berling, *Pilgrim in Chinese Culture*, pp. 12–13.
6 Martin C. Yang, *A Chinese Village: Taitou, Shantung Province* (New York: Columbia University Press, 1945), pp. 158–161.
7 Thomas J. Hopkins, *The Hindu Religious Tradition* (Belmont, CA: Dickenson Publishing, Inc., 1971), p. 1.
8 Brian Daizen Victoria, *Zen at War*, 2nd edition (Lanham, MD: Rowman and Littlefield, 2006).

Further Reading

Berling, Judith. *A Pilgrim in Chinese Culture: Negotiating Religious Diversity.* Maryknoll, NY: Orbis Books, 1997.
Cobb, John B. Jr. *Beyond Dialogue: Toward a Mutual Transformation of Christianity and Buddhism.* Philadelphia: Fortress Press, 1982.
Eck, Diana. *Encountering God: A Spiritual Pilgrimage from Bozeman to Benares.* Boston: Beacon Press, 1993.
Knitter, Paul F. *Introducing Theologies of Religion.* Maryknoll, NY: Orbis Books, 2002.
Smith, Wilfred Cantwell. *Religious Diversity.* New York: Crossroad, 1976.

4

Conversion Sought and Feared

Hans Ucko

Conversion is controversial. I am a convert and even today, more than 40 years following my conversion, I cannot just say the word without having to define what I mean or qualify what my conversion was all about. I'm almost apologetic about it. I have to say, "Well, it is not that I was or is against the religion that I left. I hardly knew that religion. I did not convert from," I would say, "I converted to."

And then there are those who will make a big hoopla about their conversion. The religion the convert left is being discarded wholesale and the religion the converted joined is presented in an apotheosis dismissing everything else. And then there are those who will look upon the convert as a traitor, someone who has joined the enemy or become a potential detractor of the old religion.

To be able to convert someone is high on the priority list for some; for others it is a day of grief when someone converts. It would be foolish not to realize the psychological aspect of it all: someone converting to my faith confirms me in my religious tradition. Someone converting from my faith seems to reject what I stand for. Even those who want others to convert will not easily accept the phenomenon of one of their own leaving their faith for another. There seems to be no logic when it comes to conversion. Conversion is indeed sought by some and feared by some.

Religious Conversion: Religion Scholars Thinking Together, First Edition.
Edited by Shanta Premawardhana.
© 2015 World Council of Churches Publications. Published 2015 by John Wiley & Sons, Ltd.

Hans Ucko

To Convert To and to Convert From

People of different faiths hold opposing views in relation to the issue and reality of conversion. Christians have fairly easy conversions into and out of the faith, although the latter may be only resentfully accepted by Christians. Jews have difficult conversions into and even more out of the faith. Muslims have easy conversions into the faith but have major difficulties with conversion out of the faith. When Dalits in great numbers decide to convert from Hinduism to Buddhism, Islam, or Christianity, it creates tensions and concerns in the Hindu community, and in some places there are calls for legislation against conversion. Theravada Buddhists set up a mission university in Myanmar to counter the incursion of zealous Christian missionaries from the West.

The issue of conversion into the faith is understood as an integral part of both Christianity and Islam. Although the concept of conversion is understood differently in Islam and in Christianity, this complex reality in both religions could make relations between Christians and Muslims converge. Both religions advocate "conversion to" but oppose in very different ways "conversion from." Christians and Muslims can refer to their religious tradition as advocating respect for the integrity of the other. Muslims point to the verse in the Qur'an that says there should be no compulsion in religion (2:256). Christians can quote verses from the Bible where it is obvious that God has other priorities for people than their religious affiliation: "What does the Lord require of you but to do justice, and to love kindness, and to walk humbly with your God?" (Micah 6:8). And yet, there are other verses or vestiges in history that speak another language, demonstrating the complexity. There are many verses in the Bible seeming to advocate that the highest goal is the conversion of the other. Those who claim this see these verses as offering them a strong warrant for missionary activities. And it has a bearing also on the involvement of Christians in interreligious dialogue. How do Christians in dialogue deal with the call for the conversion of all?

In the often troubled relationship between Christians and Muslims, Muslims are often put on the defensive. Christians claim that violence is intrinsic to Islam, and point to what is called "converting by sword" as part of the history of Islam. This is widespread and is heard both in the center and in the periphery of Christianity.

Pope Benedict had not been pope for long before he was drawn into conflict with Muslims all over the world. It happened through a lecture, which went far beyond the university campus of Regensburg, the locus of his presentation. Reference was made to Byzantine emperor Manuel II Paleologus, who said (and the Pope quoted), "Show me just what Mohammed brought that was new, and there you will find things only evil and inhuman, such as his command to spread by the sword the faith he preached."[1]

Even when talking about Islam in our own time, this argument is used: Islam spreads the faith through the sword or teaches the killing of apostates. Quotes are readily available, "If somebody discards his religion, kill him."[2] People prefer to "nail" Muslims to these quotes and neglect the contemporary work taking place in Islamic thinking, such as how to interpret the text and tradition in the complex world of our time.[3]

Conversion does not stand alone. It is interwoven with the way we understand the authority of scripture and the way we look upon the interrelationship between tradition and contemporary challenges. Conversion is intrinsic to the religious heritage. And it is in all religious traditions. The pope as well as other Christians needs to remember that there are indeed embarrassing texts in the Bible or parts of the checkered history of Christian dealings with people of other faiths.[4]

Furthermore, Jews were once upon a time active in converting Gentiles and there are Jewish communities that even today have taken it up again, trying to inject new blood into an ever-decreasing minority. But as a whole, conversion is more feared than practiced in Judaism. It is a serious threat. A convert is almost seen as a traitor. Conversion out of Judaism reduces the Jewish people, already a dwindling minority. Jewish scholar Emil Fackenheim once said that continuing Jewish life and denying Hitler a posthumous victory was the 614th commandment. Catholic theologian Gregory Baum, himself a convert from Judaism, elaborated on Christian views toward conversion and, building upon Fackenheim, said: "After Auschwitz the Christian churches no longer wish to convert the Jews. While they may not be sure of the theological grounds that dispense them from this mission, the churches have become aware that asking Jews to become Christians is a spiritual way of blotting them out of existence and thus only reinforces the effects of the Holocaust."[5]

If Christians and Muslims have a particular sense of mission in the world, other religions have other visions. There is certainly a Buddhist mission to the West, but it doesn't have that absolute ring about it as conversions to Christianity and Islam have. Other religions are either not explicitly witnessing to make people convert, they have through the course of history given it up, or they never engaged in seeking to bring the other into their community in the first place.

Obliged to Invite to Conversion?

The conversion of the other is definitely an objective in traditional Christian self-understanding. The statement by theologian Elton Trueblood is said in many different ways and by very many Christians, when the issue of mission and witness is discussed: "There is no such thing as a non-witnessing Christian." And in common parlance, witnessing is for the conversion of the other. Many Christians would be disappointed if it was said that conversion is above all about the conversion of the world to a place of justice and human dignity. It would not be enough.

The topic of conversion has today become divisive and has the potential not only to put people of different faiths against each other but also to create frictions among Christians themselves. It is a problematic issue within the church. Everyone should have the right to change his/her religion, but should we be involved in making others change theirs? There are those who feel that seeking out others and converting them from their religion is divinely ordained and nothing can thwart this heavenly injunction.

I remember one of my first experiences in Jewish–Christian dialogue, meeting a Christian theologian actively involved in the Society for Christian Mission to the Jews. I asked him if the church could honestly and with integrity continue advocating mission to Jews, considering what had happened 60 years ago in Germany and the sad history of how Jews had fared in Christian lands. Should not the Shoah rather convert the church in its relationship to the Jewish people? Could the church after the Shoah go about its business as usual? The theologian said to me: "I realize what you are saying. What happened in Auschwitz was terrible. It was an atrocity, it was dreadful, but it does not change anything. The Gospel tells us that there is no other name by which we can be saved." He told me that he might personally regret that there was no other way for him to go but to seek the conversion of the Jews. He said, "I wish it were different, I wish I could say: There will be no more mission to Jews – but I cannot." He had to obey the Gospel.

The ordinary man or woman in the street in Europe is likely to consider mission that seeks the conversion of people of other faiths as something bigoted, intolerant, and aggressive. They would say the same about any religion trying to seek the conversion of the other. According to them, it is just out of place and order. There are also Christian theologians who feel that the conversion of others is no longer the business of the church. They are seeking to formulate the mission of the church not as seeking converts but as converting our world to become a world where justice reigns and human dignity is a commandment. They prefer expounding *Missio Dei*, the mission of God, in which the church as well as people of other religious traditions may be called to participate. But such a view is controversial and contested by those who advocate mission as inviting people to convert; they would likely label it as postmodernist relativism.

Conversion through Mission or Proselytism

I cannot look upon the targeting of the other for conversion as anything else than proselytism. Many Christians will object and will claim that it is their obligation to follow the so-called Great Commission in Matthew 28:18–20: "All authority in heaven and on earth has been given to me. Go therefore and make disciples of all nations, baptising them in the name of the Father and of the Son and of the Holy Spirit, teaching them to observe all that I have commanded you; and lo, I am with you always, to the close of the age." They will say that not only do they have an obligation but also a right to seek the conversion of the other.

Am I avoiding the Great Commission? No, I am reading the same text but cannot separate these words and the effect that these verses have had in history. Conversion is not per se a result of proselytism but tensions regarding conversion are often related to proselytizing activities by another actor, individual, or organization. The word has changed meaning. A *proselytos* in the New Testament refers to a convert to Judaism hinting at a time when Judaism too was involved

49

in seeking converts.[6] The Acts of the Apostles mention the first Pentecost; there were devout Jews from every nation under heaven living in Jerusalem. One region after another in Asia Minor, Asia, and North Africa is mentioned, and finally it is said that there were also "visitors from Rome, both Jews and proselytes" (Acts 2, 10).

To proselytize has today gained a very loaded meaning. "To induce someone to conversion is to proselytize," says *Dictionary of the Ecumenical Movement*.[7] Proselytism has become such a negative word that even those who are involved in the conversion of others would prefer to use alternative words. They would name it as an invitation extended to others to join the Christian faith. They say that they do not proselytize but they have the right to manifest, the right to teach, the right to express, the right to impart religious ideas. They would also argue that the right to issue such invitations is supported by the world community having signed on to the UN Declaration of Human Rights. It is a question of freedom of religion.

The UN Declaration on Freedom of Religion or Belief

The most important international legislation on the freedom of religion or belief is Article 18 in the UN International Covenant on Civil and Political Rights (CCPR) from 1966. It in turn builds upon Article 18 of the Universal Declaration of Human Rights (DHR) from 1948, which says, "Everyone has the right to freedom of thought, conscience and religion; this right includes freedom to change his religion or belief, and freedom, either alone or in community with others and in public or private, to manifest his religion or belief in teaching, practice, worship and observance."[8]

The wording of CCPR Article 18 says:

1. Everyone shall have the right to freedom of thought, conscience and religion. This right shall include freedom to have or to adopt a religion or belief of his choice, and freedom, either individually or in community with others and in public or private, to manifest his religion or belief in worship, observance, practice and teaching.
2. No one shall be subject to coercion, which would impair his freedom to have or to adopt a religion or belief of his choice.

There can be no question about the right to communicate one's faith. And no one shall be coerced to maintain his/her religion or belief. No one should "impair" the right to change religion; yes, the state has an obligation to actively ensure the right to change religion or belief. Included in the freedom of expression is also a right to seek and to receive information. The freedom of assembly and the freedom of association are important expressions of the UN declarations.

However, those who rightly quote the right to change religion and the right to persuade others to change often forget that the UN declarations also talk about the right to maintain one's religion or belief. No one shall be coerced to change his or her religion or belief. The right to religious freedom is actually limited by other human rights. In addition, one person's religious freedom may be limited by the religious freedom of another. Thus one interesting field for exploration is the interaction between the freedom to propagate religion, on the one hand, and the freedom to practice one's religion without interference, on the other. The CCPR has in Article 17 a clause on the right to privacy, which, for instance, will protect the home from forced invasion by people seeking your conversion.

The question is, of course, how to balance the right to engage in faith persuasion against the right to maintain one's religion or belief. How do we protect the juxtaposed claims of majority and minority religions? How do we consider the relationship between material aid and missionary activities and questions of unequal distribution of material resources, sometimes along other lines than numerical minority and majority situations? It is important to remember the vital role that factors such as power (cultural, financial, mental etc.) of the proselytizer plays in the relationship with the one who is the object of faith persuasion or conversion.

Attempting to convert the other is not only jeopardizing relations between people of different faiths; it is also threatening ecumenical relations, particularly in situations when the judicial institutions in society legislate against conversion. This has been the case in India, where Christians were worried by the attempts to legislate against conversion. They felt that they themselves were the victims of what para-church groups, often with foreign funds, were involved in. Their evangelization campaigns and crusades antagonized Hindus, who either could not or would not distinguish which church proselytized and which church abstained from aggressive evangelism. People in the churches were afraid that their diaconal work – for example,

51

their schools – would be considered instruments for conversion and banned by law.

Mainline churches find themselves in a dilemma, accused by evangelicals of not fulfilling and living up to the great Commission of our Lord. Their question rings in the ear: "Does the ecumenical church still have conversion on its agenda?" Although most of the spectacular calls for conversion are made within the so-called "Evangelical" camp, it is probably not so easy for any Christian to dissociate him- or herself clearly from the proselytizing activities of other Christians. Proclamation toward conversion is, after all, a command. People of other faiths, however, see activities toward the conversion of the other, particularly the poor, as an act of Christian cowardice. Gandhi is reported to have said: "Why are you Christians converting the depressed classes? Come and convert us instead."

Aid Evangelism

The issue of conversion has in the Thinking Together discussion, often focused on so-called aid evangelism, providing help on condition that the poor convert. The relief work following the earthquake in Gujarat led to suspicions that Christian relief work was connected with conversion. At the Millennium Peace Conference in August 2000 in New York, I was part of a small group addressing the particular issue of conversion in India. We agreed upon an "Informal Working Understanding – Freedom from Coercion in Religion":

• We agree that the free and generous preaching of the Christian Gospel is welcome in India.
• We condemn proselytism; we particularly reject the exploitation of the issue of poverty in religious outreach and missionary work.
• We agree that the giving of aid to those in need is a primary commandment of all our religious and spiritual traditions; we are resolved that this act of justice should never be tied to compulsory conversion.
• We commit ourselves to a continuing dialogue in the spirit of interreligious harmony, mutual respect, and the co-operative

common effort to build a better world. In this way, we will discover trust in one another that any altruistic work will not be a means for conversion.

The issue of aid evangelism does not go away. It is not made up. It was practiced following the post-tsunami relief work in 2004 and there are many who have pointed to flagrant examples of proselytism that can only be prefaced by the word "coercive." It is coercive proselytism.

Conversion as an Issue in Interreligious Relations

In the late 1990s, staff of the Office on Interreligious Relations and Dialogue (IRRD) of the WCC and the Pontifical Council for Interreligious Dialogue of the Vatican (PCID) repeatedly heard news from our constituencies that highlighted the topic of conversion. It concerned, above all, relations between Hindus and Christians in India and Christians and Muslims worldwide. We heard the same stories about unethical conversion, about aid evangelism, about conspiracy to overturn Islam, and we realized that our counterparts in dialogue or their constituencies were not always able to distinguish between Christians in dialogue and Christians involved in what was seen as coercive proselytism. The WCC document *Ecumenical Considerations for Dialogue and Relations with People of Other Religions* articulated this dilemma:

> Although dialogue by its very nature is direct encounter, there are invisible participants on each side in every dialogue. Our dialogue partners will ever so often hold us responsible for what fellow Christians have done or neglected to do, said or not said. While this in some ways is inevitable and even sometimes understandable, we are well aware of deep disagreements within religions and we know that the dividing lines do not always go between religious communities but often within religious communities. We may for various reasons find ourselves in opposition to some of those with whom we share a common faith. We learn that religious communities are not monolithic blocks confronting each other. Plurality of positions on each side should not be ignored or suppressed while defending what is perceived to be the interest of one's community. Commitment to a faith does not entail identification with what is done or not done in its name.[9]

In an effort to address the issue, the two offices on dialogue initiated a project entitled "Interreligious Reflection on Conversion – From Controversy to a Shared Code of Conduct." Although the project was to focus mainly on "intra-discussion" among Christians on the topic of conversion, the project was initiated in May 2006 through a multi-religious hearing entitled "Assessing the Reality." What are the memories, experiences, reactions, and comments from our counterparts in other religious traditions on the issue of conversion? What are the issues? What should we as Christians bring to the table from the interreligious reality on the issue of conversion? What do Muslims and Hindus say about conversion? How do we address the fears of people wanting to become Christians but living in countries where another religion is dominating the religious landscape?

The report from the consultation "Conversion – Assessing the Reality" stated, among other things:

- That interreligious dialogue, to be meaningful, should not exclude any topic, however controversial or sensitive, if that topic is a matter of concern for humankind as a whole or for any section/s thereof.
- That freedom of religion is a fundamental, inviolable, and non-negotiable right of every human being in every country in the world. Freedom of religion connotes the freedom, without any obstruction, to practice one's own faith, freedom to propagate the teachings of one's faith to people of one's own and other faiths, and also the freedom to embrace another faith out of one's own free choice.
- That while everyone has a right to invite others to an understanding of their faith, it should not be exercised by violating others' rights and religious sensibilities. At the same time, all should heal themselves from the obsession of converting others.
- That freedom of religion enjoins upon all of us the equally non-negotiable responsibility to respect faiths other than our own, and never to denigrate, vilify, or misrepresent them for the purpose of affirming superiority of our faith.
- That errors have been perpetrated and injustice committed by the adherents of every faith. Therefore, it is incumbent on every community to conduct honest self-critical examination of its

historical conduct as well as its doctrinal/theological precepts. Such self-criticism and repentance should lead to necessary reforms inter alia on the issue of conversion.

- That conversion by "unethical" means is discouraged and rejected by one and all. There should be transparency in the practice of inviting others to one's faith.
- That humanitarian work by faith communities should be conducted without any ulterior motives. In the area of humanitarian service in times of need, what we can do together, we should not do separately.
- That no faith organization should take advantage of vulnerable sections of society, such as children and the disabled.
- That we are sensitive to the religious language and theological concepts in different faiths. Members of each faith should listen to how people of other faiths perceive them.
- That there is a need to collectively evolve a "code of conduct" on conversion, which all faiths should follow. We therefore feel that interreligious dialogues on the issue of conversion should continue at various levels.[10]

A Critical Moment on Conversion

The question of conversion emerged as a critical issue during a major interreligious event, the Critical Moment Conference organized by the World Council of Churches, held June 6–9, 2005 in Geneva. The charge was made by several participants that the WCC needed to be much clearer on the question of conversion as a problematic issue in interreligious relations. If one wanted to be serious in interreligious dialogue, one needed to speak out against those who sought the conversion of others. A Muslim woman from Egypt said:

> It is my assumption, that we have moved beyond the conversion mentality and that we share a post-conversion mentality. We believe in the freedom of religion and everybody must enjoy the freedom of expressing and practising his or her religion and calling others if he or she wishes others to do so. It is my conviction that we should recognise the conversion mentality, that either you are with me or against me as something of the past.[11]

Hans Ucko

The report from the conference addressed the issue of conversion and said:

> In our relationship in dialogue we need to address also issues of controversy as difficult as they may be. But we cannot pretend that they are not there. There is in many of our dialogues an asymmetry, which we must be aware of and attentive to.
>
> The issue of conversion remains for many an issue of pain. The question of mission and conversion is highly sensitive, yet at the centre of some religious traditions' own sense of self-understanding. Making distinctions on the issues of conversion could be a topic for interreligious dialogue. Such dialogues may help clarify what conduct should be identified as proselytism, and perhaps also lead to greater understanding as to why witnessing is so highly valued within some religious traditions. In addition, Christians and Muslims, above all implicated in mission and da'wa, might through interreligious dialogue be encouraged to pursue this question through intrareligious dialogue within their own communities.
>
> How do we balance the right to individual and collective self-understanding linked to the notion of religious freedom with that of self-defence in the name of preserving often long historical religious traditions? It goes without saying that interreligious dialogue should enable us to share fully our beliefs but we must at the same time be mindful of sharing in a way that it will not offend others. There should be no coercion in religion and we need to reflect on how to refine the ethics of conversion.
>
> Many of us feel that religions should overcome the mentality of conversion as a strategic mechanism to convince people to change religion. A mentality of conversion fails to recognise the integrity of the other and the other's religion. The subject of conversion is complex. It raises tensions within and between religious communities. Violence and anger are not uncommon results. Although our religions provide tools with which to tackle this problem (e.g., "there is no compulsion in religion", Qur'an 2:256), we have to acknowledge that conversion is a reality present in our religious histories. Conversion can however not be the goal of and is opposed to interreligious dialogue. We denounce conversion by unethical practices such as using threatening behaviour, material benefits, or any forms of coercion. Conversion does have a role in religion but historically we need to recognise the instances when it has taken place under duress.
>
> To this end, we need to emphasise less the old meaning of conversion as a change of belief, and practice instead the kind of

conversion that requires a change of heart. Without this new kind of conversion process, fears will not be overcome and the building of a stronger interreligious agenda for social transformation towards the common good will remain outpaced by the growing crises of our world. A politics of conversion of the heart is a *sine qua non* for an honest dialogue that includes the development of joint cooperation for peace and justice ....[12]

Thoughts of a Convert

What is conversion? It is the transformation of one thing into another. We find the term used in many walks of life. A particular event may result in a transformation or conversion. Europeans may have to convert from Fahrenheit to Centigrade in order to understand how hot it could be in the United States. We must be familiar with currency conversion from rupees to euros. Conversion is also understood as a spiritual enlightenment causing a person to enter another religious tradition. In psychiatry it can be understood as a defense mechanism repressing emotional conflicts which are then converted into physical symptoms that have no organic basis.

It would be interesting to discuss philosophically whether the different usages would allow us to look upon the convert, be it in relation to degrees, currency, or change of religion, as basically the same as before, only seen with other glasses or from another angle. But these may be only the naive wishes of a convert that, after all, the heat remains the same, the euro the same, etc.

The convert is looked upon with suspicion by those s/he left and those he joins. There are, of course, reasons for this. The history of Jewish–Christian relations knows of many cases where converts from Judaism to Christianity became more anti-Semitic than their new-found Gentile brothers and sisters. Anton Margarita converted from Judaism to Christianity in 1522. His book "Der gantz Judisch Glaub" ("The Whole Jewish Faith") greatly influenced Martin Luther, who cites it frequently in his late tract "Von den Juden und ihren Lügen" ("Of the Jews and Their Lies"). Margarita, the son and grandson of rabbis, had a "checkered" career, having denounced his own community to the non-Jewish authorities two years before his conversion. After his conversion he became an instructor in Hebrew at the University of Vienna. At the command of Holy Roman

Emperor, Charles V, Margarita debated with Joseph (Joselmann) b. Gershom of Rosheim, a leader of the German Jewish community, at the Diet of Worms in 1530.[13]

It is true that many converts become "more Catholic than the pope," as the saying goes. I recall Catholic priests in Sweden being not very happy with converts from the Church of Sweden, who left the Swedish Church because they couldn't deal with women's ordination. My Catholic friends said; "We don't want these converts. They are more conservative than the Vatican and are actually stuck in a pre-Vatican II spirituality."

Is a convert by definition someone who will have to prove his/ her credentials by being more Catholic than the pope or by denigrating that which she left? Is a convert necessarily a renegade, someone who looks down upon that which she has left? Isn't it quite often the case that converts usually come from the periphery rather than from the center and that their conversion is not first of all a conversion from the core of a religion but a move to a core of a religion? Of course, it is difficult to put all converts together as if they were all of one mind. Not every convert hates the religious tradition she left. She is probably more at home in what she found but not necessarily in opposition to what she left.

I mentioned earlier Gregory Baum as a different kind of convert. One could add others. There are reasons to recall the impact of converts on the change that took place in the Roman Catholic Church in relation to Jews. Many Jews, converts to Christianity, brought about the conversion of the church in relation to the Jewish people. When celebrating *Nostra Aetate*, we should remember that this document would not have existed as it is today, were it not for people like John Oesterreicher and Bruno Hussar. Has not Cardinal Lustiger in many ways supported the French bishops in their work on changing the teachings of the church in relation to the Jewish people?[14] The question is whether conversion a priori suggests that accepting one religion means rejecting another.

Can one be a convert without endorsing conversion? I would like to paraphrase a Swedish stand-up comedian, who said about the prayer, "And lead us not into temptation...," "Thank you very much, you don't have to lead me, I can very well walk myself into temptation." Applying it to conversion, I don't think I need to be converted by someone, I can convert myself. What I mean to say is, the problem with conversion is the arrogance of those who think that they have a right to convert others and particularly so when they refer to UN declarations to support their actions. Claiming the right to seek out the other for conversion is nothing else but turning the other into an object for my design. It is meeting the other as an object, not interested in the encounter and where it might take us.

There will always be people who for various reasons will want to break out and look for other pastures. One cannot erect walls high enough to prevent them from leaving. The wall isn't built that will hinder their flight. It is better to let them leave without clipping their wings. We live in a world where encounters and dialogues will lead some to seek other ways than the ones just traveled. This is the right that UN declarations talk about and this is the right of and in each of our religious traditions.

Notes

1   http://www.vatican.va/holy_father/benedict_xvi/speeches/2006/
    september/documents/hf_ben-xvi_spe_20060912_university-
    regensburg_en.html.
2   Ṣaḥīḥ al-Bukhārī, hadith collection by the Persian Muslim scholar
    Muhammad al-Bukhari,
    referred to as "The Abridged Collection of Authentic Hadith with
    Connected Chains regarding Matters Pertaining to the Prophet, His
    practices and His Times," commonly known as Bukhari, Volume 4,
    Book 52, Number 260. http://www.thereligionofpeace.com/Quran/
    012-apostasy.htm.
3   Ibrahim B. Syed, "Is Killing an Apostate in the Islamic Law?" http://
    tinyurl.com/qomuy.
4   Karen Armstrong: "We cannot afford to maintain these ancient preju-
    dices against Islam," *The Guardia*, September 18, 2006. http://www.
    guardian.co.uk/comment/story/0,,1874653,00.html. Our Islamophobia
    dates back to the time of the Crusades, and is entwined with our chronic
    anti-Semitism. Some of the first Crusaders began their journey to the
    Holy Land by massacring the Jewish communities along the Rhine
    valley; the Crusaders ended their campaign in 1099 by slaughtering
    some 30,000 Muslims and Jews in Jerusalem. It is always difficult to for-
    give people we know we have wronged. Thenceforth Jews and Muslims
    became the shadow-self of Christendom, the mirror image of every-
    thing that we hoped we were not – or feared that we were.

5 Gregory Baum (ed.), *The Twentieth Century. A Theological Overview* (Maryknoll, NY and London: Orbis Books and G. Chapman, 1999).

6 The Greek word used is how Septuagint translated the Hebrew word *ger*, "sojourner" or "resident alien."

7 *Dictionary of the Ecumenical Movement* (Geneva: World Council of Churches, 1991), p. 828.

8 http://www.un.org/en/documents/udhr/.

9 *Ecumenical Considerations for Dialogue and Relations with People of Other Religions –Taking Stock of 30 Years of Dialogue and Revisiting the 1979 Guidelines* (Geneva: World Council of Churches, 2002). http://www.wcc-coe.org/wcc/what/interreligious/glines-e.html.

10 Report from the interreligious consultation "Conversion – Assessing the Reality," organized by the Pontifical Council for Interreligious Dialogue, Vatican City, and the Office on Interreligious Relations & Dialogue of the World Council of Churches, Lariano (Italy), May 12–16, 2006. http://wcc-coe.org/wcc/what/interreligious/cd47-18.html.

11 Hans Ucko (ed.), *Changing the Present, Dreaming the Future – A Critical Moment in Interreligious Dialogue* (Geneva: World Council of Churches, 2006), p. 22.

12 Ucko, *Changing the Present*, p. 81.

13 Anton Margarita, "Der gantz Judisch Glaub: Mit sampt einer grundlichen und warhafftigen anzeigunge, aller satzungen, Ceremonie[n], gebetten, heymliche und offentliche gebreuch, dere[n] sich die Juden halte[n], durch das gantz Jar, mit schonen unnd gegrundten Argumenten wider jren glauben/durch Anthonium Margaritham Hebreischen Leser, der loblichen Universitet unnd Furstlichen Statt Leyptzigk, beschriben unnd an tag gegeben" (Frankfurt am Main, 1544).

14 http://www.jcrelations.net/en/?id=2550.

Part II

Views from Five Religious Traditions

5

Buddhists on Religious Conversion
A Critical Issue

Mahinda Deegalle

> *In Asia conversion is one of the most dominant, and also politically,*
> *extremely controversial issues. Conversion has led to confrontation*
> *and serious conflict with the older religions of Asia.*
>
> Report of the Sinhala Commission[1]

Conversion to a new faith is an inevitable result of religious
encounters in the ancient as well as in the modern world. But the
issue of religious conversion has never been so acute or publicly
contested in pluralist societies as it is today. The *Report of the Sinhala
Commission* compiled in 2001 illustrates well public awareness
of religious conversion, at least in one predominantly Buddhist
country, and the extent to which religious conversion has
become a publicly debated controversial issue. The commission
was appointed to address issues related to education, employment,
cultural heritage, and the identity of the Sinhalese, and therefore
deals extensively with issues related to the arrival of Europeans,
Christian conversions,[2] and activities of NGOs. While this report is
appreciative of earlier Christian missionary work, is highly critical
of the contemporary activities of fundamentalist or Evangelical
Christian organizations.[3]

Beyond Sri Lanka, for modern Buddhists in other Asian societies,
the issue of religious conversion, to some extent, has become a

Religious Conversion: Religion Scholars Thinking Together, First Edition.
Edited by Shanta Premawardhana.
© 2015 World Council of Churches Publications. Published 2015 by John Wiley & Sons, Ltd.

serious and critical issue as well as an obstacle often preventing them from engaging and effectively encountering non-Buddhists both in public activities and interfaith forums. Thich Nhat Hanh (b.1926), the most influential Vietnamese Zen master of our time, is highly critical of the Christian missionary involvement in Vietnam during the Vietnam War.[4]

While recognizing these specific concerns of modern-day Buddhists, this chapter primarily aims to identify traditional Buddhist perspectives on religious conversion. First, it examines the terminology involved in Buddhist discussion of religious conversion, along with the perspectives that accompany such terminology. Second, with an emphasis on primary textual resources in the Pāli canon, this chapter will locate Buddhist discourses and legends that discuss religious conversions of individuals such as Upāli in historical settings in pluralistic, ancient India. This section will stress both the historical Buddha's attitudes toward religious conversion and the type of religious tolerance and coexistence that was subsequently appreciated and adopted by influential laypersons such as the Emperor Aśoka (268–239 BCE), who had been significantly shaped and nurtured by the teachings of the Buddha, as the Aśokan inscriptions strongly testify today. Third, the chapter will identify one important modern Indian Buddhist narrative on religious conversion with a focus on "mass conversions" initiated by Dr. Bhimrao Ramji Ambedkar (1891–1956), who replanted the prospect of a thriving Indian Buddhism in 1956 by filling the gap of seven centuries of Buddhist absence as a social and religious phenomenon in its birthplace in India. Finally, the discussion on modern Ambedkar Buddhism in India leads to an analysis of the legal measures initiated both in Sri Lanka and India in legislative assemblies to curb what the proponents argued as "unethical" conversions.

Buddhist Terminology on Religious Conversion

To discuss Buddhist terminology on religious conversion, I use here a specific example taken from one traditional Asian Buddhist society. In modern Sri Lanka, there are two Sinhala expressions that Sinhala people use specifically to identify two aspects of religious conversion. The expression *āgamakaṭa härīma* signifies a voluntary action where a person chooses a religious tradition of one's own preference. In this case, religious conversion depends on one's choice. Therefore, one may not see any problem in this type of conversion since it is based on free or voluntary choice. The second expression – *āgamakaṭa häravīma* – is an involuntary action where one is forced or coerced by someone or some institution to choose the newly adopted religion. This form of conversion may use force and/or the influence of some person or institution in expediting religious conversion. This type of coercive religious conversion has come under close scrutiny and severe criticism from the Buddhists of Sri Lanka in particular. When people refer to "unethical" conversions, they are talking about *āgamakaṭa häravīma*.

The terms used for signifying a "missionary" in the Buddhist tradition needs our attention as well. In contemporary Sri Lanka, Buddhists as well as non-Buddhists often identify a Buddhist "missionary" by using the compound noun *dharmadūta* (messenger of *dharma*). The second element in this compound, "*dūta*," means "messenger or envoy." In historical literature of Sri Lanka such as the *Dīpavaṃsa*, *dūta* is used to denote political emissaries or ambassadors.[5] For example, the four emissaries sent by Emperor Aśoka to Sri Lanka are identified in the *Dīpavaṃsa* using the plural form of *dūte*.[6] This compound – *dharmadūta* – that we use today to identify Buddhist missionaries cannot be found in premodern Sri Lankan Buddhist literature or ancient Pāli literature.

No doubt, it was in much later times that the non-violent "missionary" efforts of early Buddhists, found throughout Buddhist history, have been given a name with missionary connotations. Today's researchers identify a gradually emerging notion of *dhammadūta* (Skt. *Dharmadūta*). This Pāli term means a "messenger of *dhamma*" but can also be translated as a "Buddhist missionary" if one wishes to do so. It seems that it was only in later times that the Buddhist monks and nuns who traveled by land and sea to distant and remote lands to spread the teachings of the Buddha came to be identified by using a generic term, "messengers of *dhamma*" (*dhammadūta*).

In any of the early or modern Buddhist literature, it is hard to find the term *dhammadūta*. Scholars who have researched Buddhist missions have some useful information here. To our surprise, the earliest use of the Sinhala term *dharmadūtaya* (messenger of *dharma*) can be found in *An English–Sinhalese Dictionary* (1891), compiled by Baptist missionary Rev. Charles Carter[7] who arrived in Ceylon in

1853. Carter used *dharmadūtaya* to translate the English term "missionary." In Carter's explanation, there are also two other Sinhalese expressions – *dharmadūta gamana* (a journey for [spreading] the *dharma* message) and *dharmadūta pirisa* (a group of *dharma* messengers). Carter's *A Sinhalese–English Dictionary* (1924), however, does not contain any entry related to the term *dharmadūtaya*.[8]

There is a related term – *dhammadūteyya* – found in some literary works. The term *dhammadūteyya* (duty of *dhamma* messengers) is found in the *Madhuratthavilāsinī*[9] as well as in the *Saddharmaratnāvaliya*[10] with reference to "the Buddha's Great Commission." Venerable Vidurupola Piyatissa Thera's *English–Pāli Dictionary* has noted the existence of the term *dhammadūteyya* and has presented it as a synonym for the English word "mission."[11] Yet, well-known authoritative dictionaries seem to have omitted mentioning even this related term *dhammadūteyya* (duty of *dhamma* messengers). Perhaps it is due to the fact of its late origins that important projects such as the *Sinhala Dictionary*, which began in 1937, fail to mention it. Dictionaries such as *The Pali Text Society's Pali–English Dictionary* (1921–1925) and the *Encyclopaedia of Buddhism* (1961–) fail to take these terms – *dhammadūta* and *dhammadūteyya* – into account. While these two terms and expressions are helpful to delineate "unethical conversions," one should be aware that the Buddhist view of religious conversion is quite complex and varied.

The Historical Buddha's Attitudes to Religious Conversion

In general, although Buddhism has a very positive view toward religious conversion, Buddhist views on religious conversion can vary from tradition to tradition and from country to country depending on various factors such as social and political circumstances. Because the Buddha was born in an environment of religious diversity in India at a critical moment in the history of the development of a variety of religious practices other than Brahmanic religion, at the very outset of his religious mission he encountered various conversion practices. The Buddha encouraged those who encountered him in conversation to adopt an attitude of critical tolerance toward religious faiths. By recommending critical examination and being open to new potential converts, the Buddha encouraged those he met to think again before making a crucial decision such as conversion. The freedom given to the listener and the disciple to choose the religion that one wants to adopt stands out as a critical feature in the Buddha's missions and religious encounters.

B.G. Gokhale's study of the conversion narratives of early Buddhist monks and nuns in the *Thera-* and *Therīgāthās* illustrates that "43% of the conversions were due to the *impact of the personality of the Buddha*. 24% of the conversions were due to the *impact of the personality of one of the leading disciples.*"[12] There are plenty of narratives in the Pāli canon as well as in the later Buddhist literature that testify that the Buddha himself had gone out of his way in search of would-be converts[13] in order to preach to them or discipline them if they were having difficult times. Various narratives, thus, show that the Buddha himself had taken personal interest in a disciple's conversion and created initiatives to facilitate that. One advantage that the Buddha had that others often lacked was the ability to identify those who were suitable for religious conversion; he was skillful in identifying their inclinations and facilitated their understanding of *dhamma*, enabling their progress in the spiritual path.

However, an important difference that we should note here is that the Buddha himself – and most Buddhists throughout the centuries – left the final act of religious conversion as the responsibility of the person. Religious conversion, a wholesome thing for the person as well as for the community, was regarded by Buddhists as not to be messed with, intruded upon, forced into, or compelled upon.

The key to the non-violent missionary legacy of Buddhism is the historical Buddha's own words; some early interpreters of Buddhism in the West have identified the powerful words of the Buddha, which have potential missionary implications, as "The Buddha's Great Commission." The account that explains the Buddha's advocacy appears three times in the Pāli canon: (i) The (Second) Snare Sermon (*Pāsasutta*[14]) of the *Saṃyuttanikaya*, (ii) the *Mahāvagga* of the *Vinayapiṭaka*,[15] and (iii) the *Mahāpadānasutta*[16] of the *Dīghanikāya*. At the age of 35, when the Buddha gathered his first 60 disciples, he had a compassionate and powerful message for them to carve out a missionary path to Buddhism. The Buddha instructed them:

Monks, wander around for the welfare of many, for the happiness of many, out of compassion for the world, for the benefit, welfare and happiness of deities and humans. Do not two of you go the same way.

> Monks, preach the *dhamma*, which is lovely at the beginning, lovely in the middle, lovely at the end, and rich in content and form. Publicise the pure holy life, which is fully complete. There are beings with little passion in their natures who are languishing for not hearing the *dhamma*. Monks, there will be those who understand it.[17]

This maiden instruction of the Buddha to his first disciples had a significant effect in shaping his teaching, which later was identified as Buddhism and came to represent itself as a religion, which spread so fast in later centuries. No doubt, this "willingness to share the *dhamma* [teachings] with others" is the explicit missionary zeal in Buddhism. This zeal, however, quite different from other world religions, is well orchestrated in a non-violent mission purely on the basis of voluntary conversion of converts. Though this is a mission,[18] it is a different type of mission with a distinctively non-aggressive notion of religious conversion on the basis of individual choice.

The historical Buddha strongly believed that religious seekers should listen to criticisms made by fellow religious practitioners. As listeners, they should examine those criticisms and determine whether they were grounded on facts or were just mere accusations. Once, the Buddha addressed the monks highlighting the importance of paying attention to criticism and advised them not to become angry when hearing it:

> Bhikkhus, if others should speak ill of me or of the doctrine, or of the order, you should not on that account either bear malice or suffer dejection or become unhappy. If you, on that account, would be angry, and hurt, it will be a danger to yourselves. Bhikkhus, if when others should speak ill of me, or of the doctrine, or of the order, you feel angry and hurt, would you know whether what they say is appropriate or not?[19]

This toleration of criticism and the appreciation of the freedom to criticize became the cornerstone of the Buddhist attitude toward other religions in the very early stage of Buddhist missions. This attitude of critical tolerance may have facilitated interreligious communication in Indian society. Because of both this spirit of tolerance and its capacity to coexist with other systems of beliefs and practices, Buddhism spread beyond the Indian subcontinent to other parts of Asia, and in the nineteenth century it reached Europe and North America.[20]

In the course of the expansion of Buddhism to the rest of Asia, Buddhism was able to adapt to diverse cultural and socioreligious environments. Unlike many contemporary religious teachers mentioned in the Buddhist literature, it is hard to maintain that the Buddha was solely interested in converting others or expanding his following by approaching them using inappropriate means. As an illustrative example, it is worth drawing attention to a conversation that the Buddha had with a wandering ascetic named *paribbājaka* Nigrodha. As recorded in the *Udumbarika-Sīhanāda Sutta*, the Buddha said to Nigrodha:

> May be, Nigrodha, you will think: the Samana Gotama has said this from a desire to get pupils; but you are not thus to explain my words. Let him who is your teacher be your teacher still. May be, Nigrodha, you will think: Samana Gotama said this from a desire to make us secede from our rule; but you are not thus to explain my words. Let that which is your rule be your rule still ... May be, Nigrodha, you will think, the Samana Gotama has said this from a desire to detach us from such points in our doctrines as are good, reckoned as good by those in our community; but you are not thus to explain my words.[21]

The Buddha directs attention to the potential impact that a doctrine or religious teaching can have on public and private lives:

> Let those points in your doctrines which are good, reckoned to be good by those in your community, remain so still ... But O Nigrodha, there are bad things not put away, corrupting, ... and it is for the putting away of these that I teach the Norm, according to which if ye do walk, the things that corrupt shall be put away, the things that make for purity shall grow and flourish, and ye shall attain to and abide in, each one for himself even here and now, the understanding and the realization of full and abounding insight.[22]

In this conversation with Nigrodha, the Buddha gives a personal touch to the subject of religious encounters and attempts at measuring the relative merits of each religious faith, and illustrates that giving up certain things enhance human welfare. Human welfare achieved through religious practice seems to be the main focus of the Buddha's teachings. This conversation with Nigrodha suggests that the Buddha was not preoccupied with gaining followers like most of his contemporaries, or rejecting their doctrines for the sake of argument, but that he aimed to show the path to freedom. Though Nigrodha expressed great admiration for the teachings of the Buddha, neither he nor his disciples made any significant move toward religious conversion to Buddhism.

The Buddha's approach to those who encountered him in religious conversation was distinctive. On many occasions, the Buddha suggested that people whom he met retain their former teachers, rules, and good behavior. For example, the Buddha's meeting with the Jain follower Upāli was an important one. The householder Upāli lived at Nālandā and was a follower of Nigaṇṭha Nātaputta. According to the *Upāli Sutta*, after a conversation with the Buddha, Upāli decided to accept the Buddha's teachings and become a follower. When Upāli requested to be converted to Buddhism, the Buddha advised him three times to reconsider whether he should become a lay follower (*upāsaka*) of the Buddha. In the case of religious conversion, what is striking is the Buddha's advice regarding one's former teachers. To the surprise of Upāli, the Buddha advised him not to abandon support for his faith, Jainism. Seeing the Buddha's open-mindedness, Upāli was surprised and remarked:

> I, revered Sir, am even exceedingly pleased and satisfied with that which the Lord has said to me: "Now, householder, make a proper investigation. Proper investigation is right in the case of well-known men like yourself." For if I became a disciple of another sect, they would have paraded a banner all round Nālandā, saying: "The householder Upāli has joined our disciplehood."[23]

In the cases of both Nigrodha and Upāli, the Buddha set an example of how a religious teacher should approach followers of other faiths. From the Buddha's perspective, such religious encounters should aim for better understanding and realization between the participants rather than persuading someone to side with one particular religious teacher.

By defending the freedom to choose a religious order, by advising a follower of another religious faith to patronize his former order, and by tolerating the opinions of other religious faiths, the Buddha asserted the need for a tolerant attitude toward other religions. Seeing the possible dangers for coexistence and religious harmony, the Buddha opposed the ridicule of any religious teacher or doctrine and recommended harmony with other religious teachers and doctrines. The Buddha's tolerant attitudes toward other religions had significant influence on some later rulers of India. His tolerant attitude toward other religions is well reflected in some of the inscriptions of Emperor Aśoka (268–239 BCE).

Today, it is widely held that Emperor Aśoka was influenced by Buddhist teachings. In Minor Rock Edict I, Emperor Aśoka stated that after going to the *sangha* he made a lot of progress. The Nagalisagar Inscription mentions Emperor Aśoka's pilgrimage to Buddhist sites, and his visit to the Buddha's birthplace, Lumbini, is mentioned in the Rummindei Inscription. As a lay Buddhist follower, Emperor Aśoka acknowledged the importance of religious tolerance, and appreciated wholeheartedly the coexistence of all religions. He encouraged religious harmony through the promotion of mutual understanding among religious groups. As an open-minded ruler, he supported all religions, dedicating caves even to non-Buddhist ascetics.[24] He further asserted that all Brāhmins and renouncers deserved respect. The teachings and the life of the Buddha probably fostered the Emperor Aśoka's sympathetic attitude toward other religions.

The Rock Edict XII of Emperor Aśoka is a good illustration how his public policy toward religious faiths was influenced by Buddhist attitudes:

> One should not honour only one's own religion and condemn the religions of others, but one should honour others' religions for this or that reason. So doing, one helps one's own religion to grow and renders service to the religions of others too. In acting otherwise one digs the grave of one's own religion and also does harm to other religions. Whosoever honours his [her] own religion and condemns other religions, does so indeed through devotion to his own religion, thinking "I will glorify my own religion." But on the contrary, in so doing he injures his own religion more gravely. So concord is good: Let all listen, and be willing to listen to the doctrines professed by others.[25]

From the Buddhist point of view, if a Buddhist disparages or discriminates against a follower of another religion, he/she would be violating the fundamental principles of Buddhism.

In terms of religious conversion, the Buddha's critical attitude to religions is also important. In the midst of the cultural and religious pluralism of India, the Buddha taught in a pragmatic and rational way by appealing to reason. In the *Kālāma Sutta*, the Buddha strongly criticized traditional means of knowledge as unsatisfactory and emphasized the importance of rational understanding, critical examination, and personal verification. The Buddha encouraged seekers of truth to test and verify any religious doctrine by means of direct personal experience (*pratyaksa*) and granted immense freedom to religious seekers. The Buddha advised: "O Kālāmas, you have a right to doubt or feel uncertain for you have raised a doubt in a situation in which you ought to suspend your judgement."[26] The Buddha's criterion for choosing a religious path was one's own experience and critical judgment. The Buddha rejected the validity of 10 traditional means of knowledge[27] by privileging the practitioner's experience:

> Come now, Kālāmas, do not accept anything on the grounds of revelation, tradition, or hearsay. Do not accept these things because they are mentioned in the collections of the scriptures … But, O Kālāmas, when you know for yourselves that certain doctrines are unwholesome [*akusala*], wrong [*sāvajjā*], and bad, then give them up … and when you know for yourselves that certain doctrines are wholesome [*kusala*] and good, then accept them and follow them.[28]

With reflections on problematic issues of pluralism, I can note here that the *Kālāma Sutta* presents a common situation that a seeker of truth faces in any religiously pluralistic society. An attitude similar to that of Kālāmas can be found among people in any pluralistic society today, in particular where religious persuasion is used for religious conversion while accepting that different religions might preach different ways to truth and salvation. In a complex and diverse environment, it is rather difficult to find and choose one's own path. The advice of the Buddha to Kālāmas to verify any religious opinion according to one's own personal experience becomes very meaningful in this context.

The *Alagaddūpama Sutta*[29] is an important early Buddhist scripture that deals with the emotional involvement or attachment that religious followers develop toward their traditions. In this *sutta*, the Buddha compared his teachings (*dhamma*) to a raft, which served only for crossing a stream; although his teaching helped one to cross over the stream of *saṃsāra* (the cycle of births and deaths), one should not identify with the teaching (*dhamma*) or become emotionally involved with it. The Buddha compared misuses of religion to "catching a snake by the tail."[30] Both educated and uneducated people misuse religion either for the purpose of disparaging others' religion or for defending their own. Such personal attachments and inclinations to favor certain views generate negative qualities such as hatred. Since such favoritism hinders spiritual progress and prevents cultural and religious pluralism by closing doors to diversity, Buddhism attempts to awaken wisdom in human beings and recommends an attitude of detachment even toward Buddhist teachings. This attitude of detachment helps Buddhists live in a pluralistic society with tolerance for other religions; their beliefs and practices become neither obstacles to cultural and religious pluralism nor potential threats to diverse faiths.

Mass Buddhist Conversions: The Case of Dalits

On October 14, 1956, in a public ceremony held in Nagpur, India, massive conversions of Dalits (traditionally known as "untouchables" within the caste structure, or "scheduled caste" in the Constitution of India) to Buddhism took place. It was the 2500th year of Buddha Jayanti. Two months before his death, Dr. Bhimrao Ramji Ambedkar (1891–1956), who was a Dalit himself and the leader of Indian Dalits, chose Buddhism as his religion of choice after years of deliberation. Ambedkar's conversion to Buddhism paved the way for millions of Dalits to choose Buddhism as their religion. The raison d'etre of mass conversions for Dalits is basically a desire to regain their humanity and claim a sense of dignity, which was denied to them in the Hindu caste structure.[31]

In the case of Ambedkar, the embracing of Buddhism took place as a result of certain practical concerns in his own social background. Ambedkar himself was born into the Mahar caste in Maharashtra, the area of geographical concentration of Dalit Buddhists. His low social location, according to religious canons of the day, was unsatisfactory and Ambedkar wanted to find self-respect and dignity for his people by abandoning the oppressive Hindu caste ideology.

Writing a book entitled *The Untouchables*[32] in 1948, Ambedkar advanced an explanation claiming that the untouchables of India were descendants of the few Buddhists who survived when Buddhism was wiped out from India. From this point of view, the untouchables converting back to Buddhism was a return to the original religion of the untouchables.

Due to Muslim aggression and attacks of the Turk Mohammad Ghuri on prominent Buddhist universities such as Nālandā (1197 CE) and the gradual assimilation of Buddhism into Hinduism, Buddhism as a social, philosophical, intellectual, and cultural movement disappeared from India by the end of the twelfth century. Now, as a result of the mass conversions organized by Dalits, once again Buddhism is becoming visible in the religious landscape of India. The 1951 Census estimated the total number of Buddhists in India to be 180,823. By the time of 1991 Census, the number of Buddhists had grown to 6,431,900. The sudden increase in the number of Buddhists in the birthplace of Buddhism is increasingly due to the influence of Dr. Ambedkar's conversion. The 50th anniversary of Dr. Ambedkar's death (2006) was an important moment for massive conversions to Buddhism.

Conversions of untouchables to Buddhism still pose a threat to the caste-based social order of India. Therefore, as a response to untouchable conversions, the Bhāratiya Janatā Party (BJP) amended[33] its 2003 anti-conversion bill, The Gujarat Freedom of Religion (Amendment) Bill 2006, to enable "conversions between different sects of the same faith as well as between Hinduism, Buddhism and Jainism."[34] The amendment redefined "conversion" as meaning "to make one person renounce one religion and adopt another; but does not include one who renounces one denomination and adopts another denomination of the same religion."[35] This classification of Buddhism and Jainism as branches of Hinduism makes conversion from Hinduism to Buddhism legal while proscribing conversions to Christianity and Islam illegal.

Recent Buddhist Responses to Religious Conversions

The year 2004 was a significant milestone with regard to understanding recent Buddhist responses to religious conversions. That year saw a heightened awareness among Buddhists in Sri Lanka regarding the issue of religious conversion. Some activist Buddhist monks who were affiliated with a newly established organization named Jātika Saṅgha Sammēlanaya (National Saṅgha Assembly) became ardent protesters who drew attention to the issue of "unethical" conversion.[36] Their political agenda, which eventually led some Buddhist monks to be elected as members of the Sri Lankan parliament, was heavily influenced by the notion of "unethical" conversion. The *Report of the Sinhala Commission* has explained what an "unethical" religious conversion might entail from a Buddhist perspective: "This sudden rise in Evangelical activity in Sri Lanka has intrigued many people ... These new Evangelists are well provided with foreign money and are using this money to buy up the poorer disadvantaged villagers ... They are in fact engaged in buying new converts, saving souls, and making Christianity another business."[37] On the basis of this document, a definition of "unethical conversion" can be advanced as *using material support and providing tangible and intangible resources for vulnerable and disadvantaged social groups in an exploited, abusive and degraded manner for the sake of intensifying religious recruitment from another religion or religious denomination.*

Concentrated research on the issue of unethical religious conversion in Sri Lanka can illustrate further. Even before the public articulations of unethical conversions by the monks of the Jātika Saṅgha Sammēlanaya, the *Report of the Sinhala Commission* (2001) had already recommended to the Sri Lankan Government to: "[M]onitor the activities and the foreign funds used by evangelical groups engaged in unethical conversions to various Christian creeds and put a stop to such illegal activities by passing the necessary legislation."[38]

Over a couple of years, Jātika Saṅgha Sammēlanaya successfully, however, developed very well articulated arguments for a political platform to raise issues related to unethical religious conversions. The public awareness on unethical conversions generated by these monks partly led to the formation of "Buddhist monk only political party," Jātika Hela Urumaya (National Sinhala Heritage),[39] in mid-February 2004, a few weeks before the general election held in April 2004. They successfully demonstrated in public both in emotional tones and in legislative forms the need to take action against unethical religious conversions.

The impact of the Jātika Hela Urumaya's political agenda against unethical religious conversion is clearly visible in the birth of two parliamentary bills presented to the Sri Lankan parliament in 2004 for approval. These legislative measures also reflect the wider political and interreligious climate in South Asia in response to the wide spread of Evangelical Christianity and the immediate influence of the Anti-Conversion Ordinance of Tamil Nadu State passed on October 5, 2002, which made converting "someone to another religion through force, fraud or allurement" illegal.[40]

Responding to public Buddhist sentiments raised over religious conversions carried out primarily by some recently arrived Protestant Evangelical groups, two draft parliamentary bills were drafted in 2004. The Parliamentary Select Committee again presented to parliament the anti-conversion draft bill on January 6, 2009.[41] Due to strong pressure from national and international church bodies,[42] international aiding agencies, human right activist groups,[43] and most recently by the United States Congress,[44] these bills are still waiting in draft forms seeking parliamentary approval; but they point to critical concerns about interreligious dialogue and harmonious coexistence.

On May 6, 2005, the Jātika Hela Urumaya political party introduced its anti-conversion bill to the Parliament. It recommended punishment of up to five years' imprisonment for the crime of "attempted conversion."[45]

On June 27, 2005, the government of Sri Lanka published its anti-conversion bill entitled: *Freedom of Religion: A Bill.*[46] Any action or speech that "indirectly influences" a person to convert from one religion to another could result in fines or up to seven years' imprisonment. The bill defines unethical conversion as follows:

> "Unethical" means the use of any procedure contrary to accepted norms of ethics that may be used to propagate a religion." "Conversion to another religion" means any direct or indirect action or behaviour designed to cause a person to embrace a religion or religious practice, or religious philosophy to which he does not subscribe or to attempt to cause a person to do so.
>
> No person shall convert or attempt to convert another person to another religion, and no person shall provide assistance or encouragement towards conversion to another religion.

Prior to these two bills, even in 2001, the *Report of the Sinhala Commission* had recommended criminal punishment for unethical conversion.[47]

As the All Ceylon Buddhist Congress report suggests, thorny issues arise when business investment visas are used for setting up educational establishments.[48] These educational institutions have been subsequently used for the propagation of religion. The anti-conversion bill of the government of Sri Lanka aims to address these issues and rectify the situation.[49] Buddhist perceptions of religious conversion now have directed attention to Buddhist institutions.

The most recent development and Buddhist response to the issue of unethical conversion is the All Ceylon Buddhist Congress Commission Report[50] published in 2009.[51] In June 2006, the All Ceylon Buddhist Congress, which was founded in Colombo in 1918 by leading Buddhist elites, appointed a nine-member commission to examine the ways in which Buddhists are converted to other religious faiths using unethical and cunning ways.[52] Over four decades ago, in 1956, when the Sri Lankan state was emerging from colonialism, the All Ceylon Buddhist Congress also published *Buddhist Commission Report*[53] evaluating the status of Buddhism in Sri Lanka under colonial governments.

With a focus on Buddhist teachings and practices, this chapter has presented a broad socioreligious context in order to understand today's most critical interreligious issue of religious conversion. By presenting a close analysis of Buddhist scriptural foundations and modern narratives, this chapter has illustrated a non-intrusive missionary zeal at work in the Buddhist tradition while it maintains a very positive and proactive standpoint toward religious conversions, simultaneously safeguarding individual freedom to choose. Though there are debates in contemporary Buddhist communities about "unethical" conversions and resulting political demands for legislative measures to curb them, it must be stated explicitly here that Buddhism is not against voluntary religious conversion. When religious conversion is accompanied by the use of force or coercive means – for example, providing material benefits to new converts – and when vulnerable groups such as the sick and children are involved in the conversion process, along with other co-religionists such as Hindus, Buddhists have raised "ethical" issues – rightly, as responsible citizens who care about their communities and are concerned with the flight of their members who are constantly subjected to forced religious conversion. It cannot be stated explicitly, however, that Buddhism operates as an "evangelizing" missionary religion in the same way that Christian and Islamic traditions have historically functioned as missionary religions. Though these three world religions – Buddhism, Christianity, and Islam – share some superficial similarities in terms of their geographical spread from the land of their births to distant, remote places in the globe, and subsequently bear some trans-local qualities as global religions, the missionary strategies that they use to recruit new members are not the same and motivations behind such religious conversions also significantly differ. In Buddhist traditions, by far the most democratic and voluntary mechanisms operate in the religious conversion process as well as in the methods adopted in recruiting new members.

Notes

1 *Report of the Sinhala Commission: Part II* (Colombo: The National Joint Committee, 2001), p. 285.
2 Specific references to Christianity and religious conversions can be found in several places in the *Report of the Sinhala Commission: Part II*, pp. 6–10, 30–41, 70–72, 97–131, 137–140, 147–197, 284–294, 303.
3 *Report: Part II*, pp. 97–113.
4 Thich Nhat Hanh, *Vietnam: Lotus in a Sea of Fire* (New York: Hill and Wang, 1967), p. 28.
5 See the *Cūlavaṃsa* (100: 112) for a reference to "royal envoys." Wilhelm Geiger and C. Mabel Rickmers (trans.), *Cūlavaṃsa: Being the More Recent Part of the Mahāvaṃsa* (London: The Pali Text Society, 1929), p. 283. This very common term is also used to identify the leaders of the fifteenth-century Burmese embassy to Sri Lanka recorded in the Kalyāṇi Inscription.
6 *"caturo dūte"* (11:29) in Herman Oldenberg (ed.), *The Dīpavaṃsa: An Ancient Buddhist Historical Record* (London: Williams and Norgate, 1879), p. 61.
7 Charles Carter, *An English–Sinhalese Dictionary* (Colombo: M.D. Gunasena & Co., Ltd, 1965 [1891]), p. 300.
8 Charles Carter, *A Sinhalese–English Dictionary* (1924).
9 The exact wording is: *"karontā dhammadūteyyaṃ …"* I.B. Horner (ed.), *Madhuratthavilāsinī nāma Buddhavaṃsaṭṭhakathā of Bhadantācariya Buddhadatta Mahāthera* (London: PTS, 1978), p. 19.
10 The thirteenth-century Sinhala text, Dharmasēna Thera's *Saddharmaratnāvaliya* (Colombo, Sri Lanka Oriental Studies Society, 1985), records: *"vidhātuṃ dhammadūteyyam vissajjesi tahiṃ tahiṃ,"* p. 22.
11 Venerable Vidurupola Piyatissa, *The English–Pali Dictionary* (Colombo: The Colombo Apothecaries' Company, Ltd., 1949), p. 411.
12 Quoted in Torkel Brekke, "Conversion in Buddhism?" in R. Robinson and S. Clarke (eds.), *Religious Conversion in India: Modes, Motivations, and Meanings* (New Delhi: Oxford University Press, 2003), p. 188.
13 The most popular Buddhist narrative on religious conversion, in which the Buddha himself had taken a personal interest in the

conversion and retransformation of the murderer Angulimāla (the one who wears a necklace of fingers) to his former, pure, non-harming Ahiṃsaka (the one who does not harm) status. For a detailed textual analysis of this religious conversion narrative, see Mahinda Deegalle, *Popularizing Buddhism* (Albany, NY: State University of New York Press, 2006), pp. 86–92.

14 S.I.106.
15 *Vinaya* I.21.
16 D.II.6–54.
17 *Vinaya* I.21.
18 For an extensive study of Buddhist missions, see and Egil Lothe, "Mission in Theravada Buddhism," MA Thesis, University of Oslo, 1986.
19 The *Dīghanikāya* I.2–3.
20 The formal introduction of Buddhism to the United States and the West can be traced to the World's Parliament of Religions held in Chicago in 1893. For a recent evaluation of the World's Parliament of Religions in general, see Eric J. Ziolkowski (ed.), *A Museum of Faiths: Histories and Legacies of the 1893 World's Parliament of Religions* (Atlanta, GA: Scholars Press, 1993). For a specific evaluation of Dharmapāla's role in it, see Mahinda Deegalle, "Dharmapala and the World's Parliament of Religions in Chicago," World Fellowship of Buddhists Review 32.4 (1995): 54–58.
21 *The Dialogues of the Buddha* III.51–52.
22 *The Dialogues of the Buddha* III.51–52.
23 The *Middle Length Sayings*, trans. I.B. Horner (London: PTS, 1954), II.44.
24 Barabara Inscription; Richard F. Gombrich, *Theravada Buddhism* (London: Routledge and Kegan Paul, 1988), p. 130.
25 Quoted in Walpola Rahula's *What the Buddha Taught* (New York: Grove Press, 1974), p. 4.
26 The *Aṅguttaranikāya*, ed. Richard Morris (London: PTS, 1885), I.189; K.N. Jayatilleke, *The Buddhist Attitude to Other Religions* (Kandy: Buddhist Publication Society, 1975), p. 18.
27 See K.N. Jayatilleke, *Early Buddhist Theory of Knowledge* (London: George Allen & Unwin, 1963), p. 175.
28 Morris, *Aṅguttaranikāya*, I.189; Jayatilleke, *Buddhist Attitude*, p. 18.
29 *Parable of the Snake*, trans. Jotiya Dhirasekera (Colombo: The Ministry of Cultural Affairs, 1983), p. 9.
30 The *Majjhimanikāya*, ed. V. Trenckner (London: PTS, 1888), I.133. *Parable of the Snake*, trans. Jotiya Dhirasekera, p. 9.
31 "'Untouchables': Undergo Mass Conversion to Buddhism," October 13, 2006. http://www.buzzle.com/articles/112259.html.
32 B.R. Ambedkar, *The Untouchables: Who Were They and Why They Became Untouchables* (New Delhi: Amrit Book Co., 1948).

33 "'Untouchables': Undergo Mass Conversion to Buddhism"; "Written Evidence Submitted by Christian Solidarity Worldwide," October 2006. http://www.parliament.the-stationery-office.co.uk/pa/cm200607/cmselect/cmfaff/55/55we12.htm.

34 "Gujarat Anti-Conversion Amendment," 20 September 2006. http://christianpersecutionindia.blogspot.com/2006_09_01_archive.html.

35 "Gujarat Anti-Conversion Amendment."

36 Mahinda Deegalle, "Buddhist Ethics in Politics of Religious Conversion," *International Research Seminar on Buddhism: Truthful Knowledge and Quality of Life* (Ayutthaya, Thailand: Buddhist Research Institute, Mahachulalongkornrajavidyalaya University, 2009), pp. 153–161; Mahinda Deegalle, "Contested Religious Conversions of Buddhists in Sri Lanka and India," in Lalji Shravak and Charles Willemen (eds.), *Dharmapravicaya: Aspects of Buddhist Studies* (Delhi: Buddhist World Press, 2012), pp. 71–101.

37 *Report: Part II*, pp. 116–117.

38 *Report: Part II*, p. 303.

39 For a detailed treatment of Jātika Hela Urumaya, see Mahinda Deegalle,"JHU Politics for Peace and a Righteous State,"in Mahinda Deegalle (ed.), *Buddhism, Conflict and Violence in Modern Sri Lanka* (London and New York: Routledge, 2006), pp. 233–254.

40 "Anti-Conversion Ordinance Passed in Tamil Nadu, India." http://www.press-release-writing.com/distribution1/gospelasia-pr5.htm.

41 "Anti Conversion Draft Bill Presented to the Parliament." http://www.archdioceseofcolombo.com/DraftBill_2009.01.06S.php.

42 "Christians Protest Anti-Conversion Bill," January 29, 2009, http://www.persecution.org/suffering/newssummpopup.php?newscode=9399; "Sri Lanka Attempts to Ease Fears over Anti-Conversion Bill," http://www.lankalibrary.com/phpBB/viewtopic.php?f=23&t=221; "USCIRF Expresses Concern Over Sri Lanka's Forced Conversion Bill," *Christian Post*, July 15, 2005, http://www.wwrn.org/article.php?idd=17891&sec=59&con=29.

43 For example, the Sri Lankan ambassador received a letter signed by 20 human rights activists representing Jewish, Muslim, Christian, Baha'i, and interfaith organizations in Feburuary 2009, "U.S. Congress Pressures Sri Lanka on Anti-Conversion Law," February 5, 2009, http://www.archdioceseofcolombo.com/USonAntiConBill_05.02.2009.php.

44 In February 2009, the Sri Lankan ambassador in Washington, DC received a letter signed by 15 congressmen requesting shelving the anti-conversion bill, "U.S. Congress Pressures Sri Lanka on Anti-Conversion Law," February 5, 2009, http://www.archdioceseofcolombo.com/USonAntiConBill_05.02.2009.php.

45 "(3a) Whoever converts any person from one religion to another either by performing any ceremony by himself for such conversion as a facilitator or by taking part directly or indirectly in such ceremony shall, within such period as may be prescribed by the Minister, send in an intimation to that effect to the Divisional Secretary of the area ..."
"(4b) Whoever fails, without sufficient cause, to comply with the provisions of section 3 (a) and (b) above shall on conviction before a Magistrate be punished with imprisonment for a term not exceeding five years or with a fine, not exceeding rupees one hundred and fifty thousand."

46 *The Gazette of the Socialist Republic of Sri Lanka*, Part II of June 24, 2005 Supplement (issued on 27.06.2005) *Freedom of Religion: A Bill.*

47 *Report: Part II*, pp. 151–152.

48 Mahinda Deegalle, "Buddhist Protests over Non-Buddhist Evangelism: All Ceylon Buddhist Congress Commission Report on 'Unethical' Conversion," International Journal of Buddhist Thought & Culture 22 (2014), 65–86.

49 Ibid.

50 *Śrī Laṅkāvē bauddhayin sadācāra virōdhi hā kūṭa upakkrama mangin anyāgamvalaṭa harava gänīma pilinbandava pariksā kara balā vārtā kirīma sandahā pat karamu läbū komisan sabhā vārtāva 2552/2009* [Report of the Commission Appointed to Examine and Report on the Conversion of Sri Lankan Buddhists to Other Religions by Employing Unethical and Crafty Means (Colombo: All Ceylon Buddhist Congress, 2009), xiv+303, plus an appendix pp. i–cxvi.

51 Janaka Perera, "Launching Report on Unethical Conversions," *Asian Tribune*, January 6, 2009, http://www.asiantribune.com/?q=node/15031. See also "Buddhist Commission on Unethical Conversions: Pressurizing the Government to Pass the Anti-Conversion Bill," January 25, 2009, http://www.archdioceseofcolombo.com/AntiConv Commiss_25.01.2009.php.

52 Members of the commission are (i) Sarath Gunatilaka (former High Court Judge?), (ii) Ariyaratna Lankachandra (former Director of Education), (iii) Pannadas Gardiye Punchiheva (former civil servant), (iv) Gamini Gunawardhana (former senior assistant Chief of Police), (v) Disanayaka Mudiyanselage Jayatilaka Disanayaka (former Director of Education), (vi) Somaratna Kariyavasam (former commissioner of Buddhist Affairs), (vii) Budagoda Arachige Don Alfred Vijewardhana (former assistant Chief of Police), (viii) Katriaracchige Srimati Citra Vijesekara (Sri Lanka Educational Administrative Service), and (ix) Karuna de Silva. The original commission members were modified on October 8 since the last member, Ms. Karuna de Silva, was planning to go abroad. Three new members were added: Vatutantrige Hubert de

Alwis (former commissioner of Surabadu), Samaratunga Devage Chandradasa (former Sri Lanka Civil Service), and Sinnakarupan Suppayiya Rajalingam (Buddhist social worker). Finally, the commission included one female and one Tamil member.

53 The commission was appointed on April 2, 1954 and the *Buddhist Commission Report* (Colombo: All Ceylon Buddhist Congress, 1956) was published on February 4, 1956. A special reprint of the report was brought out in 2006 (Colombo: Visidunu Prakasakayo) on the occasion of 2550 Buddha Jayanti.

Further Reading

Brekke, Torkel. "Conversion in Buddhism?" In *Religious Conversion in India: Modes, Motivations, and Meanings,* edited by Rowena Robinson and Sathinathan Clarke. Oxford and New York: Oxford University Press, 2003, pp. 181–191.

Deegalle, Mahinda. "Buddhist Ethics in Politics of Religious Conversion." *International Research Seminar on Buddhism: Truthful Knowledge and Quality of Life,* Buddhist Research Institute, Mahachulalongkornrajavidyalaya University, Ayutthaya, Thailand, 2009, pp. 153–161.

6

A Christian Perspective on Conversion

Jay T. Rock

"Conversion" in Christian contexts refers most importantly to the Christian's life of faith. The word speaks of a longed-for change of heart or inner transformation, and an external change of loyalty and belonging usually expressed in communal forms. But "conversion" is also an issue in the practice of Christian evangelization, both in regard to the many difficult problems that create tension and conflict when people change from the practice of one religious tradition to another, and in relation to the approach and intentions of evangelists.

I write as one who is himself a convert to the Christian way of life, to which I came as an adult out of a secular North American background, the child of parents who no longer practiced the different religious traditions into which they were born. Because of this, I have long been aware that many Christians and Christian communities – though by no means all – view people of other religions and cultures as somehow different in kind, or less in quality, than they themselves. Some Christians carry subtle prejudices against, and misinformed stereotypes of, their non-Christian neighbors. These attitudes and ideas infect Christian thinking and affect the practice of evangelization among people of other religious traditions.

Though I begin and end this chapter with explorations of Christian self-understanding and practice, for which the idea of "conversion" has its greatest relevance for Christian life, the larger part of the

Religious Conversion: Religion Scholars Thinking Together, First Edition.
Edited by Shanta Premawardhana.
© 2015 World Council of Churches Publications. Published 2015 by John Wiley & Sons, Ltd.

chapter deals with Christian evangelization. Too many Christians assert, wrongly, that conversion is the proper aim of evangelism. To the extent that it is true that Christians aim to convert people at any cost, Christian evangelism is degraded, and deeper, more significant commitments of Christian faith are trammeled.

A Religion of Converts

Many members of the Christian community have begun their journey into Christianity from another faith, or from none; and we commonly speak of this group of people as "converts." By this language we are referring both to the process of change that such a person experiences as she embraces Christ and enters the Christian community, and also to a category of believers – that is, those who entered from another realm or way of thinking into the Christian way. It is not unusual to hear Christians in any part of the world identify into what "generation" they fall since one of their forbears became a follower of Christ.

Even though many Christians have grown up completely within the religion, with little or no understanding of life apart from Christian community, it is nevertheless accurate to describe Christianity as a religion of converts. This is reflected in the prominence the tradition gives to Abraham, as one willing to leave all behind to follow God's command; to Noah, the one who chose righteousness in an evil age; to Ruth, who yearned to join God's people; and to the many stories of Jesus welcoming outcasts of various sorts into fellowship and the work of realizing God's kingdom. From its earliest days, Christianity has asserted that no ethnic, national, gender, or linguistic factors confer or deny membership to anyone in the community of God's people. For Christians, all that separates human beings from God is removed in and through Jesus. Entry into the community, even for those who have grown up within the tradition, depends on a willing embrace of Jesus as one's own Lord, and of the practices and disciplines of the community as one's own.

The "membership ritual" for the Christian community is the sacrament of baptism. In baptism, Christians understand that one dies to the past, and enters into the new life of Jesus, the Christ, marked as one of God's own. We who are Christians affirm in the sacrament that those becoming a part of the community, whether as infants or adults, die a death like his – that is, embrace with Jesus a life given over fully to God, even to the point of death – and enter into resurrection life with him. Baptism is the point of leaving the past behind, including one's religious past, and allowing oneself to become a new creation.

Being a Christian involves, then, giving allegiance to God rather than to any other power. It involves a transfer of loyalties – shifting one's adherence away from "Caesar," in whatever form that political or social power may take, away from Mammon, and away from idols. In addition, becoming a Christian means changing the community within whose norms one is living, in order to embrace and take part in the Christian community and its life. We are a community whose people-hood is constituted by our common loyalty to Jesus. We take our place within that community as God's people, who together engage in the ongoing effort to hear what God is saying in the scriptures and to live in the way of Jesus. These changes are all part of "conversion" to Christ.

It is hard to overestimate this understanding of "conversion" for the Christian community. Conversion in this sense is a part of our identity: we are a community of people who understand ourselves to have been changed in relation to God, and to be on a journey of further transformation as people of faith.

Of course, since Christians are so diverse, it is no surprise that "conversion" is experienced in many different ways. Some Christians know it through direct experience of the Holy Spirit, as do our Pentecostal sisters and brothers. Some speak of an encounter of a life-changing or "saving" kind, with Jesus himself. This encounter is experienced by some as a sudden and dramatic event, but by others as a very slow process. Others find that their practice of Christian discipleship – that is, their experience and participation in Christian community and in following the way of Jesus – changes them in a deep way. (This is how I talk about my own experience of "conversion.") Still other Christians think of their conversion more along the lines of Paul's injunction in Romans (12:2): "Do not be conformed to this world, but be transformed by the renewing of your minds, so that you may discern what is the will of God – what is good and acceptable and perfect." Common to all of these descriptions of "conversion" is some experience in one's life of the transforming power of God.

85

Jay T. Rock

Evangelism and Conversion

This experience of conversion, in its various forms, together with the injunctions of the gospels and apostolic letters of Scripture, have led Christians in many times and places to share the good news of Jesus. To paraphrase a popular song from Christian youth camps in North America, once you have experienced new freedom, acceptance, and transformation in Christ, "you want to pass it on." Joy overflows and invites sharing. Evangelism, for Christians, is a sharing of hope, and a part of a believer's calling. With the experience of conversion so much at the heart of Christian self-understanding, sharing the faith often takes on a particular urgency.

Evangelization takes many shapes. How individuals and groups share the good news differs, depending on their theological understanding, primary biblical referents, and on how they think about the many peoples and cultures of the world. Especially within Protestant traditions in the West, most forms of evangelism involve a kind of fervor or enthusiasm, which makes it important that the methods and thinking embodied in how evangelism is done be carefully and regularly examined. In sharing the gospel, Christians must ensure that the attitudes and practices involved cause no harm to others, but are shaped by respect for, and honoring of, them.

Unfortunately, Christian mission history offers many examples of evangelization carried out with little genuine regard for the people "targeted," and in ways that have been very aggressive toward them. In case after case, sharing of "good news" has been done disrespectfully, and in ways that have been damaging to the people on the receiving end.

Christian missions have often arrived in specific countries along with commercial or colonial ventures, the goals of the missionaries intertwined with the goals of those trying to control trade or access to local resources and labor. Thus, evangelism has often been an accompaniment to the imposition of outside power in the contexts in which people live. As a result, too often evangelists have offered their good news in situations marked by tensions, unrest, the fracturing of local cultures and authority structures, etc. At the worst, Christians have offered education and evangelization as a kind of ameliorating factor to people being enslaved, without awareness of their resulting complicity in the process of enslavement. People in poverty or on the margins of their society have embraced conversion to Christianity in some cases in order to receive food, or because they perceived that this community gave them access to economic and educational advantages that they would otherwise not have. In such cases religious conversion becomes entangled in the reshaping of social structures, and with seeking a better life for self and children. Even the delivery of outside aid to people displaced by natural or man-made disaster is used as an opportunity for evangelization, one in which an invitation to become a Christian cannot be received on its own terms because of the destruction and social disequilibium of the situation.

In addition, many traditional forms of mission and evangelism have devalued the spiritual experience and ways of life of their audience. Evangelists and mission workers have focused narrowly on belief in Christ, seeking conversion of heart and mind to Christ, acceptance of the Jesus of the gospels, and participation in the believing and worshiping Christian community. Often, such presentations of what is needed to become a Christian have been accompanied by a demand that new believers forsake all that is contrary to, or different from, Christian faith as the evangelizers understand it (that is, the "old," "sinful" indigenous forms of life must be left behind).

Those who have been violated by evangelization of this kind, as well as those who have seen and heard their cultures and religions stigmatized, belittled, or undermined by Christian missionaries have naturally reacted negatively, and challenged the mission enterprise. Others, including those who became part of the Christian community in response to Christian mission, have raised serious questions about its approaches.

Traditional summaries of the call to evangelize, and how to do so, leave many questions unanswered. For example, look at the thoughtful presentation in the Book of Order of my own Presbyterian Church (USA):

a. *The Church is called to tell the good news of salvation by the grace of God through faith in Jesus Christ as the only Savior and Lord, proclaiming in Word and Sacrament that*
   1. *the new age has dawned.*
   2. *God who creates life, frees those in bondage, forgives sin, reconciles brokenness, makes all things new, is still at work in the world.*

b. *The Church is called to present the claims of Jesus Christ, leading persons to repentance, acceptance of him as Savior and Lord, and new life as his disciples.*
c. *The Church is called to be Christ's faithful evangelist*
    1. *going into the world, making disciples of all nations, baptizing them in the name of the Father and of the Son and of the Holy Spirit, teaching them to observe all he has commanded;*
    2. *demonstrating by the love of its members for one another and by the quality of its common life the new reality in Christ; sharing in worship, fellowship, and nurture, practicing a deepened life of prayer and service under the guidance of the Holy spirit;*
    3. *participating in God's activity in the world through its life for others by*
        i. *healing and reconciling and binding up wounds,*
        ii. *ministering to the needs of the poor, the sick, the lonely, and the powerless,*
        iii. *engaging in the struggle to free people from sin, fear, oppression, hunger, and injustice,*
        iv. *giving itself and its substance to the service of those who suffer,*
        v. *sharing with Christ in the establishing of his just, peaceable, and loving rule in the world.*

The Church is called to undertake this mission even at the risk of losing its life, trusting in God alone as the author and giver of life, sharing the gospel, and doing those deeds in the world that point beyond themselves to the new reality in Christ.[1]

This definition tells us that our task in evangelization is to be witnesses, teachers, practitioners, givers, those who engage in the struggles of life, and extend the invitation to become disciples to all others among whom we live. The description is theological, and specifies the content of the message to be shared in terms that refer to Jesus' announcement, living demonstration, and invitation to take part in establishing the Reign of God in the world. It refers specifically to Matthew 28:18–20: "And Jesus came and said to them, 'All authority in heaven and on earth has been given to me. Go therefore and make disciples of all nations, baptizing them in the name of the Father and of the Son and of the Holy Spirit, and teaching them to obey everything that I have commanded you.'" However, the summary does not offer much guidance regarding the methods and practices to be used, nor does it reflect on differences in contexts for evangelism. And it does not have a word to say about whether, and how, God might already be present in the lives of those among whom one is to be "Christ's faithful evangelist."

A Reshaping of Evangelism

It is clear that more significant thinking has long been needed regarding the issues, biblical roots, and theology that should shape, or reshape Christian mission, and, in particular, the practice of evangelization.[2]

One strand of the ongoing conversation among (primarily) Protestant, or Evangelical, Christians has focused on the purpose of sharing the good news, and in particular on a theological re-evaluation of God's relation to mission. In the 1930s, for example, many Presbyterian mission leaders, and others, sought to shape a mission enterprise that was less focused upon salvation from the world and more committed to transformation of the world.[3] A new approach was emerging, that lifted up not the mission of the church, but the church's participation in God's mission. In this view, mission is understood as being derived from the very nature of God. Biblical history is viewed as the story of the unfolding of God's saving purpose, God's plan to bless all of the peoples of the earth through his Son. A primary biblical reference here, rather than the so-called "Great Commission" of Matthew 28, is Ephesians 1:8b–10: "With all wisdom and insight he has made known to us the mystery of his will, according to his good pleasure set forth in Christ, as a plan for the fullness of time, to gather up all things in him, things in heaven and things on earth." The focus of the church's sharing of the gospel is, in this understanding, on the kingdom of God, not the church. What God is doing in the world determines what the church must do. The practice of mission, following this line of thinking, is based not on how to "take" the gospel to the world, nor how to make converts, but how to discern where God is already at work and to join God there. The mission is God's mission (*Missio Dei*), and the church is called to join in it.

A second line of thinking has lifted up the practice of Jesus himself as the guide for evangelization. The text which in many circles has now replaced Matthew 28 as a formative mission text is John

20:21, "As the Father has sent me, so I send you." Jesus not only sends his followers into the world, but teaches them, through the demonstration of his own ministry, the manner by which they should go.

> Our obedience in mission should be patterned on the ministry and teaching of Jesus. He gave his love and his time to all people. He praised the widow who gave her last coin to the temple; he received Nicodemus during the night; he called Matthew to the apostolate; he visited Zacchaeus in his home; he gave himself in a special way to the poor, consoling, affirming and challenging them. He spent long hours in prayer and lived in dependence on and willing obedience to God's will. An imperialistic crusader's spirit was foreign to him.[4]

As Rob Weingartner, the Director of the Presbyterian Outreach Foundation observes,

> The point is that those who share the gospel should consistently relate to others in a manner which reflects the grace and goodness of God that they bear witness to. Evangelism, if it is to be done in Jesus' way, must be invitational without being coercive, passionate without being manipulative, confident without being triumphalistic. Too often, the good news has been made to sound like bad news, the church's witness to the gospel has been crippled by those who express towards others a spirit of judgment and hostility that is inconsistent with the grace that they themselves profess to have found through faith in Jesus.[5]

A third strand of reflection on Christian mission rejects the practice of dividing evangelism from compassion and social action. No such division is possible if one takes Jesus seriously. "A proclamation which does not hold forth the promises of the justice of the kingdom to the poor of the earth is a caricature of the gospel. A Christian participation in the struggle for justice which does not also point to God's gracious offer of reconciliation and salvation to the poor is likewise a caricature."[6] This insistence on the indivisibility of proclamation and action leads away from the narrow view of the salvation of souls as the end of evangelism. Those who would speak of love must seek to love, and work alongside, the people among whom they live, for social righteousness. "It is ... impossible to talk about God's love for the poor, the outcast, the marginalized, and not to incarnate that love in the ways that demonstrate that God's kingdom is, in fact, coming now. One cannot communicate a gospel of love without letting that love become the dominant agenda of one's own life and the life of the community."[7]

Finally, insights regarding the relationship between gospel and culture have suggested further ways in which Christian mission needs to be reshaped. This view points to the particularity of the incarnation of Jesus as a Jew in Roman Palestine, and finds such concrete embodiment to be an important dimension of God's engagement with humanity, teaching us that any and every culture can be a fit vehicle for the expression of the gospel. Western churches often have arrogantly conflated the gospel with Western culture, or with democratic capitalism, consumerism, patriotism, or some other -ism. But the incarnational nature of the Christian faith demands that the gospel be transmitted, and allowed to grow, in forms and ways that develop out of other cultures and in the ways of living of other peoples. As D.T. Niles put it,

> The Gospel is like a seed, and you have to sow it. When you sow the seed of the Gospel in Palestine, a plant that can be called Palestinian Christianity grows. When you sow it in Rome, a plant of Roman Christianity grows. You sow the Gospel in Great Britain and you get British Christianity. The seed of the Gospel is later brought to America, and a plant grows of American Christianity. Now, when missionaries come to our lands [in Asia] they brought not only the seed of the Gospel, but their own plant of Christianity, flower pot included! So, what we have to do is to break the flower pot, take out the seed of the Gospel, sow it in our own cultural soil, and let our own version of Christianity grow.[8]

Christian mission has to face the challenge to embrace and love other cultures as vessels every bit as suitable as the missionary's own to receive God's presence.

In terms of evangelization among men and women of other religious traditions, these critiques are very helpful. When evangelists begin to think positively of each culture, learning about others, and from others, regarding how they live and how God is known by them becomes a value and a practice. If the evangelists' practice is to actively and concretely love others, and to do so as a primary purpose, free from ulterior motive, then genuine engagement with neighbors and mutual sharing become possible. Making the

91

commitment to pattern Christian mission more and more on the model of Jesus' own ministry invites Christians to meet and embrace persons as they are, and to engage with them in the establishing of God's kingdom in this world. And the ideas of *Missio Dei* affirm that God is not absent from the lives of any of our neighbors, and suggest that God is also present in their religious lives, in ways that it is for us to discover with their help.

If we are to discern and join in God's mission – the power of God's transforming presence among all human beings and in all of life – then it also becomes clear that it belongs not to us but to God to "reach" people, to be the one that heals or frees, to change or "convert" individuals and empower communities. The task we are given as disciples of Jesus is to be witnesses of transformation; to make the good news apparent and available to others both through what we say, and in how we live; to be ambassadors representing the One who reconciles all humanity to one another and to God. "Conversion" is a gift of God and an act of God's Spirit in human lives, and not something that we can export or implant or do through any of our own designs. When sharing the gospel aims to "convert" others, it usurps the role of God, can be dangerous, and must be confronted by other Christians.

An additional corrective to the practice of evangelization and Christian mission comes from the churches' now long experience of interreligious relationships and dialogue. We have enough experience to know that dialogue among people of different religious traditions is not an alternative to mission, nor a preparation for mission. To be authentic, dialogue cannot expect a certain answer to be its outcome. Dialogue means a mutual, open exchange of experience, of witness to what God has done and is doing in the lives of those on both "sides" of the conversation; it includes listening and questioning. Part of the purpose of interreligious conversation is to grasp more fully God's concern and love for all humankind, even as manifested and known through different revelations and religious traditions. It involves acknowledging and receiving the rich insights that come from the cultural and religious traditions and lives of others, in part, so that the message of each tradition can be clarified and known more deeply. Can we believe, then, that a proper witness to God is not announcing an exclusive claim to truth, but a witness to be made and shared and contemplated together with people of religious traditions other than our own?

Maryknoll Missioner William T. Knipe has written that one theological and practical way to find our way among these issues is to practice "Mission in Dialogue," a living together with people of other religions as neighbors and friends, to "search for the ways we can learn from others how God has operated among them, share with them our own Christian faith experiences, and journey together towards the ultimate truth." He gives us a picture of how this would work:

> the purpose of mission-in-dialogue is to mediate the love of God to the world. The proclamation of the gospel would depend for its credibility on being alive in the lives of the Christians ... Every Christian would be a missioner, and the total life witness of the local community would be a proclamation of the gospel. Every Christian would be a missioner engaged in the mission of dialogue, listening and learning, speaking and sharing: an unconditional act of love, not expecting anything in return ... The doing of mission would always include the proclaiming of the gospel in witness and in dialogue, but together with the ministry of reconciliation, the doing of justice for people, the loving of one another as people, the creation of a peaceful and harmonious world, the realization of the Kingdom of God: all of this by Christians and Muslims [and others] together.[9]

Such practice of Christian mission is possible, if hard to achieve. We Christians do have an internal struggle to wage to be sure that our witness to what gives us hope and abundant life does not become a source of further strife and damage in the world, but is based on respect, openness, willingness to learn from and live with others, and desire to enter into relationships of love across the barriers we so easily erect to separate us.

Conversion of the Heart

"Conversion" is best understood, as mentioned earlier, as a basic dimension of Christian life and practice. The dynamic of "conversion" is an essential element of who we are as Christians. This understanding has been most helpfully developed for me in the thinking of the ecumenical Groupe des Dombes, in *For the Conversion of the Churches* (1993).

The Groupe points out that, contrary to what we might think, "there is no [Christian] identity without conversion; a fortiori

Christian identity could not be constituted and sustained, either personally or ecclesially, without constant and continued conversion" (p. 4). "Conversion is constitutive of the church" (para. 8), they say, because,

> Existentially, Christian identity is not static but dynamic. It is a shifting of the centre, an exodus, a transition, a paschal movement. Christian identity is always a Christian becoming. It is an opening up to an eschatological beyond which ceaselessly draws it forward and prevents it from shutting itself up in itself. Thus it is a radical opening up to others beyond all the walls of separation. In its very essence it therefore contradicts the fixed or intransigent need for a secure identity. The existence in the church of the living Tradition, which is creative in its very faithfulness, has illustrated this constantly through the centuries. (#19)

> Christian identity rests on a basic conversion: "The kingdom of God has come near; repent, and believe in the good news" (Mark 1:15). This conversion is required by the coming and the resurrection of Jesus Christ. Its absolute nature opens onto a process which is never accomplished fully in this world. This conversion is initiated and celebrated in baptism. Thus it includes an "already" and a "not yet". It is a grace which opens onto a task. It leads into an existence which must undergo continual conversion." (para. 39)[10]

This vision of conversion at the heart of what it means to be the church may be startling, but it is in fact what we remember at every baptism, and whenever Christians renew their baptismal vows. "Do you not know that all of us who have been baptized into Christ Jesus were baptized into his death? Therefore we have been buried with him by baptism into death, so that, just as Christ was raised from the dead by the glory of the Father, so we too might walk in newness of life. For if we have been united with him in a death like his, we will certainly be united with him in a resurrection like his" (Romans 6:3–5). To be Christian is to be a people being continually converted, always further transformed, radically open to "an eschatological beyond," to a "new creation" that is other than who and what we now are.

The struggle for Christians is to remain open to this reality of God's interaction with us. Internally, we often find ourselves wanting to stop this process of ongoing conversion, to stop the exodus, the transition, the movement from death to resurrection in our lives. Resistance to the changes it asks of us is common, and not surprising. As for community life, Christians, like other human beings, often want things to stay the same; we do not always welcome the changes that God is bringing about. Christians find themselves wanting to pin down the Spirit of God; we want her to speak to our community in some ways and not in others, saying some things, and not others. We often do not want to devote much if any time to discerning what the Spirit is saying to us and to the churches. We struggle to embrace this life of continual conversion.

In the relations of Christians with others, this same dynamic can be seen at work. Our engagement in ecumenical relationships as Christians aims to move the community beyond simply understanding one another, or becoming able to tolerate one another. Ecumenical relations call the community to hear, in our encounter, how the Spirit of God is asking us to change our practice of the faith. Our ecumenical relationships are "for the conversion of the churches"; ecumenical engagement calls us to make actual changes in our life and practice.

The same may be said of our interreligious relations, as the Groupe des Dombes notes:

> In a category of its own, which is not part of the ecumenical process in the strict sense, the Assisi encounter (1986), in which the representatives of the great religions of humanity met together to pray for peace in the world, was also a common gesture of conversion. For Christians also have to experience together a conversion of charity and respect towards their brothers and sisters who are believers of other faiths. (para. 138)

For Christians, engagement with neighbors of other religious traditions is not understood rightly if it is understood as something that has the goal of "converting them." That is not the goal of such engagement, though entering into relationships of friendship and sharing is a part of a Christian's authentic response to the gospel. Interfaith engagement is part of a Christian's calling as a disciple of Jesus, for the sake of building one beloved human community, for the purpose of mutual witness, and for our own conversion.

When Christians meet with women and men who root their lives in religious traditions other than our own, we are given an opportunity to come to know them, and also to talk with one another, from different traditions, about our own religious practices and beliefs. This two-way sharing of faith is what I and many other Christians call "mutual witness." It involves making our witness with respect, openness, and honesty, in our actions as well as in our words. And it also involves receiving the witness of the person or persons we are meeting with respect, attention, and the conviction that we can learn from them about God and God's ways with humanity.

In these interreligious engagements Christians are given the opportunity to reflect on our own faith and religious practice. We receive the gift of seeing ourselves and our way of living and communicating "from the outside," "in a different mirror," from a different perspective. Through this we have the opportunity to see how we are falling short of faithfulness to our own tradition; to see ways that we can change our practice to be more faithful. We can experience not only a "conversion of charity and respect" toward our neighbors, but also a deeper conversion in our own Christian life and faith.

Notes

1   The Constitution of the Presbyterian Church (USA) (Louisville: Office of the General Assembly, 2003–2004), G-3.0300–3.0400.
2   I am especially indebted, in what follows, to "A Presbyterian Understanding of Evangelism" by Robert J. Weingartner, in Joseph Small (ed.), *Let Us Reason Together: Christians and Jews in Conversation* (Louisville: Witherspoon Press, 2010). Much more should be said about the vigorous critique and efforts to reformulate the task of evangelization in other parts of the world!
3   Milton J. Coalter, John M. Mulder, and Louis B. Weeks, *The Re-Forming Tradition: Presbyterians and Mainstream Protestantism* (Louisville: Westminster/John Knox Press, 1992), 99.
4   "Mission and Evangelism: An Ecumenical Affirmation," World Council of Churches (Geneva: World Council of Churches, 1982); "Turn to the Living God: A Call to Evangelism in Jesus Christ's Way," A Resolution Adopted by the 203rd General Assembly of the Presbyterian Church (USA), (1991).
5   Weingartner, "A Presbyterian Understanding of Evangelism."
6   "Message" of the San Antonio Conference on World Mission and Evangelism of the World Council of Churches, quoted in "Turn to the Living God," 22.

7   Darrell L. Guder, "Incarnation and the Church's Evanglelistic Mission," International Review of Mission 83.30 (1992), 424.

8   Cited by Paul-Gordon Chandler, *God's Global Music* (Downers Grove, IL: Intervarsity Press, 1997); by C. Michael Hawn, *Gather Into One: Singing and Praying Globally* (Grand Rapids, MI: Eerdmans Press, 2003), and elsewhere.

9   William T. Knipe, M.M., "A Christian Approach to Muslims," in *Dialogue with People of Other Faiths*, a compilation of presentations by the Division of Overseas Ministries, National Council of Churches of Christ in the USA, 1986.

10 Groupe des Dombes, *For the Conversion of the Churches* (Geneva: World Council of Churches, 1993).

Further Reading

Bria, Ion. *Go Forth in Peace: Orthodox Perspectives on Mission.* Geneva: World Council of Churches, 1986.

Jones, E. Stanley. *Conversion.* New York: Abingdon Press, 1959.

Muck, Terry and Frances Adeney. *Christianity Encountering World Religions: The Practice of Mission in the 21st Century.* Grand Rapids, MI: Baker Publishing, 2009.

Rivera, Luis N. *A Violent Evangelism: the Political and Religious Conquest of the Americas.* Louisville: Westminster/John Knox, 1992.

Thangaraj, M. Thomas. *The Common Task: A Theology of Christian Mission.* Nashville: Abingdon Press, 1999.

Wickeri, Philip L. (ed.). *The People of God Among All God's Peoples: Frontiers in Christian Mission.* Hong Kong: Christian Conference of Asia, 2000.

Witte, John, Jr. and Richard C. Martin. *Sharing the Book: Religious Perspectives on the Rights and Wrongs of Proselytism.* Maryknoll, NY: Orbis Books, 1999.

7

Conversion from a Hindu Perspective
Controversies, Challenges, and Opportunities

Anantanand Rambachan

Introduction

The phenomenon of religious conversion has become the single most important source of tension, controversy, and violence between Hindus and Christians in India.[1] It is a highly combustible issue that ignites intense emotions on both sides, exploding swiftly into conflict that engulfs communities and leads to the tragic destruction of life and places of worship. Hindu concerns about conversion have led to historically unprecedented efforts to enact legislation in various Indian states in order to prohibit conversions through coercion, allurement, and fraud. In the words of the Rajasthan Anti-Conversion Bill (2006), "No person shall convert or attempt to convert either directly or otherwise any person from one religion to another by the use of force, or by allurement or by any fraudulent means nor shall any person abet such conversion."[2] Although this bill and others like it do not make the act of converting from one religion to another illegal, consensus on the meaning of terms like "force," "allurement," and "fraudulent" is

Religious Conversion: Religion Scholars Thinking Together, First Edition.
Edited by Shanta Premawardhana.
© 2015 World Council of Churches Publications. Published 2015 by John Wiley & Sons, Ltd.

impossible. The threat of "divine displeasure," for example, is included in the definition of force, highlighting the deep differences over this matter.

Hindus, on the whole, have the perception that mission is the single and most important concern of Christianity. They understand it to be a compulsion that is fed by the nature of Christian theological claims. Chowgule's understanding is typical of this Hindu generalization:

> Christianity believes in exclusivism. It says that Christ is the only Son of God, and was sent to this world to lead the people to him. Upon the death of Christ, this task was given to the Church set up in the name of Christ. The present inheritors of Christ are the Popes, the Cardinals, the Bishops, the priests, etc. Furthermore, Christianity believes that Christ has commanded his followers that it is their duty to convert others to their system. Many have interpreted this command to imply that one could use physical violence as a means to achieve the objective.[3]

Swami Dayananda Saraswati, a leading Hindu spokesperson, founder of Arsha Vidya Pitham and convener of the Hindu Dharma Acharya Sabha, classifies the world's religions as aggressive and non-aggressive.[4] Non-aggressive religions, as he classifies Hinduism, Judaism, Shinto, and Taoism, do not seek to win converts. Aggressive religions, on the other hand, like Christianity, are "zealous in their mission of preaching and conversion. In their zeal, the end more often than not justifies the means."[5] More importantly, Swami Dayananda understands conversion to be a form of violence that generates violence:

> Religious conversion by missionary activity remains an act of violence. It is an act of violence because it hurts deeply, not only the other members of the family of the converted, but the entire community that comes to know of it. One is connected to various persons in one's world. The religious person in every individual is the innermost, inasmuch as he or she is connected to a force beyond the empirical. That is the reason why the hurt caused by religion can turn into violence. That is why a religious belief can motivate a missionary to be a martyr. When the hurt of the religious becomes acute, it explodes into violence. Conversion is violence. It generates violence.[6]

At its very first meeting in Chennai (2003), the Hindu Acharya Sabha spoke out against conversion and called upon the state governments of India to follow the example of Tamil Nadu and Gujarat and implement legislation to ban conversion by "force, fraud or allurements, overt and covert and implement the legislation vigorously."[7] Conversion was condemned again at conventions of the Hindu Acharya Sabha in Mumbai (2005) and Chunchanagiri (2008).

Christians, on the other hand, reject the equation of conversion with violence and emphasize the human rights dimension of the issue. They argue for the freedom to change one's religion and for the public manifestation of faith and practice that they understand to be enshrined in the Universal Declaration of Human Rights (1948): "Everyone has the right to freedom of thought, conscience and religion; this right includes freedom to change his religion or belief, and freedom, either alone or in community with others and in public or private, to manifest his religion or belief in teaching, practice, worship and observance." Dalit Christians see conversion as the opportunity for freedom from the hierarchically oppressive structures of caste and for entry into a new religious community that affirms their individual and social worth and dignity. They are convinced that such dignity cannot be professed within the boundaries of the Hindu tradition.

Such different understandings of conversion generate deep suspicions and mistrust and underline the need for deeper dialogue aimed at clarifying concerns, building trust, and allaying fears. The challenges are urgent in the face of the reality and lurking threat of violence. My aim is to identify major Hindu concerns about conversion, as articulated by a few of its prominent spokespersons. The reader should not construe this as indicating support for these positions. My own critical perspectives and my differences from the positions articulated by some of these spokespersons will be apparent in the course of our discussion. This analysis necessarily involves generalizations about Hinduism and Christianity and the diversity of both must not be overlooked. Hinduism may be thought of as a family name that embraces an astonishing diversity of beliefs and practices reflecting the cultural, linguistic, and geographical richness of the Indian subcontinent. The tradition resists homogeneity and this holds true also for attitudes to conversion.

Exclusive Theology, Community, and Conversion

Tensions between Hindus and Christians about conversion reflect varying understandings of community, ways of professing religious claims, and attitudes to religious difference.

Before clarifying these, we should note that the Hindu tradition is not averse to the sharing of religious wisdom and, in fact, commends such sharing. The often-cited Rg Veda (1.89.1) text, "Let noble truths come to us from all sides," expresses the deep and ancient Hindu value of sharing and receiving wisdom. At the conclusion of the Bhagavadgita (18:67–71) the teacher, Krishna, commends the sharing of his teachings. He characterizes the sharing of wisdom as the dearest form of service and the teacher as dearest to him among human beings (18: 69):

> One who reveals this supreme secret to those who have offered me their love,
>   Enacting the highest offering of love for me – that one shall certainly come to me, without doubt.
>   And among humans, there is no one whose acts are more dearly loved by me than that one,
>   Nor shall there be any other on earth who is more dearly loved by me than such a person.[8]

The motivation for such sharing is the conviction that these teachings are universally relevant and conducive to human well-being. The sharer hopes that the consequence of such sharing is that the other is persuaded to embrace these teachings by awakening to their truth and beauty. In addition, varying truth claims are vigorously argued, advocated, and defended among the multiple perspectives (*sampradayas*) comprising the family of Hindu traditions.[9] In the late nineteenth century, Swami Vivekananda undertook the hazardous and pioneering journey from India to the United States, inspired by the conviction that the message of the Vedanta tradition was needed by and was good for persons in the West. His path continues to be followed by a line of distinguished Hindu teachers. Hindu traditions, therefore, are not unfamiliar with the religious motive of sharing one's conviction, and debating and persuading others about its validity. To claim otherwise is not be faithful to important strands of Hinduism. Having noted this, however, it may

101

be misleading to employ the term "conversion" to describe such movements since the term carries its own assumptions about the nature of religion and religious identity.

Along with identifying the changing of religious commitment and the obligation to share religious wisdom, we must note the distinctive ways in which this sharing occurred. The absence of institutionalization and centralization meant that there were no consistently organized and systematic efforts to supplant different viewpoints. Hindus become uneasy and suspicious of grand plans, programs, and resources aimed at conversion and of the development of missionary strategies targeting particular religious communities. They join Buddhists, for example, in expressing disapproval for the late Pope John Paul II's declaration of the intention of the church, in the third millennium, to plant the cross in Asia, after doing so in Europe in the first millennium and in North and South America in the second millennium. Such planned and programmatic efforts at conversion cause Hindus to feel under attack and lead to defensive attitudes. Even when numbers do not justify it, there is a fear of religious and cultural extinction as expressed in the comment below:

> When I visited Egypt a few years ago, I asked the Egyptologist who was with me, if I could see the people belonging to the cultural tradition that made the pyramids, the Egyptologist replied that there was not a single person to be found. The culture was totally wiped out. The ancient Greek culture, the South American culture, and other indigenous cultures are all gone. All over the world, the indigenous traditions not given to expansionism through conversion programs are slowly disappearing.[10]

Although there is significant diversity of belief and practice within the family of traditions constituting Hinduism, there are important shared teachings that may include the doctrine of *karma*, the belief in rebirth (*samsara*), the value for a teacher (*guru*), and an Ultimate Reality that is both immanent and transcendent. In a context where religion and culture are inseparable, a shared religious worldview was only one aspect of a common identity. A widely shared understanding of the limits of human reason and symbols resulted in the understanding that truth always exceeded the comprehension and description of any one tradition and justified relationships of theological humility. A truth whose nature and essence could be fully revealed in words or contained within the boundaries of the human mind would not be the absolute truth.

There was no persistent and widespread negativization or problematization of the fact of religious diversity and no systematic effort at homogenization. Religious diversity was seen as reflecting the diversity of human nature and experience. The street-corner fire and brimstone denunciation of other traditions was absent. The development of the idea of the *ishtadevata* (chosen God) oriented Hindus to understanding the deities of the Hindu tradition, Vishnu, Shiva, and Shakti (Goddess) as different names and forms of the one infinite God and not as rival Gods. Regional, family, or personal needs determined one's choice, but one did not think of the other as choosing a rival or false God. Such attitudes have become even more important today.[11]

Sharing in the Hindu tradition occurred in response to a request for religious teaching made by a student to a teacher. It was always felt that this teaching spoke meaningfully to the person who had examined life's experience and discovered that finite or created ends such as power, fame, or pleasure are ultimately unfulfilling. A religious need, in other words, must be established and not presumed. It is the function of the teacher to validate this need and to impart wisdom through words and example. The qualified teacher is one who knows the sacred texts and methods of imparting wisdom and whose life is firmly rooted in God. Hindus regard religious teachers with profound respect and honor. Religious teaching is liberating only when shared by a qualified teacher to a receptive student who is devoted to ethical values, who practices sense-control and is calm in mind. The dissemination and receipt of religious teaching is a demanding and transformative process that requires commitment.

Into this evolved ethos, proselytizing religions such as Christianity and Islam entered, with historical exceptions, as partners in political empire-building adventures.[12] We have already noted that, prior to the advent of Islam and Christianity, there existed the reality, in India, of change in religious commitments. This must not, however, obscure the fact that Islam and Christianity introduced new dimensions to this phenomenon. Because of an alliance with empires, these traditions came to be associated with the imperialist attitudes of the colonizer and the explicit disdain for India's religious expressions. Imperialist political claims were seen as finding echo in exclusive theological claims to truth, revelation, and salvation and in the proclaimed hope to replace the traditions of Hinduism. Christian theology in relation to Hinduism was and remains largely mission oriented.

Christian missionaries understood quickly the inseparability of religion and culture in India. The fear that converts might revert to traditional practices led to systematic efforts to define a Christian identity over and against the prevailing Hindu ones. Christian converts took on new names from the biblical texts, renamed villages to reflect their new faith, constructed churches following the architectural models of Europe, and adopted new musical forms. In many cases, converts also adopted new forms of dress and cuisine. Such forms of self-definition help a community, especially a minority one, to maintain its new identity. In the case of the Dalit Christians, such changes signified the opportunity to create new communities where oppressive caste identities could be overcome and collective freedom affirmed.

At the same time, such deliberately sharp distinctions between self and other are a source of tension and resentment. This is especially so when the basis of such distinction is the claim also to religious superiority and when the other (Hindu) is seen as fallen and in need of religious rescue. The nature of the Christian church as a voluntary association with membership implied and necessitated boundaries and also a sharp distinction from Hindus.[13] This significant dimension of identity was absent entirely from Hinduism and engendered also a sharp sense of difference between self and other. The tearing apart of family and community is one of the effects of conversion that concerns Hindus who think that Christian missionaries care little about this outcome.

Christian fears about the unity of religion and culture and their efforts to create a new Christian identity by shedding all symbols of Hindu culture are seen from the Hindu side as a part of the effort to destroy its ancient heritage:

> A committed Christian will not wear a tilakam, much less have rangoli in front of the house. If there is no rangoli at the entrance to a Tamil Nadu house, we immediately know that it doesn't belong to a Hindu. A converted Christian woman ceases to wear Indian traditional clothes, like saris, etc. No Christian woman will wear a nose ring. It is amazing how easily cultures disappear by the program of conversion through various means, leaving only dead monuments to be preserved for posterity.[14]

Mahatma Gandhi articulated Swami Dayananda's concerns in the early twentieth century when he described his childhood encounter with Christianity:

> In those days Christian missionaries used to stand in a corner near the high school and hold forth, pouring abuse on Hindus and their gods. I could not endure this. I must have stood there to hear them once only, but that was enough to dissuade me from repeating the experiment. About the same time, I heard of a well-known Hindu having been converted to Christianity. It was the talk of the town that, when he was baptized, he had to eat beef and drink liquor, that he also had to change his clothes, and that thenceforth he began to go about in European costume including a hat. ... I also heard that the new convert had already begun abusing the religion of his ancestors, their customs and their country. All these things created in me a dislike for Christianity.[15]

In the words of Gandhi we hear many of the continuing concerns of Hindus about Christianity and proselytization. These include the a priori and aggressive denunciation of Hindus and their object of worship, the abandonment of traditional cultural symbols, changes in dress and eating habits, and hostility to family and community. The issue of nationalism is one to which we will return.

In spite of the fact that Christianity, especially the mainline churches, has made some revisions in its theological response to Hinduism and continues to discuss and assess its relationship with other religions, such theological movements have had a minimal impact on the way in which most Hindus think about or encounter Christianity. These have not transformed, I may also add, the thinking of most Christians about Hinduism. The South Baptist Mission Board, for example, in a 1999 pamphlet, "Prayer for Hindus," spoke of the "900 million people ... lost in the hopeless darkness of Hinduism." Hindus are represented as steeped in superstition and idolatry, worshiping out of fear, not love and never experiencing joy or forgiveness.[16] The consequence is that Hindus continue to imagine and encounter Christianity as an exclusive religion which is not genuinely open to the religious claims and experiences of others and which is concerned primarily with increasing its institutional power and domination through evangelization and conversion. It is still seen as an ally of Westernization. Such perceptions and experiences induce uneasiness, defensiveness, and, on occasions, hostility.

Hindus have the perception that mission continues to be the most important concern of Christianity and do not distinguish between mainline and so-called fringe churches: "The 'mainline churches' have the same ethos as 'fringe churches,' that is Jesus Christ is the ONLY son of god, and that salvation is not possible to those who do not accept this exclusivity. The 'mainline churches' have not given up their objective of conversions, except that they pretend to do in a subtle way."[17]

It is important for Christians to understand and take seriously the historical and experiential concerns that Hindus have about Christian mission and consider the reasons why its theological exclusivity is received with a defensive attitude on the Indian subcontinent and elsewhere.

Caste and Conversion

Hindu concerns about proselytization, some of which have been identified above, must not obscure or ignore the opportunity for self-critical reflection that conversion demands. It appears to me that there are few serious attempts on the Hindu side to understand the meaning and attraction of Christianity to the convert. It must be instructive that the largest numbers of converts from Hindu traditions to Christianity come from the so-called untouchable castes. They experience the tradition as oppressive and as negating their dignity and self-worth. For such persons, the Christian message of the inclusive love of God and acceptance in a community where human equality and value are affirmed is liberating. In a social context where occupation may still be determined by caste and where the ability to change one's identity and work must await future birth, the opportunity for a new identity, which may afford dignity, choice, and better economic opportunities, is compelling. For such persons, the argument that the religion into which one is born is best only adds to the oppression and is seen as part of a deliberate effort to deny them freedom and control over their lives. Hinduism must be challenged by conversion to understand the many ways in which the tradition is failing to meet the legitimate needs of those who are born into its fold for a religious and social system that attests to their dignity and self-determination.

The absence of such self-critical reflection is, in part, the consequence of the fact that Hindu leadership is still dominated by male persons from the upper castes who have always experienced power and privilege within the tradition. Having never experienced religiously justified oppression and injustice, they assume wrongly that the tradition that has been good to them is good for all born within its fold. They resist the overturning of a system that guarantees them power and privilege. Conversion is a challenge but also an opportunity for Hindu leaders to consider the relationship between religious doctrine, and especially the theological assumptions of caste, and systemic social and economic structures that condemn millions to lives of poverty, indignity, and marginalization. The tradition needs to stop treating the convert as a childlike individual who needs to be always protected from the lures and deceptive practices of missionaries. This is a demeaning condescension that denies them agency and self-determination.

It is unfortunate that some Christians see all Hindu concerns about conversion as disguised efforts to preserve the privileges and power relationships inherent in the caste system. Such a perception reflects a monolithic and stereotypical view of Hinduism, not unlike the Hindu perception of Christianity as a tradition concerned only with increasing power through conversion. It ignores the controversial nature of the caste structure in Hinduism and the history of challenge to the system by distinguished Hindu leaders and movements. It also ignores the fact that even the Christian Church in India has not been able to free itself from the social inequities and expressions of caste, pointing to caste as a phenomenon that is capable of transcending a specific religious doctrine. This must by no means be employed as a Hindu argument to justify caste. Too often Hindus cite caste-like structures in other societies to mute interrogation about caste. Conversion is a loud cry to Hinduism to investigate the relationship between theological teachings about human nature and systemic structures of oppression. Hindus must be attentive to and respectful of the voices of Dalit Christians and their experiences of the tradition. Conversion is also a call for interreligious and intra-religious dialogue and action on a pervasive and persistent social phenomenon that is capable of crossing religious boundaries. The Hindu tradition does have theological visions that affirm the equal worth and dignity of all human beings and their freedom for self-determination. These visions must be the location from where the hierarchies of caste must be repudiated and where we advocate for alternative communities of human equality, justice, and non-violence. Hindus cannot expect others to become aware of such an alternative vision unless they themselves embrace, embody, and work for its realization in community.

Social Service and Conversion

Another dimension of the controversy over conversion, where there are significant tensions and differences of approach between Hindus and Christians and where the need for dialogue exists, concerns the provision of social service. Hindus have grown increasingly suspicious of Christian motives in offering service, seeing such work as a part of the overall strategy of proselytization: "The objective of the social service is to get an access to the people who are targeted or conversion. Once the missionaries come close to the people, and the latter become obligated to them, the 'benefits' of believing in Christ are explained to them."[18]

There are several issues underlying this suspicion. The Hindu tradition has a deep value for service and Hindus are encouraged to be generous in gifts (*dana*) to the needy. Chapter 17 of the Bhagavadgita discusses appropriate and inappropriate ways of serving others. The text commends service that is motivated by a belief in the intrinsic value of serving, that is without expectation of reward, and that is offered to a needy person at a proper place and time. Less commendable is service that is reluctantly offered, with the aim of receiving something in return. When there is a link between social service and conversion, Hindus are troubled by what is contrary to their tradition's emphasis on *nishkama karma* (service without expectation of reward). This becomes even more difficult when the motive of proselytization is covert.

It is not true that Hindus are inactive when it comes to social service. One difference is that Hindu activity in this area has a less visible or proclaimed religious character. At the same time, it is wrong for Hindus to see all social service activity by Christians as a guise for proselytization. Social service, inspired by the perspective of Christian liberation theology, is less concerned with conversion and more with the transformation of society through the practice of justice, the overcoming of suffering, and the transforming of structures of oppression. This must be a shared concern of Hindus and Christians. Traditionally, the Hindu quest for liberation (*moksha*) occurred after a life of success in the world and the fulfillment of material (*artha*) and pleasure (*kama*) needs. The path to liberation was associated with renunciation and disinterest in the world. In those forms of Christianity which emphasize the role of Jesus as social prophet and his criticism of systems of domination, liberation is construed not only as the overcoming of estrangement from God, but also as liberation from systems of domination and the creation of a just and inclusive social order. Activity directed toward this end, such as the provision of education, health care, housing, food, and clothing, is seen by Christians as an inextricable expression of the meaning of their religious commitment and the quality of human relationships that this commitment requires. Hindus will benefit from dialogue with Christians about the meaning of liberation and the work to transform social systems.

Mutual mistrust is also evident in the quite different perceptions of indigenization. Many Christians understand such efforts as genuine attempts to move away from Western cultural forms and to root their tradition in local customs and traditions. Hindus, on the other hand, think of indigenization as mere tactical strategies in the mission battle. For example, Swami Jayendra Saraswati, Sankaracharya of Kanchi, in a media release after an interreligious meeting with Cardinal Jean-Louis Pierre Tauran of the Vatican's Pontifical Council for Interreligious Dialogue, requested that the church in India "stop forthwith the use of Hindu religious words, phrases and symbols like Veda, Agama, Rishi, Ashram, Om and other such in what is referred to as 'inculturation' tactics, but which are only intended to deceive the vulnerable sections of our people who are the intended targets for religious conversion."[19] The relationship between religion and culture, like conversion and aid, need to be addressed and mutual concerns taken seriously. Hindus must take seriously the more comprehensive understanding of liberation exemplified in Christian communities concerned with justice and the dismantling of oppressive structures. Both traditions can speak in unison against the exploitation of those who are vulnerable, economically and otherwise, for the purpose of conversion. Aloysius Pieris has lamented also the failure of the church to seek development programs that have an Asian character. This may be one of the promising fruits of cooperation between Hindus and Christians in India.[20]

Hindus and Christians could agree that it is wrong to use material rewards as means of enticing another to join one's religion. Meaningful faith is not awakened and nurtured by exploiting others in times of vulnerability and need. Hindus need also to refrain from sweeping generalizations about the significance of charitable works in the lives of Christians and to understand better why, under conditions of oppression and deprivation, the caring face of God attracts. There is a lot of Christian humanitarian work, both past and present, which is not linked to conversion, but this commendable expression of Christian values is made suspect by those who use works of charity to win converts. This controversial matter can be addressed, in part, by Christians cooperating with people of other traditions in bringing relief to the poor and dispossessed. Such joint effort will build trust and help to make the point that it is the overcoming of suffering and not conversion which is the primary concern of religious persons. We need a more comprehensive understanding of the sources of human suffering and the role of religion in the midst of injustice and oppression. Both Hindus and Christians can benefit immensely from such a discussion and from common action.

Conversion, Human Rights, and the State

I started by noting the tendency, from the Christian side, to discuss the issue of conversion as one of human rights and freedom of religion. Let me return now to this issue. Hindus and Christians must agree about religious freedom as a fundamental human right and with the definition of it as including freedom of practice and the freedom to freely change one's faith. Such language becomes particularly important for those who struggle with the oppressive faces of religion that prescribe social and economic possibilities on the basis of birth and limit freedom to self-determination. The language of human rights becomes an important resource to articulate their demands and struggle.

Recognizing this fact, it is important still to ask if the language of human freedom and rights is appropriate in the context of propagating one's faith to others. Does the use of such terms imply that this is a right and freedom equal to those listed in the Universal Declaration of Human Rights, such as the right to life, liberty, and security of person or the right to freedom of movement? Should we continue with the use of this language or should we search for an alternative discourse? Swami Dayananda articulated the problem in the following terms:

> In all conferences I have attended, I am asked to help with the committee that drafts resolutions. I always have asked for the term "mutual respect among all religions" to be included as one of the resolutions, but always this mutual respect clause is struck down, and is replaced by "freedom of religion." The freedom of religion is understood by some as the freedom to preach and convert with an evangelistic program.[21]

From the Hindu perspective, there are four issues worthy of consideration when Christians insist that proselytization and conversion are essentially human rights issues.

First, it is important to remember that religious claims, despite protestations to the contrary, are essentially faith claims that are meaningful in the context of the history, doctrine, and practice of specific communities. Although such claims may be made available to persons outside of these communities, it seems inappropriate to equate such sharing with fundamental freedom and rights such as the right to life, liberty, and security of person. Faith claims can only be professed and shared in humility, but the language of rights can too easily mask arrogance in relation to other faith claims, especially when faith claims are professed in an exclusive manner that implies the negation of other claims.

Second, those who assert it almost never qualify the language of freedom and right in relation to propagating one's faith to others. Freedom, as we know well, is not intrinsically valuable. For many in the world today, a free market is anything but free. They find it exploitative and oppressive. Some of the greatest historical atrocities have been committed in the guise of exercising freedom. If we argue for freedom to propagate our faiths as a fundamental right, we must also, at the same time, articulate the moral content and limits of that freedom. Why is this freedom so important and to what end is it being exercised? What are its constraints in religiously diverse communities? How can this freedom be exercised responsibly and with attentiveness to the concerns of Hindus?

Third, the representation of the issue as one of religious freedom objectifies the one who is the intended recipient of conversion efforts and transforms him or her into a passive entity. The language of rights, especially when employed in the sphere of human relations, is not usually mutual and overlooks obligations. The fact that the other is also a person of living faith with a tradition that speaks profoundly of God, and with whom one can enter into a mutually enriching relationship of learning and sharing, is ignored. I cherish the freedom to share my faith with others, but this sharing should be a response to the interest of the other and with openness to his sharing. We clearly need a language that emphasizes mutuality rather than rights since we are all spiritually poorer without the freedom to share our faiths with each other.

Fourth, the language of freedom and rights is meaningful in a context where these are or can be curbed. Freedom is sought from that which constrains it and rights asserted against those who seek to infringe their exercise. When we assert the freedom to propagate the teachings of our religion to people of other faiths as a right, who or what are we seeking this freedom from? In other words, who is the agent likely to constrain religious freedom? If it is the state, why should not all religions find consensus in ensuring limits on state power? Why are some religions feeling the need for state action? If, on the other hand, rights are asserted against persons of other faiths, this only reflects a broken relationship that will not be healed by the assertion of rights. Like a marriage in difficulty, the profession of rights is symptomatic of a rupture that may be healed only by treating the deeper issues.

Conversion and Hindutva

The issue of conversion has, in more recent times, taken on a new dimension and complexity with the rise of the ideology of Hindutva, an ideology of Hindu identity articulated by Vinayak Damadar Savarkar (1883–1966) in his influential work entitled *Hindutva*.[22] Savarkar contended that Hindus were the original indigenous people of India and constituted one single nation (*rashtra*). Hindus constitute not only a nation, but also a race (*jati*) with a common origin and blood. Savarkar defined Hindus as those who consider India their holyland (*punyabhumi*) and the land of their ancestors (*matribhumi/ pitribhumi*).[23] One of the important distinctions made by Savarkar is between "Hinduism" and "Hindutva (Hinduness)." In his understanding, "Hinduism" refers only to religious beliefs and practices. It comprises only a small part of the totality of "Hindutva." "Hindutva" refers to the historical, racial, and cultural factors constituting the Hindu nation. It is the unifying sociocultural background of all Hindus. In Savarkar's view, Sikhs, Jains, and South Asian Buddhists are Hindus. By defining a Hindu as one who regards India as both fatherland and holyland, Savarkar excludes East Asian Buddhists, Western converts to Hinduism and, most importantly, Indian Muslims and Christians. For Savarkar, Muslims and Christians were essentially alien communities in India. A contemporary exponent of the Hindutva perspective expressed it in the following way:

> Non-Hindus can join to create a Hindustani unity, but first they must agree to adhere to the minimum requirement: that they recognize and accept that their cultural legacy is Hindu, or that they revere their Hindu origins, that they are as equal before the law as any other but no more, and that they will make sacrifices to defend their Hindu legacy just as any good Hindu would his own. In turn the Hindu will defend such non-Hindus as they have the Parsis and Jews, and accept them as the Hindustani *pariwar* [family].[24]

One can easily appreciate the fear and confusion that such a view stirs. It is quite capable of provoking hostile attitudes toward those who are seen as not satisfying the criteria of Hindutva and, in fact, has contributed to the atmosphere of mistrust and antagonism.

While the advocates of "Hindutva" appear to suggest a distinction between "Hindutva" and "Hinduism," this distinction is, in reality, very difficult to make. The insistence on "Hindutva" as a requirement for participation in the national life of India denies the freedom of cultural and religious self-definition to those communities who find "Hindutva" to be incompatible with their core beliefs and values. This controversy is an opportunity for the Hindu tradition to reflect more critically on its own relationship with culture, nationalism, and ethnicity. V.D. Savarkar's parochial identification of Hinduism with what he refers to as nation, race, and culture makes it difficult for Hinduism to proclaim itself as a world religion. It cannot do this while clinging to the particulars of territory, race, and culture. If the Hindu tradition claims universal validity for its insights, these must, of necessity, transcend the specificities prescribed by Savarkar. The readiness to completely equate Hinduism with Indian culture makes it difficult also for the religion to offer a detached critique of cultural traditions that may be inconsistent with its core claims and values.

There is an ancient and persisting hospitality to religious diversity in India that made it possible to accommodate a wide variety of religious beliefs and practices and to offer shelter to persecuted religious groups for centuries. Legitimate Hindu concerns about conversion must not result in abandoning or compromising this precious perspective. Although no political system can afford to ignore the concerns of its majority community, if the Hindu tradition backs a form of majority rule that is unable to accommodate plural identities, it will be unhealthy for India and will send a tragic message to other nations struggling with issues of religious difference.

Conclusion

Diana Eck has argued that minority consciousness is not just a matter of number. A majority can have a minority consciousness. In support of her argument, Eck cites the example of the Buddhist Sinhalese majority in Sri Lanka. Eck's argument also holds true for the Hindu majority in India who feel "that they have no power in their own land because of a proliferation of special privileges and reservations given to minorities."[25]

In the case of conversion, Hindus have a sense of being engaged in a battle with highly organized, well-funded, and aggressive forces intent on religious conquest. Such fears must not be summarily dismissed as unfounded because Hindus constitute a majority in India. Some Hindus frame the issue as one of unequal combatants:

> In any tradition, it is wrong to strike someone who is unarmed. In the Hindu tradition, this is considered a heinous act, for which the punishment is severe. A Buddhist, a Hindu, a Jew, are all unarmed, in that they do not convert. You cannot ask them to change the genius of their traditions and begin to convert in order to combat conversion. Because it is the tradition of these religions and cultures not to convert, attempts to convert them is one-sided aggression. It is striking the unarmed.[26]

It is this sense of helplessness and inequality that explain, in part, the appeal to the state for protection against what is perceived to be unethical and unfair methods. It also explains international appeals for support for the preservation of disappearing cultures and traditions, likening their significance and value to ancient monuments that are part of the common human heritage.

Hindus have been vocal in opposing conversions achieved by " fraudulent" methods and have lobbied for legislation against these. It is not always clear, however, whether the Hindu objection is to conversion that it considers the result of improper methods or if the opposition is against all conversion. Agreement on what constitutes fraudulent methods is extremely difficult. One attempt to clarify acceptable conversion still leaves the issue ambiguous. These are described as "spiritual conversions," resulting from self-inquiry into another tradition: "True spiritual conversion implies that a person not only understands the new religion well, but also that he is well-acquainted with his present one. In this way, he will be able to understand why the religion of his forefathers does not give him the spiritual satisfaction that he will find in his new religion."[27]

Such an inquiry, it is also specified, can only be done by one who is "materially contented," and "has the necessary education to make the inquiry." Although these specifications highlight various Hindu concerns about aggression and the exploitation of poverty and religious illiteracy, discussion and clarification on what constitutes understanding of one's own and another tradition, material contentment, and a self-initiated inquiry are still necessary. Hindus must be clear that under the label of "fraudulent" conversion they are not, in fact, failing to recognize the freedom that human beings must have to embrace other traditions and understand the valid reasons that may cause them to do so.

Conversion offers a special historical opportunity for the Hindu tradition, especially in the case of the Dalit Christians, for critical examination of those elements of its theological worldview that deny the equal worth, dignity, and freedom of others through the pervasive institution of caste and leave them with no choices but the complete rejection of such a worldview and the embrace of another. This is an opportunity also for Hindus to identify with those core and life-giving teachings that, without compromise, proclaim the equal worth and freedom of all human beings and to labor for the creation of communities that embody these teachings in the character of human relationships. At the heart of such a redeeming theological vision is the understanding that God is present equally and identically in every human being and the implications of this for social egalitarianism. Unless Hindus admit the oppressive interpretations of the tradition and the injustices of caste and do so by committing themselves to its redemptive vision, they cannot expect others to recognize this liberating face of the tradition. The Dalits have not experienced it and are rightly skeptical.

While rightly suspicious of any Hindu resistance to conversion that may be motivated by desires to preserve the power and privileges of caste through the subjection and servility of the Dalits, Christians must recognize and regard seriously Hindu concerns about conversion. Are there questionable methods and assumptions in some forms of Christian proselytization that Christians may recognize and address? Or do we persist with dismissing all such concerns as internal Hindutva colonialization? I have tried, in this contribution, to highlight some of the Hindu questions about conversion, while calling the tradition to self-critical reflection and attentiveness to the voices and experiences of suffering and protest coming from the Dalits. Hindus and Christians may not find consensus in all matters relating to conversion and this may be the consequence of deep-seated theological differences.[28] Respect for such difference by reasonable Hindus and Christians will go a long way to ensure that dialogue is mutually enriching and that relationships are non-violent.

Notes

1 An earlier version of this article was published in Christine Lienemann-Perrin and Wolfgang Lienemann (eds.), *Crossing Religions Borders: Studies on Conversion and Religious Belonging* (Wiesbaden: Harrassowitz Verlag, 2012), pp. 575–589.
2 See www.cswusa.org/filerequest/1124.pdf (accessed February 11, 2015).
3 Ashok V. Chowgule, *Christianity in India: The Hindutva Perspective* (Mumbai: Hindu Vivek Kendra, 1999), p. 10.
4 The Hindu Dharma Acharya Sabha, founded in 2003, is an umbrella organization of over 125 leaders of various Hindu traditions in India. See http://www.vivekanandagospel.org/renaissance.htm (February 11, 2015).

5 Swami Dayananda Saraswati, "Conversion Is an Act of Violence." http://www.jaia-bharati.org/anglais/swami-conviolence.htm (August 3, 2009). This rigid classification overlooks the historical occasions when these traditions have been employed to sanction violence.

6 Ibid. Of course, the assumption here is that all conversions involve the use of force upon the unwilling. This simplifies the complexity of the reasons for conversion, especially in the case of marginalized and oppressed groups who see conversion as liberation.

7 See http://www.vigilonline.com/index.php?option=com_content&task=view&id=562&Itemid=103 (accessed February 11, 2015).

8 Graham M. Schweig (trans.), *The Bhagavadgita* (New York: HarperSan Francisco, 2007).

9 It is wrong to describe the Hindu tradition as proposing that all truth claims are valid equally.

10 Swami Dayananda Saraswati, "Plenary Address Delivered at the World's Religions After 9/11," Montreal, Canada. http://www.acharya sabha.org (accessed August 5, 2009).

11 This is not to deny the historical moments when rivalries existed. On the whole, contemporary Hindus think of the various names and forms of God as complementary and as expressing one absolute being.

12 As we reflect on this issue, we must be cognizant of both the antiquity and diversity of Christianity. The Christian tradition in India has a long history. The Eastern Orthodox churches, for example, trace their arrival to the first century and have a history that is not connected with the colonial enterprise. The first Protestant teachers came against the wishes of the colonial authorities. Many have encountered the Christian tradition through fellow Indians and not Western missionaries.

13 I am indebted to Thomas Thangaraj for helping me to understand better the process of Christian identity formation in India. He traced some of the elements of this process in an unpublished paper entitled, "Who is the *Other*? – An Indian Christian Perspective," delivered at a World Council of Churches "Thinking Together" Consultation, Tampa, December 2003.

14 Swami Dayananda Saraswati, "Conversion Is an Act of Violence." Many Christians will contest vigorously Swami Dayananda's description here. What is significant is the fact that many Hindus continue to think of Christianity as hostile to Hindu culture.

15 M.K. Gandhi, *An Autobiography* (Harmondsworth: Penguin Books, 1983), pp. 46–47.

16 See www.missionindia.org (accessed August 6, 2009).

17 Hindu Vivek Kendra, *Religious Conversions* (Mumbai: Hindu Vivek Kendra, 1999), 13.

18 Hindu Vivek Kendra, *Religious Conversions*, p. 15. See also Chowgule, *Christianity in India*, pp. 67–69.
19 Nitin Sridhar, "Inculturation: Fooling the Hindu Masses." www.vijay vaani.com (accessed August 10, 2009).
20 Aloysius Pieris, *Love Meets Wisdom* (New York: Orbis Books, 1988), pp. 39–40.
21 Swami Dayananda Saraswati, "Plenary Address Delivered at the World's Religions After 9/11." www.acharysabha.org (accessed August 7, 2009).
22 Vinayak Damadar Savarkar, *Hindutva* (New Delhi: Bharti Sahitya Sadan, 1989).
23 Savarkar, *Hindutva*, pp. 102–116.
24 Subramanian Swamy, *Hindus Under Siege: The Way Out* (New Delhi: Har-Anand Publications, 2006), p. 41.
25 Diana Eck, *Encountering God* (Boston: Beacon Press 1993), p. 177.
26 Swami Dayananda Saraswati, "An Open Letter to Pope John Paul II." www.swamij.com (accessed August 10, 2009).
27 Hindu Vivek Kendra, *Religious Conversions*, p. 8.
28 See Sebastian C.H. Kim, *In Search of Identity: Debates on Religion Conversion in India* (Delhi: Oxford University Press, 2003), pp. 197–200.

8

Islamic Perspectives on Conversion
Aid Evangelism and Apostasy Law

A. Rashied Omar and Rabia Terri Harris

Introduction

In the spring of 2006 an Afghan citizen, Abdul Rahman, who had converted from Islam to Christianity, was arrested under local Shari'a law. That law mandates the death penalty for apostasy. As a result of international pressure, Abdul Rahman was released and given asylum in Italy.[1] This widely publicized incident highlighted the urgent need for Muslims to seriously re-examine existing Shari'a rulings on leaving the religion.

The task is daunting, but it is already underway. The results, as they accumulate and take on collective force, are likely to be immensely beneficial. Such a re-examination strikes at the heart of much contemporary Muslim malaise, for it requires the deployment of an interpretive methodology that takes history and humanity seriously, while distinguishing the limited and circumstantial from the eternal will of God. The foundations of such a methodology have been under construction by "progressive" Muslims for decades now.[2] What is urgently required is coherent, deep, and detailed application of those insights to the real issues that confront us – and apostasy is one of the most important of those issues. As is always the case when change is afoot, there is resistance to such a project, but there is also substantial support. Many Muslims were appalled

Religious Conversion: Religion Scholars Thinking Together, First Edition.
Edited by Shanta Premawardhana.
© 2015 World Council of Churches Publications. Published 2015 by John Wiley & Sons, Ltd.

by the mechanical brutality of the Abdul Rahman sentence. What most of us lack is a compelling religious argument for the legitimacy of our dismay.

It is far from impossible to build one. The distractions, however, are formidable. It is unfortunate, for instance, that the Abdul Rahman case took place in the ravaged context of Afghanistan, where relief aid for the victims of war is dispensed by foreign Christian agencies, some with a primarily evangelistic agenda. A similar program of aid evangelism has been undertaken in war-torn Iraq. In such circumstances, conversion appears as either a hypocritical maneuver for advantage or an outright capitulation to despair. Many Muslims are appalled by such exploitation of suffering. And in these situations, it is *force majeure* that has ignored the legitimacy of our dismay.

For any progress to be possible in such a standoff, it is important to realize that both "gut reactions" of horror spring from the same origin. The Prophet Muhammad taught that all human beings have an intrinsic spiritual compass that points toward the right: *dîn al-fitrah*, natural religion. And in both these cases that compass points toward the principle enunciated in the Qur'an (2:256) as *lâ iqrâha fîd-dîn*: there must be no compulsion in religion.

This chapter argues that both the prevailing Muslim positions on apostasy and Christian engagement in aid with the primary intent of evangelism are morally indefensible and generate significant harm. It concludes by challenging Christians and Muslims committed to interreligious dialogue to move from cloistered conference declarations to creative community action.

It might be useful to commence by revisiting the question of religious conversion in the context of interreligious dialogue. The problem of the right to religious conversion and the ethics of Christian mission and Islamic *da'wah*[3] has been a longstanding topic of debate in scholarly dialogue circles. The subject was considered at length during a meeting between Christian and Muslim scholars and leaders in Chambesy, Switzerland in 1976.[4] Since then, the issue has been raised intermittently, most notably at a "Christian–Muslim Consultation on Religious Freedom, Community Rights and Individual Rights" sponsored by the Office of Interreligious Relations and Dialogue of the World Council of Churches (WCC) at the Duncan Black MacDonald Center for the Study of Islam and Christian–Muslim Relations in Hartford, Connecticut, in 1999.[5] More recently, the question has resurfaced at a number of interreligious forums. For example, at the "Critical Moment in Interreligious Dialogue" conference convened by the WCC in Geneva, June 7–9, 2005, the twin problems of religious conversion and the ethics of mission were raised as one of the most divisive issues between religious communities.[6]

Both Christian and Muslim scholars of interreligious relations share concerns over the right to conversion and the ethics of mission. Elizabeth Scantlebury, for example, has argued that the matter of Christian mission and Islamic *da'wah* is central to the negative model of interaction between the followers of the two religions.[7] Similarly, the Muslim thinker and scholar Seyyed Hossein Nasr observed that "one of the most contentious issues in the dialogue between Islam and Christianity is missionary activity." He goes on to describe it as one of the obstacles and outstanding problems in Islamic–Christian dialogue.[8] Therefore, we begin with asking the question: How does Christian mission today actually compare to Islamic *da'wah*?

Christian Mission and Islamic *Da'wah*: A Comparative Perspective

Renowned scholar of Christian–Muslim relations David Kerr correctly argues that "little scholarly attention has yet been given to the comparative study of Islamic da'wa and Christian mission"[9] (the 1976 Chambesy meeting stands practically alone). Yet despite the paucity of comparative studies, a noticeable trend emerges. Non-Muslim scholars such as William Wagner,[10] J. Dudley Woodberry,[11] and to a lesser extent Antoine Wessels[12] have highlighted the parallels between Muslim *da'wah* and Christian mission. Muslim scholars, on the other hand, have been eager to point out significant differences. Three renowned Muslim scholars who have emphasized these differences are the Pakistani economist and thinker Khurshid Ahmad; the late Sayed Zainul Abedin, founder of the Institute for Muslim Minority Affairs; and the late Palestinian-American scholar Isma'il Raji al-Faruqi.[13]

In his editorial to the published proceedings of the 1976 Chambesy Consultation, Ahmad, for example, called attention to differences in the way Muslims and Christians "offer their message to others and at a deeper level, in the way they concern themselves with the world."[14] In particular, he drew a sharp distinction between the methods of doing *da'wah* and what he called "the widespread abuse of Christian *diakonia*."[15] Ahmad's position was reflected in the final declaration of the Chambesy Consultation, which condemned in clear terms the misuse of *diakonia* (caritative service and support), and strongly urged Christian churches and organizations to suspend their misused *diakonia* activities in the world of Islam.[16] Although representatives of two of the leading Christian bodies – the Pontifical Council for Interreligious Dialogue and the Inter-religious Office of the WCC – endorsed the Chambesy declaration, it subsequently became clear that not all Christians agreed with the strong stance that was adopted. And some Christian scholars have since made similar charges of Muslim organizations' offering monetary enticements to Christians in exchange for their conversion to Islam.

Abedin takes Ahmad's critique even further and proposes that *da'wah* means witness borne to the truth solely by means of the exemplary lives of individuals and communities. He contends that making religious conversion the explicit and measurable objective of *da'wah* violates both the prerogative of God, who alone changes the hearts of human beings, and humanity's God-given freedom of choice, without which the call of Islam to faithful submission would be meaningless.[17] Abedin also draws a sharp distinction between *da'wah* and dialogue. He defines interfaith dialogue as different from evangelism and mission, and sees its primary function as that of social solidarity, joining hands in equality and respect to fashion a better world.[18] Abedin's definitions of *da'wah* and its methodology are idiosyncratic, but they may provide us with a useful clue for the development of an ethic of mission and *da'wah*.

Among these three Muslim scholars, Faruqi in particular has accentuated *da'wah*'s divergences from Christian mission. During his presentation at Chambesy he defined *da'wah* as "ecumenical *par excellence*. All religious traditions," he proposed, "are *de jure*," by which he means that "they have all issued from and are based upon a common source, the religion of God which he planted equally in all men ... *din al-fitrah*." While committed to religious pluralism in principle, Faruqi opposes relativism and what he describes as "kitchen cooperation," a kind of lazy ecumenism. Based on this novel outlook on religious mission, Faruqi views Islamic *da'wah* as "an ecumenical cooperative critique of the other religion *rather than its invasion by a new truth*" [our italics].[19]

The tension between Christian and Muslim scholarly perspectives on their common commitment to mission is usefully illustrated by J. Dudley Woodberry when he claims that Faruqi's conception of the nature and ethics of *da'wah* "shows considerable parallels with Christian mission, though he does not recognize it."[20] Woodberry's assertion suggests a significant gap in understanding between many Christians and Muslims on the way in which they perceive their respective missions.

David Kerr is one of the few scholars who have been attentive to this tension. Kerr develops a conceptual distinction between what he calls the "sending notion" of Christian mission and the "calling notion" of Islamic *da'wah*. "The former," Kerr suggests, "entails a centrifugal process while the second is centripetal."[21] He is acutely aware that these theological concepts are shaped by historical experience and actual practice. He furthermore proposes that Christian–Muslim reflections on mutual understandings of mission and *da'wah* may find renewed consensus in the Eastern Orthodox Church's concept of "witness" (Greek *martyria*). The concept resonates with the Qur'anic concept of *shahâda* and may provide a way of clarifying intentions and avoiding the malpractices of proselytism.[22] The ongoing challenge for Muslims and Christians is to find an ethical consensus on what Woodberry usefully describes as "mutual respectful witness."[23] We shall look again at the Islamic implications of witness later in this chapter.

Partly in recognition of the pressing nature of this challenge to interreligious dialogue, Dr. Hans Ucko, of the WCC's Office on Interreligious Relations and Dialogue, called on the Pontifical Council for Interreligious Dialogue to join the WCC in assuming responsibility to address what he described as "one of the most controversial issues in interreligious relations: conversion."[24] But why have the questions of religious conversion and the ethics of mission and *da'wah* re-emerged as critical issues for interreligious dialogue at this time?

The Context for the Re-emergence of the Debate

We argue that geopolitics is the key source of renewed interest in the right to religious conversion and the ethics of mission and *da'wah*. In support of this claim we draw on the theoretical insights offered by Elizabeth Scantlebury. In a seminal article published exactly two decades after the Chambesy dialogue, Scantlebury argued that the contestation of the two faiths to gain converts at the other's expense always takes place within specific social and historical contexts, which in turn significantly affect the way those involved interpret the situation.[25] The sociopolitical context may account for why many Christians and Muslims see the relationship between mission and *da'wah* differently. The negative experience of Christian mission as a facilitator of colonialism may propel Muslims to idealize their understanding of *da'wah* in order to distance it from the historical practice of Christian mission in Muslim contexts. And following Scantlebury, we contend that questions of comparative conversion ethics have drawn new energy among Christians from an uneasy sense of Christian vulnerability to Islam after 9/11, along with the aggressiveness of certain Christian aid agencies accompanying the US-led wars in Afghanistan and Iraq.

In this latter regard it may be expedient to note, for example, the views of the American evangelical scholar Charles Marsh. Marsh brought the problem of war as a context for proselytization into sharp relief in an editorial in the *New York Times* of January 21, 2006.[26] He contends that not only did "[A]n astonishing 87% of all white evangelical Christians in the United States" provide overt religious legitimation for the American invasions of Afghanistan and Iraq, but some of their most prominent leaders, like Franklin Graham [27] and Marvin Olasky,[28] drummed up support for the wars through Sunday congregational sermons touting such conflicts as creating "exciting new prospects for proselytizing Muslims."[29]

Yet the issue of Christian proselytization was already a vexed question in Afghanistan before war was declared. In August 2001, the Taliban charged eight members of a German aid agency, Shelter Now, with promoting Christianity under the cover of relief efforts. The workers were all later rescued by a US helicopter. This incident was touted as yet another example of the lack of religious freedom in Muslim countries,[30] and the freeing of the aid workers was greeted with great fanfare by certain Christian groups. That false pretenses might indeed be involved, that the Shelter Now strategy of dissimulation might be offensive, or that in the Afghan context conversion might function as subversion, was nowhere considered. Therefore it is scarcely surprising that, almost four years after the US invasion, the right to convert to Christianity found its "poster boy" in Afghan national Abdul Rahman.

There have been many other similar cases, frequently charged under the Taliban's harsh "blasphemy laws." But whether Christian mission is well or ill intentioned, and whether explicit conversion initiatives are socially destabilizing or not, such laws generate grave religious problems of their own.

The Conflict between Religious Freedom and Islamic Apostasy Law

Abdul Rahman converted to Christianity in 1990 while working as a medical assistant for a Christian non-governmental aid group in Peshawar, Pakistan. Sixteen years later, in February 2006 (during the protracted Western military presence in Afghanistan), he was arrested and charged with apostasy under what were interpreted to be traditional Shari'a laws. The case received worldwide publicity, with an Afghan court threatening to execute Abdul Rahman if he did not repent. As the direct consequence of a vociferous international outcry, the judge dismissed the case on the traditional ground of insanity. Despite his acquittal, the defendant was forced to leave Afghanistan and was given asylum in Italy for fear of social recriminations.[31]

Whatever its political context, Abdul Rahman's story is also a simple human tragedy, and we must take this tragedy seriously.

It is not good enough for Muslims engaged in interreligious dialogue to skirt the issue by hiding behind their support for the Chambesy statement affirming "the right to convince or to be convinced."[32] A close reading of the Chambesy discussions discloses that, despite their support for the declaration, the Muslim interlocutors were equivocating. At one point in the discussions, Bishop Kenneth Cragg felt compelled to spell out unambiguously the Christian concern about the Muslim position on religious freedom in the following manner: "... we are not talking about freedom of belief, or of religious practice, but the freedom of movement of belief and there is a radical difference between these two. A faith which you are not free to leave becomes a prison, and no self-respecting faith should be a prison for those within it."[33]

The equivocation of liberal Muslim academics is grave enough. Yet graver is the fact that "the right to be convinced" and therefore to convert from Islam to another religion, even as a theoretical possibility, is supported by only a minority of Muslim scholars, past and present. Most classical and modern Muslim jurists regard apostasy (*riddah*), defined by them as an act of rejection of faith committed by a Muslim whose Islam had been affirmed without coercion, as a crime deserving the death penalty. Almost all traditional books of Islamic jurisprudence (*fiqh*) deal extensively with the penalties to be imposed on apostates. These include the disposition of apostates' property and inheritance and the dissolution of their marriages.[34] The preponderance of classical Islamic positions proscribing apostasy makes all too understandable the harsh recent responses to Abdul Rahman. But these classical positions are political rulings articulating the laws of treason, of willful betrayal of the community for ulterior motives. They never entertain the notion that a rational, sincere change of views might not only be possible, but sometimes even healthy for the community as a whole.

Islam is designed to be a religion of conviction. When one utters the *shahâdah*, the profession of faith that makes one a Muslim, it is not sufficient to say, "There is no god but God. Muhammad is the servant and messenger of God." Before each of these statements it is necessary to declare, "I bear witness." Conscious assent is the foundation of faith. But consent cannot be forced. Not only is it religiously impermissible (*lâ iqrâha fîd-dîn* – "there must be no compulsion in religion") but it is actually impossible. As a famous *hadîth* puts it, "the heart is between the two fingers of the All-Compassionate God, and God turns it howsoever God pleases." Our state of heart, or conscience, is the direct business of God. And a *shahâdah* of the tongue that is not a *shahâdah* of the heart is inadmissible according to religious law.

Islam, as a converting religion, rests its whole structure upon the interior change of hearts. This change is documented in story after story of the early Companions of the Prophet. Since that time, however, the vast majority of Muslims have inherited their Islam as a social "given." They seldom encounter Islam as a spiritually transformative force, but rather as rote custom, the rationale of the *status quo*. Rote custom easily becomes a degenerate condition. And rote custom *of any kind* is coercive by default, especially when that custom includes few emergency mechanisms for permitting change. The tyranny of custom essentially violates the basic principle of *lâ iqrâha fîd-dîn* – there must be no compulsion in religion. When that custom is punitively enforced, whether socially or legally, the violation doubles. Given this reality, it stands to reason that some people will be unable to recover the spiritual gift at the core of the tradition of their birth, and must seek guidance elsewhere. One might hope that eventually their growth would permit them to "arrive where they started, and know the place for the first time," as T.S. Eliot said in the *Four Quartets*. But in any case it is important for each of us to be able to bear witness to whatever it is we actually see. That alone is sincerity, and sincerity is religion. The Qur'an calls its teaching *dîn al-haqq*, the religion of truth. But a *shahâdah* of the tongue that cares nothing for the heart is the institutionalization of a lie.

Acknowledging all this, in modern times a number of Muslim scholars have argued for more lenient and humane positions on apostasy, and they have marshaled strong support. (The web site http://apostasyandislam.blogspot.com/ has already accumulated 104 scholarly voices on the topic, and the number is growing.)[35] The viewpoint issued by Louay Safi of the Islamic Society of North America (ISNA), in the context of the Abdul Rahman furor, is representative of this trend. Safi declares unequivocally that a "Muslim who converts to Christianity is no more a Muslim, but a Christian, and must be respected as such."[36]

Notwithstanding the growing strength of tolerant Islamic positions on religious conversion, Muslims engaged in interreligious dialogue need to be more honest and forthcoming about the enormous challenge they are accepting in seeking to reform the hegemonic traditional Muslim position on apostasy. Indeed, the reintroduction of the notion of freedom of conscience into Islamic discourse is nothing less than an intellectual revolution in progress.

It appears to us that there are two major obstacles this revolution must overcome. The first is a widespread misdirection of loyalty. The second is the broad generalization of a sense of threat. Both these mechanisms are common human phenomena, brought to a point of particular poignancy among Muslims by the course of recent history. Readers may well recognize them from other religious contexts. Our particular responsibility as Muslims, however, concerns their presence within Islam.

Loyalty to past scholars' opinions, and to established custom, is equivalent in many Muslim minds to loyalty to the religion itself, and loyalty to the religion of Islam is equivalent to loyalty to God. In the name of these conflated loyalties, contemporary Muslim jurists uncritically impose upon present-day realities medieval legal positions that were negotiated in radically different circumstances. To these jurists, it seems obvious that the great past was right, while the miserable present is wrong. The re-establishment of divine order therefore requires the heroic *denial of significance* to lived experience. In the name of these conflated loyalties – that is to say, in the name of conflated loyalties – such faithful give up their own inner "freedom of movement of belief." This sacrifice of one's own lived experience comes at high emotional cost, and the nobility of such painful loyalty must be vigorously defended. How else is one to explain the broad attachment to the death penalty verdict among traditional Muslim scholars and the social ostracization meted out to so-called apostates – the unashamedly and ultimately "disloyal" – in many Muslim societies?

The situation is exacerbated by the shattering trauma inflicted by European colonialism upon those societies. It has barely registered on most of the subjugated peoples of the world that they have, in fact, survived, and that imperialism itself is in a long, slow process of implosion. The pain has simply been too great. Nor is that pain likely to end tomorrow. It still feels, in many places, as if the suffering goes on forever. Radical measures of community self-defense may well seem rational in such circumstances. Yet the Qur'an (79:25–26) is quite clear that by the very nature of things, every pharaoh is doomed to fall. With upwards of one billion Muslims in the world, Islam is scarcely in any danger. And God, of course, is never in any danger, and requires no defense.

Muslims are eloquent in their condemnation of the empires of the West. We like to believe, however, that our own empires were far superior and, reconstructed somehow, would still be far superior today. There is precious little evidence of that. Meanwhile, as long as empire, in whatever form, occupies the horizon of human political imagination, all of our religions remain in serious trouble.

Mission and *Da'wah* in a War Context

Both Christians and Muslims have historically been implicated in spreading their faiths through wars and conquests, though this is not the complete story of the growth and expansion of these world traditions. In fact, more peaceful and humane methods predominate as ways in which Christianity and Islam have historically been transmitted. The problem, however, is the romanticization of our

128

imperial legacies and the consequent denial that abuses ever occurred – a tendency that is compounded by polemical scholarship which attempts to show that one religion has been more culpable than the other. Such dispositions stand in the way of serious efforts at seeking interreligious coexistence and sustainable peace building in the contemporary era. Our times demand, instead, sincere acts of contrition and the cultivation of forgiveness to heal the memories of our sufferings and trespasses. Even more critical is the interreligious challenge of together finding ways to prevent such atrocities from ever occurring again.

This being said, it remains a fact that despite the fear and damage intentionally generated by small-group efforts toward Islamic imperial resurgence, there has been no Muslim empire in existence for nearly a century now, while "Christian" empire, unevenly secularized, is vastly mighty and just beginning to ebb. Christian efforts toward the conversion of Muslims are correspondingly strongly resourced, and often aggressive, whereas Muslim efforts toward the conversion of Christians are weakly resourced, and often defensive. Each power position generates distinctive attitudes and strategies, regardless of who holds it. Globally, however, the two positions have clear occupants at present.

We must look more closely, therefore, at the sad complementarity of modern Muslim apostasy cases and Christian evangelical exploitation of social crises. The fiercest of these crises is war, and the most shameful of exploitations are those that take place under cover of wars instituted by "Christian" (or "Judaeo-Christian") nations.

In April 2003, almost exactly one month after the United States of America launched a pre-emptive war against Iraq, *Time* magazine reported that two Christian aid organizations, the International Mission Board of the Southern Baptist Convention and Samaritan's Purse, were waiting on the border between Jordan and Iraq for a green light from the US military command. They intended to enter Iraq in order to engage in what they called "aid evangelism." The Reverend Franklin Graham, son of the influential evangelist Billy Graham and head of Samaritan's Purse, justified his objective by claiming that the goal of the aid ministry in Iraq was "to heal people, and hopefully they will see God."[37]

The controversial context and insensitive timing of the Samaritan's Purse proselytization program was not accidental: it was a deliberate and well-orchestrated strategy. Samaritan's Purse and its leader have been some of the most ardent religious supporters of the US war in Iraq. Moreover, this was not the first time in recent history that Christian evangelists had used war as a means for spreading the gospel. It is well known that during the 1991 Gulf conflict, Reverend Franklin Graham's organization gave US soldiers 30,000 Arabic Bibles for distribution in Iraq and the neighboring Muslim-majority countries.[38]

The basic principle of respect for the religious other has been flagrantly missing from the rhetoric, as well as the actions, of many prominent evangelical leaders who have turned their attention to the Muslim world. Franklin Graham,[39] Jerry Falwell, Pat Robertson, and Jerry Vines have all made astonishingly derogatory statements. Graham, for example, famously called Islam "a very evil and wicked religion."[40] And in a recent book, *Secrets of the Koran*, evangelical missionary Don Richardson claimed, "The Koran's good verses are like the food an assassin adds to poison to disguise a deadly taste."[41] Major evangelical churches and church organizations, such as the Southern Baptist Convention, regularly convene seminars and lectures on Islam that characterize the religion as regressive and violent.[42] It is therefore not surprising that the vice president for governmental affairs of the National Association of Evangelicals, Reverend Richard Cizik, is on record as saying, "Evangelicals have substituted Islam for the Soviet Union," and that "The Muslims have become the modern-day equivalent of the Evil Empire."[43]

All of this raises two pertinent and interrelated questions. First, might the evangelical outreach to Muslims properly be grasped as a new crusade against Islam, however unintentional? Might one even discern in this practice the recurring colonial theme of Christian mission and Western military dominance joined at the hip? Second, is it ever ethical to use philanthropic activities and humanitarian service to support proselytism among victims of war? The answers will have important implications for conflict transformation and interreligious peace building.

Misled by Dialogue

As has already been noted, aid evangelism was one of the key questions addressed by the 1976 Chambesy dialogue, and the conference took a firm position. It strongly condemned any *diakonia* (service) undertaken for any ulterior motive and not as an expression of *agape* (love).[44] The conference urged Christian churches and religious organizations to immediately suspend such efforts in the Muslim world. It was indeed a courageous and ambitious resolution, and raised high expectations. These expectations were grievously disappointed.

Perhaps it was naive of the Muslim participants to believe that their Christian interlocutors had the authority, within their institutions, to implement the Chambesy agreements. Yet such hope existed. Five years after those deliberations, the UK-based Islamic Foundation published a report declaring that "The misused *diakonia* ties in the world of Islam not only have not been discontinued, but in fact expanded since 1976, on a vast scale and with the knowledge and participation of the very same institutions whose members were participants at Chambesy."[45] The trigger for this report was the discovery by Foundation researcher Ahmad von Denffer of a multi-million-dollar campaign launched by the Lutheran Churches in Germany, an affiliate of the WCC, to evangelize Fulani Muslims all over West Africa using *diakonia* as a cover.[46] The Islamic Foundation republished the proceedings of the Chambesy dialogue in protest.

It is against this backdrop that the interreligious movement needs once again to address the question of aid evangelism. There does not seem to be any overall Christian consensus with regard to the ethics of the practice. The one-time consensus expressed at Chambesy has clearly been ignored.

To their credit, both the WCC and the Pontifical Council on Interreligious Affairs have, since Chambesy, consistently reaffirmed their commitment to eschewing unethical forms of mission, including aid evangelism. In fact, during the 1999 WCC-sponsored "Christian–Muslim Consultation on Religious Freedom" held at Hartford Seminary, Connecticut, the participants recommitted themselves to "the relevance and value of the 1976 Chambesy statement" and affirmed the importance of distinguishing between proselytism and witness, as the WCC has done within the Christian context. Participants also emphasized the necessity for elucidating an ethics of mission and *da'wah* to which both Christians and Muslims can agree.[47] More recently, Archbishop Michael Fitzgerald, then President of the Pontifical Council for Interreligious Relations, proposed that "Christians do not engage in works of mercy as a pretext for preaching about Jesus Christ but, like the Good Samaritan, out of compassion for those who are suffering. So it can be said that interreligious dialogue is not aimed at bringing the partner in dialogue into the Catholic Church."[48]

Unfortunately, this Catholic understanding of the Christian narrative of the Good Samaritan is not shared by the evangelical relief organization bearing the same name. The international director of projects for Samaritan's Purse, Ken Isaacs, interprets his divine calling as connecting the physical care of Iraqi Muslims to their spiritual salvation. In response to concerns raised about the ethics and strategic wisdom of his organization's relief efforts in Iraq, he responded, "We do not deny the name of Christ. We believe in sharing him in deed and word." Such an entrenched disrespect is as difficult to endure as it is to dislodge.[49]

During the Vietnam era, hungry people in the war zone who "accepted Christ as their personal savior" in order to be fed came to be known as "rice Christians." The cynicism of their religion was legendary. Whether such converts are of any real value to Christianity is problematic. Meanwhile, desperation demands compassion. But what if the carrot dangled by the missionary is less survival than advantage? In time of war and brutal cultural domination, changing religion really may mean changing sides, and apostasy really may mean treason. What then?

A number of Muslim scholars, such as Mahmoud Ayoub, have pointed out that apostasy has been an explicitly political problem in both early and later Muslim societies, and that the problem has increased with the advent of colonialism and the expansion of Christian missionary activity.[50] While it would be incorrect to suggest that the harsh Shari'a views on apostasy were first formulated in the colonial era, there can be no doubt that colonial-era Christian missions generated a harsher interpretation of the Shari'a law. Similarly, the recent debate triggered by the legal persecution of Abdul Rahman emerged from a context where relief aid for war victims was dispensed by agencies linked to the perceived aggressors. We contend that the Abdul Rahman furor did not occur in a social vacuum but in a concrete political context, and was, not surprisingly, magnified by it.

There are, of course, many religious conversions that do not take place through aid evangelism or under other forms of pressure or temptation, yet still incur religious persecution in Muslim societies. However, these cases are regrettably overshadowed by the other variety. We need to learn how to distinguish conversions that validate conscience from those that violate it, and to determine truly equitable responses in either case. For this we must use all the resources of *fiqh*, of Islamic legal thinking. That few have attempted this project until recently is a historical distortion that must be corrected. But the correction is in process.

Strengthening the Muslim case for the reform of traditional apostasy law will require some Christian help. Without a moratorium on inappropriate Christian proselytization, as recommended by the Chambesy declaration, it will be difficult to convince Muslim hardliners that apostasy reform is anything but groundwork for Christian opportunism. Our Christian interlocutors may need to labor hard in order to persuade their co-religionists to leave such "opportunities" alone.

Religious Freedom and Community Solidarity in Islam: A Way Forward

This chapter is not the place to launch a fully developed formal argument for the rethinking of classical Islamic apostasy law. Furthermore, our space allotment is insufficient, a great deal of preliminary explanation would be required for the uninitiated, and those with the deepest involvement in the issue are unlikely to consult this volume. We can, however, speaking from our experience as an imam and a theologian, suggest some materials relevant to the construction of such an argument, present them here and elsewhere, and pray that God will place them in the most expert hands.

Islamic legal reasoning is strongly based on original precedent. The texts that set our norms are, in order of authority, the Qur'an, reports of the words and actions of the Prophet (*hadîth*), reports of the words and actions of the Prophet's intimate followers or Companions, and the dominant opinions of our various legal schools. Of these sources, the last, school opinion, is maintained by intellectual consensus only: its authority continues only to the extent that consensus about its value continues. The authority of the Companions, however, is based on statements of the Prophet. The authority of the Prophet is based on statements of the Qur'an. And the authority of the Qur'an is based on the mercy and wisdom of God, who alone is the ultimate authority.

133

Relying on that mercy and wisdom, and joining a growing chorus of voices, we suggest that contemporary Muslims put aside the existing school positions and reconsider the evidence presented at higher levels of authority.

The Qur'an. While the Qur'an warns that those who profess Islam and then leave it attract divine displeasure and will be held accountable in the next life, it nowhere states that such people are liable to worldly penalty. This silence is significant in itself, since the text deals closely with social transgressions that are potentially capital offenses. We therefore know immediately that leaving the religion cannot be among these. Meanwhile, the basic principle of *lâ iqrâha fîd-dîn* – there should be no compulsion in religion – may not be controverted.

Hadîth. The strongest root of the classical position is a *hadîth* relating that the Prophet said, "Whoever changes religion should be killed." Contemporary European Islamic thinker Tariq Ramadan has questioned the authenticity of this *hadîth*. Such questioning is a traditional route for legal revision, since if there is doubt concerning the attribution of a statement to the Prophet, that statement cannot be used to construct a norm. However, Ramadan provides only partial evidence for his position, while this *hadîth* is included in widely respected collections. It may be that closer examination will allow it to be discounted. However, if it cannot be discounted, then given its dissonance with general Qur'anic principle, it must be carefully contextualized. Since it is fundamental that there can be no disharmony between Revelation and Prophetic example, any seeming disharmony must result from the unique requirements of a limited case.

So if the Prophet indeed made this statement, then when did he make it? If specialists have uncovered that information, it has not yet reached us. In its absence, though, we can venture a hypothesis. The statement may have reference to the particular constraints under which the earliest Muslims waged war against the Makkans, who wished to obliterate them. The rules of engagement of the Muslim community required that if a battlefield opponent in single combat declared "I bear witness that there is no god but God," thereby affirming Islam, his Muslim co-combatant had *immediately* to lay down arms. Against complaints from his army that such utterance from the opposition was nothing but a tactic to allow escape, Muhammad insisted that only God could judge hearts. This decision leaves the problem of opponents who might utter the profession of faith and then re-enter the battlefield against the Muslims, whether during the same encounter or later. It would be absurd and militarily disastrous to treat them as anything but open enemies. It is in such circumstances that the statement reported takes on logical consistency.

Should our hypothesis prove insufficiently convincing by itself, it is also possible to offer a counter-report that argues against the generalization of the *hadîth* in question. Ramadan points out that the earliest biography of the Prophet, the *Sîrah* of Ibn Hisham, offers just such a report. The *Sîrah* relates that during an early sojourn of the core Muslim community in Abyssinia, long before the Muslims relocated from Makka [Mecca] to Madina [Medina], one of them,'Ubaydullah ibn Jahsh, embraced Christianity. He remained in Abyssinia when the others returned, and stayed a Christian until his death. Although in the process of conversion 'Ubaydullah divorced his Muslim wife, neither the Prophet from Makka nor any of the emigrant Muslims around him called for penalties against him or condemned him in any way. This report deserves just as much respect, and careful examination, as does the first.[51]

Example of the Companions. The most important precedent at this level for the formation of classical opinion is the example of Abu Bakr, first caliph of the post-Prophetic community, who declared war against a number of Bedouin tribes that attempted to withdraw from the Muslim confederation after the Prophet's death. The *Riddah* (or Apostasy) Wars forcibly returned these to the fold. The classical argument is that, therefore, all seceders must forcibly be returned to the fold. We believe this is a false generalization.

The Bedouin tribes who joined the confederation during the Prophet's last days did not become Muslim individual by individual, after the fashion in which the core community had formed and grown over many years, through the transformation of hearts. Instead, their tribal Islam was a political pledge of allegiance, taken corporately, and motivated at least in part by a keen sense of the main chance. We may presume it was met with something of the same skeptical spirit that greeted those earlier battlefield opponents who made tactical *shahâdah* when the going got rough. When the Prophet's passing led these tribes to expect a power vacuum, they were prompt in looking for opportunities elsewhere. This could well have unraveled the fragile new society. Abu Bakr did not make war on them because they had undergone a change of heart. He made war on them because they had *broken their given word*: they had violated a treaty. The thing that most concerned him was that they were refusing to pay *zakah*, the alms share due to the poor, as they had previously promised. So he took action against them until they did.

This episode had little to do with freedom of conscience, and much to do with social responsibility. Exemplifying the Qur'anic ethic, the Prophet was emphatic about keeping one's word and emphatic about caring for the poor. Abu Bakr followed his priorities, and so should we. Adhering to this principle leads us toward a different generalization.

Of course there are many born Muslims who are deeply committed. Yet many more are not. Muslims who do no more than inherit their Islam and "go along with the crowd" have made no binding personal pledge. If it so happens that their consciences lead a few of them outside their traditional religion, that is irrelevant to the jurisdiction of Abu Bakr's decision, for it is impossible to break a promise that was never given. The position of such people resembles the position of single members of the late-affiliating Bedouin tribes. To the extent that contemporary societies have specifically accepted a Muslim identity, it is these *societies* that have made the promise of Islam, at the corporate level. And if these societies refuse to support the poor, they have broken their word, and have refused Islam after publicly affirming it. This leads us to the surprising conclusion that action undertaken to *make* them support the poor might be religiously required – a conclusion that must be complemented by a second conclusion, about active non-violence, that falls beyond our particular interests here.

In support of our contention that individual members of Muslim societies are free to choose where they belong, we add an example from the next higher level of authority. When the Prophet signed a truce with the people of Makka – a truce that led, within three years, to a Muslim victory without bloodshed – he agreed to terms that surprised and troubled his advisors. He said that Makkans who left their city to join the Muslim community in Madina would be returned to Makka – a very painful decision. And he said that Muslims who gave up the community in Madina to rejoin the old life at Makka could remain where they had gone.

We have no record that any Muslim fled. That speaks to the difference between the Prophet's community and our own. Were we truly what we aspire to be, no one would choose to leave us, either. Given where we actually are, it's not surprising that some do. We could take that difference as a metric measuring the state of Muslim societies. Just as those who travel into the community tell us what is good about ourselves, those who travel out of it tell us what needs mending. We need that information, if we are sincere. The ones who leave for conscience are communicating with the Muslim conscience. We should not treat them as the Makkans did, demanding them back against their will. It is in our own best interests that the Prophet's decision should stand.

Conclusion

To sum up, it seems clear that while Christians disagree about the ethics of aid evangelism in the context of war, Muslims are close to united in condemning it. The reverse is the case on the question of the right to religious conversion. While Muslims are ambivalent about the right of their co-religionists to change religions, Christians affirm Muslim conversion as a human right. (We have not heard enough Christian thinking about *Christians* who change faiths.) Of course the different theological postures adopted by Christian and Muslim scholars are profoundly influenced by historical reality and power relations, as was so impressively illustrated by Elizabeth Scantlebury. Honest dialogue can only begin with a clear recognition of this reality. A joint Christian–Muslim assessment of power imbalances should include not only misuses of mission and *da'wah*, but also a strong rejection of all forms of violence and terrorism, including state terror. The belligerent environment resulting from these acts of barbarism threatens the relations of Christians and Muslims around the world.

The current authors hold that both aid evangelism and apostasy punishments are forms of coercion that do violence to the human soul.

We advise Muslims to heed the late Professor Isma'il al-Faruqi's call for the understanding of *da'wah* as an "ecumenical cooperative critique of the other religion." For Christians we recommend the invitation of Father Henri Sanson, SJ, of Algiers. Father Sanson asks Christians to reflect on their vocation toward Muslims "in the mirror of Islam." That is, they should take into account at every step the corresponding missionary vocation with which their Muslim partners in faith know themselves to be charged.[52] And for both communities, we commend J. Dudley Woodberry's recognition that there are times when only the deed is appropriate – as was the case when Jesus healed a leper and then instructed him to tell no one.

The deeper challenge for both Christians and Muslims committed to interreligious dialogue and peace building is to go beyond mere *declarations* of the right of any individual to change his or her religion, the easy decrying of inappropriate means to entice persons to switch faiths. Instead, Christian and Muslim interreligious leaders and activists need urgently to find creative ways of making such positive affirmations effective within our own communities, establishing them as a key part of the *modus vivendi* of convivial relations between us. May God, the best of knowers, open the way!

Notes

1 For a detailed account of the Abdul Rahman conversion and trial in Afghanistan see http://en.wikipedia.org/wiki/Abdul_Rahman_ (convert) (accessed January 2010).

2 For a useful definition of "progressive" Muslims, see Omid Safi (ed.), *Progressive Muslims: On Justice, Gender, and Pluralism* (Oxford: Oneworld Publications, 2003).

3 *Da'wah* is an Arabic word meaning "call" or "invitation," and the noun form, *da'i* (plural *du'at*), refers to "one who calls or invites to Islam." We will discuss its nature more extensively later in this chapter.

4 For the full proceedings of the Chambesy meeting, see *Christian Mission and Islamic Da'wah: Proceedings of the Chambesy Dialogue Consultation* (Leicester, UK: Islamic Foundation, 1977). Hereafter *Proceedings*.

5 For the final report on this conference see *Current Dialogue* (34), February 2000 (Geneva: World Council of Churches). http://www.wcc-coe.org/wcc/what/interreligious/cd34-19.html (accessed March 2006).

6 For a brief report see World Council of Churches, *From Harare to Porto Alegre 1998–2006: An Illustrated Account of the Life of the World Council of Churches* (Geneva: 2005), p. 89. For more details on the "Critical Moment in Interreligious Dialogue Conference," see http://wcc-coe.org/wcc/what/interreligious/cd45-01.html (accessed February 17, 2015).

7 Elizabeth Scantlebury, "Islamic Da'wah and Christian Mission: Positive and Negative Models of Interaction between Muslims and Christians," *Islam and Christian–Muslim Relations* 7.3 (1996), 253–269.

8 Seyyed Hossein Nasr, "Islamic–Christian Dialogue: Problems and Obstacles to Be Pondered and Overcome," *Islam and Christian–Muslim Relations* 11.2 (2000), 213–227.

9 David A. Kerr, "Islamic Da'wa and Christian Mission: Towards a Comparative Analysis," *International Review of Mission* 89.353 (2000), 150–171. For the full proceedings of the Chambesy meeting, see *Proceedings*.

10 William Wagner, "A Comparison of Christian Mission and Islamic Da'wah," *Missiology* 31.3 (2003), 339–347.

11 J. Dudley Woodberry. "Toward Mutual Respectful Witness," unpublished paper delivered at the Conflict Transformation Project: Interfaith Dialogue, Fuller Theological Seminary and Salam: Institute for Peace and Justice, Rockville, Maryland, USA, April 22–23, 2005.

12 Antoine Wessels, "Mission and Da'wah: From Exclusion to Mutual Witness," *Church and Society* 84.1 (1994), 101–112.

13 For a discussion of these differences, see Ataullah Siddiqui, *Christian–Muslim Dialogue in the Twentieth Century* (Basingstoke, UK: Palgrave Macmillan, 1997).

14 Khurshid Ahmad, "Editorial," *Proceedings*.

15 Ahmad, "Editorial," *Proceedings*, p. 101.

16 Sayed Zainul Abedin, "Da'wa and Dialogue: Believers and Promotion of Mutual Trust," in *Beyond Frontiers: Islam and Contemporary Needs* (London: Mansell, 1989).

17 Abedin, "Da'wa and Dialogue."

18 Abedin, "Da'wa and Dialogue," p. 54.

19 Isma'il Raji al-Faruqi, "On the Nature of Islamic Da'wah," *International Review of Mission* 65.260 (1976), 391–400. See also Isma'il Raji al-Faruqi, *Islam and Other Faiths*, edited by Ataullah Siddiqui (Leicester, UK: Islamic Foundation, 1989), p. 312.

20 J. Dudley Woodberry, "Toward Mutual Respectful Witness," in Mohammed Abu-Nimer and David Augsberger (eds.), *Peace-Building by, between, and beyond Muslims and Evangelical Christians* (New York: Lexington Books, 2009).

21 Kerr, "Islamic Da'wa and Christian Mission," p. 153.

22 Kerr, "Islamic Da'wa and Christian Mission," p. 163.

23 Woodberry, "Toward Mutual Respectful Witness."

24 Hans Ucko, "Pontifical Council for Interreligious Dialogue 40 Years." *Current Dialogue* (45), July 2005 (Geneva: World Council of Churches). http://wcc-coe.org/wcc/what/interreligious/cd45-03.html (accessed March 2006).

25 Scantlebury, "Islamic Da'wah and Christian Mission," p. 253.

26 Charles Marsh, "Wayward Christian Soldiers," *New York Times*, January 21, 2006.

27 The Reverend Franklin Graham delivered the invocation prayers at the inauguration of President George W. Bush.

28 Marvin Olasky is the editor of the conservative *World* magazine and a former advisor to President Bush on faith-based policy.

29 Marsh, "Wayward Christian Soldiers." Marsh is professor of religion at the University of Virginia and is author of *The Beloved Community: How Faith Shapes Social Justice, from the Civil Rights Movement to Today* (Basic Books, 2006).

30 For a report about this incident see http://www.pbs.org/wnet/religionandethics/week505/news.html.

31 For a detailed account of the Abdul Rahman conversion and trial in Afghanistan see http://en.wikipedia.org/wiki/Abdul_Rahman_(convert).

32 *Proceedings.*

33 *Proceedings*, p. 92.

34 For a useful summary of the classical Muslim position on apostasy, see Yohanan Friedmann, *Tolerance and Coercion in Islam* (Cambridge University Press, 2003), pp. 121–159.

35 For a survey of some modern discussions of the topic, see Abdullah Saeed and Hassan Saeed, *Freedom of Religion, Apostasy and Islam* (Ashgate Publishing, 2004). See also Mohammad Hashim Kamali, *Freedom of Expression in Islam* (Cambridge: Islamic Texts Society, 1997); Abdullahi Ahmed An-Na'im, "Islamic Law and Apostasy and Its Modern Applicability," *Religion* 16 (1986), 197–224; and Mahmoud Ayoub, "Religious Freedom and the Law of Apostasy in Islam," *Islamochristiana* 20 (1994), 73–91.

36 Louay Safi, "Apostasy and Religious Freedom." http://louaysafi.com/index2.php?option=com_content&do_pdf=1&id=54 (accessed February 17, 2015).

37 Johanna McGeary, "A Faith-Based Initiative," *Time Magazine*, April 21, 2003.

38 Graham explained his motive: "By helping refugee families ... we'll be earning the right to preach Christ to these families and their Muslim neighbors." http://www.inminds.co.uk/occ-articles.html.

39 Franklin Graham's statement was carried very widely in the media. See Nicholas Kristof, "Bigotry in Islam – And Here," *New York Times*, July 2, 2002.

40 Laurie Goodstein, "Seeing Islam as 'Evil'. Evangelicals Seek Converts," *New York Times*, May 27, 2003 at A3.

41 Goodstein, "Seeing Islam as 'Evil,'" at A3.

42 Goodstein, "Seeing Islam as 'Evil,'" at A3.

43 Goodstein, "Seeing Islam as 'Evil,'" at A3.

44 Siddiqui, *Christian–Muslim Dialogue*, p. 101.

45 Ahmad von Denffer, "Preface," in Ataullah Siddiqui (ed.), *Christian–Muslim Dialogue in the Twentieth Century* (London: Macmillan Press, 1997).

46 Ahmad von Denffer, *The Fulani Evangelism Project in West Africa* (Leicester: Islamic Foundation, 1980).

47 "Report from the Consultation on 'Religious Freedom, Community Rights and Individual Rights: A Christian Muslim Perspective," *Current Dialogue* (34), February 2000 (Geneva: World Council of Churches). http://www.wcc-coe.org/wcc/what/interreligious/cd34-19. html (accessed March 2006).

48 Unpublished keynote address delivered by Archbishop Michael Fitzgerald at a conference titled "In Our Time: Interreligious Relations in a Divided World," sponsored by Brandeis and Boston College, March 16–17, 2006. Just before addressing the conference Archbishop Fitzgerald was appointed by the Vatican as its Nuncio to the Arab League in Egypt.

49 Bible Brigade, *The New Republic*. http://www.tnr.com/article/bible-brigade.

50 Mahmoud Ayoub, "Religious Freedom and the Law of Apostasy in Islam," *Islamochristiana* 20 (1974), 75–91.

51 Tariq Ramadan, *In the Footsteps of the Prophet: Lessons from the Life of Muhammad* (Oxford University Press, 2009).

52 For a useful discussion of this challenge, see Christian W. Troll, "Witness Meets: The Church's Mission in the Context of the Worldwide Encounter of Christians and Muslim Believers Today," *Encounters* 4.1 (1998), 15–34.

Further Reading

Mohammed Abu-Nimer and David Augsberger eds. *Peace-Building by, between, and beyond Muslims and Evangelical Christian*. New York: Lexington Books, 2009.

Christian Mission and Islamic Da'wah: Proceedings of the Chambesy Dialogue Consultation. Leicester, UK: Islamic Foundation, 1977.

Mohammad Hashim Kamali, *Freedom of Expression in Islam*. Cambridge: Islamic Texts Society, 1997.

Abdullah Saeed and Hassan Saeed, *Freedom of Religion, Apostasy and Islam*. Ashgate Publishing, 2004.

Ataullah Siddiqui, *Christian-Muslim Dialogue in the Twentieth Century*. London: Macmillan Press, 1997.

9

Jewish Perspectives on Conversion

Amy Eilberg

In seeking to articulate a Jewish view of conversion, I am aware of a variety of reactions in me, ranging from puzzlement and lack of understanding to instinctive fear and anger. Puzzlement because, for the most part, Jewish communities have not engaged in mass attempts to convert others, so that I cannot fully understand the religious impulse that underlies mission. Fear and anger, because attempts to convert Jews have often been associated with contempt, prejudice, even expulsion and violence. Feelings about my people's historical experience still live in me.

As Rabbi Jonathan Sacks put it so eloquently in his remarks at the Lambeth Conference in July, 2008,

> As I prepared for this lecture, within my soul were the tears of my ancestors. We may have forgotten this, but for a thousand years, between the First Crusade and the Holocaust, the word "Christian" struck fear into Jewish hearts. Think only of the words the Jewish encounter with Christianity added to the vocabulary of human pain: blood libel, book burnings, disputations, forced conversions, inquisition, auto-da-fe, expulsion, ghetto and pogrom. I could not stand here today in total openness, and not mention that book of Jewish tears.

Sacks suggests that we must not only honor our painful historic memory, but use that memory for the good of the world. In that

Religious Conversion: Religion Scholars Thinking Together, First Edition.
Edited by Shanta Premawardhana.
© 2015 World Council of Churches Publications. Published 2015 by John Wiley & Sons, Ltd.

spirit, I seek to explore Jewish ambivalence about the enterprise of conversion in order to contribute to the interfaith conversation on the matter of mission in our time. I hope that the negative ways in which conversionary activity has affected Jews and other groups throughout history can serve as a cautionary tale as we seek to define a wholesome, ethical, and respectful way of sharing faith with others.[1]

A Brief History of Jewish Engagement in Conversionary Activity

With a few notable exceptions, the conversion of others to Judaism has not been a central preoccupation of Jewish communities throughout Jewish history. Historians note there was significant conversion to Judaism during the Second Temple period, including one period of large-scale forced conversion of the Edomites by Hasmonean leader John Hyrcanus (second century BCE). The Gospel of Matthew suggests significant proselytization by the Pharisees, and some sources indicate that there were incidents of collective conversion to Judaism, as in the fourth-century conversion of kings of the Himyarite Kingdom in southern Arabia, and the upper classes of the Khazars in the eighth century.[2] There is also evidence to suggest that Yusuf As'ar Yath'ar Dhu Nuwas, a sixth-century convert to Judaism and Himyarite king of Yemen, conducted a policy of forced conversion to Judaism in his kingdom, including annihilating several local Christian populations.[3]

But the sources of rabbinic literature reflect an ongoing internal debate among the rabbis regarding even the acceptance of proselytes who voluntarily seek conversion to Judaism, much less organized efforts to convert others. For example, one view encouraged non-Jews to join the Jewish people, as in the teaching, "When a proselyte comes to be converted, one receives him (or her) with an open hand so as to bring him (or her) under the wings of the Divine Presence" (Leviticus Rabbah 2:9).[4] On the other hand, many sources emphasize that rabbis are to actively discourage would-be converts. For example, "Our Rabbis taught: One who comes to convert, they say to him (or her): 'Why did you come to convert? Do you know that Israel at this time is afflicted, oppressed, downtrodden, and rejected, and that tribulations are visited upon them?' If he (or she) says, 'I know, but I am unworthy,' they accept him immediately ..." (Babylonian Talmud, *Yevamot* 47a).[5]

The latter statement became codified as the normative response to persons interested in converting to Judaism. To this day, rabbinic law stipulates that when a person comes to a Jewish authority seeking training for conversion, the rabbi is to "repel the person with both hands," trying three times to dissuade the person from joining the Jewish people before agreeing to accept him or her as a candidate for conversion.

A number of historical realities presumably led the rabbis to this negative attitude toward conversion. As early as the Maccabean era (second century BCE), converts to Judaism were said to have turned against the Jewish community in wartime, criticizing their chosen religion, and aiding foreign rulers in their designs against the Jewish community. Thus, Jewish leaders became suspicious of the motives of potential converts and wary of their long-term loyalty.

From the time that the practice of Judaism was forbidden in the Byzantine Empire, large waves of forced conversions spread over Christian Europe, continuing all the way into the early modern period. In one country after another, Jews were forcibly converted, or "chose" to convert under threat of violence, death, or expulsion. Christian rulers opposed conversion to Judaism, at times persecuting such proselytes. Hence, the Jewish leadership warned against accepting converts, fearing reprisal attacks on the Jewish community.

The reality of persecution of Jewish communities in Christian Europe exerted a formative impact on Jewish self-understanding, which in many ways continues to this day. The reality of anti-Semitism not only led Jews to refrain from proselytizing, but reinforced an already existing Jewish narrative that regarded the Jewish people as a perpetual minority, radically separate from the outside world, a "kingdom of priests and a holy people," wholly apart from significant contact with its neighbors. With such a self-understanding, small numbers of converts could be accepted, but were rarely sought. Conversion from Judaism was seen as a tragedy and a betrayal, a threat to a people that considered itself to be vulnerable and chronically endangered. (It has been customary, even into the modern era, for some Jewish families to perform mourning rituals for family members who have converted to other religions, signifying that the "apostates" were no longer "alive" for their families, or for the Jewish community.)

Conversion from Christianity to Judaism was not forbidden ṇ. Muslim lands; there is some evidence that such conversion may have been common among Christian servants serving in Jewish homes. Jews generally fared better in Muslim lands, under *"dhimmi"* ("protected") status, than under Christian rule, but the Jewish communities in Muslim lands remained a minority population, at times vulnerable to persecution and violence.

The Enlightenment threw open the doors of the European ghettos, and the Jews (particularly of Western and Central Europe) enthusiastically joined Christian society, eagerly seeking the Western education and social acceptance that had previously been denied to them. For many, Enlightenment principles reinforced traditional Jewish ideals of tolerance and open inquiry. There arose an apologetic and widely believed view of Jewish history, according to which Jews had never engaged in conversionary activity.

Jewish Opposition to Mission

Thus, for many contemporary American Jews, conversionary activity is seen as negative for four primary reasons:

1. *Nature of Judaism.* For historical if not philosophical reasons, Judaism has generally not seen itself as a universal religion. Jews have understood their religion as a particular way of life for the Jewish people rather than as a world religion to be shared with the peoples of the world.[6] Others could choose to join us, but there was rarely an assumption of universality, or an expectation that this particular way of life would be spread to the peoples of the world. In fact, the *Tosefta*[7] records an opinion that the righteous of all peoples have a place in the world to come,[8] and this becomes the accepted view.

   That said, there is a stream within Jewish tradition that sees the Jewish people as charged with a mission to bring the world to the knowledge of God and to commitment to justice. This vision finds expression in God's original call to Abraham, "All the families of the earth will be blessed through you" (Genesis 12:3), and elaborated eloquently by the biblical prophets. The primary Jewish task, in this view, is to be "a light unto the nations, opening eyes deprived of light, rescuing prisoners from confinement, from the dungeon those who sit in darkness" (Isaiah 42:6–7). The Jewish people is to serve as a model of righteous living, and a vehicle by which others will come to know God and the imperative of building a just society. How the world will reach that blessed moment in history is left squarely in God's hands.

Interestingly, this view is reflected in the writings of Ahad Ha'am (1856–1927), the father of cultural Zionism, as in the following passage:

> The Jewish people as a whole has always interpreted its "mission" simply as the performance of its own duties, without regard to the external world ... The Prophets no doubt gave utterance to the hope that Judaism would exert an influence for good on the moral condition of the other nations; but their idea was that this result would follow naturally from the existence among the Jews of the highest type of morality, not that the Jews existed solely for the purpose of striving to exert this influence.[9]

2. *Memory of persecution.* Historically, efforts to convert Jews to Christianity have been a natural outgrowth of a supersessionist theology, denying the validity of Judaism, and preaching contempt for Jews, all of which all too often led to violence. Thus for many Jews, mission, particularly by Christians, evokes the collective memory of forced conversions, persecution, expulsion, and genocide of Jews in Christian Europe.

3. *Minority consciousness.* Jews, representing a tiny minority of the world's population, have historically seen themselves as an "ever-dying people,"[10] endangered by hatred in many eras, and by assimilation in our own. As such, the loss of individuals to conversion and intermarriage is experienced as threatening to the size and strength of the community.

4. *Principle of religious tolerance.* A great majority of Jews, believing strongly in Enlightenment ideals of tolerance, tends to find aggressive mission to be disrespectful of others' religions, and therefore deeply offensive. Some ultra-Orthodox Jews, by contrast, engage in energetic and well-funded efforts to "convert" non-Orthodox Jews to their form of Jewish practice. These efforts, too, are widely seen by other Jews as offenses against individual religious privacy and freedom. The entire mainstream

Jewish community tends to regard communities of "messianic Jews" with distaste, regarding their mission as deceptive and coercive efforts to lure poorly educated Jews into Christianity.

Jewish Teachings on Religious Tolerance and Their Implication for Conversion

In addition to the historical circumstances discussed above, several principles embedded in Jewish theology are antithetical to proselytization. I offer here a set of such principles, drawn from Jewish sources, that may help to define a mode of missionary activity that is ethical, respectful, and appropriate for an ever-shrinking world of religious plurality.

Personal and theological humility

There is in Jewish theology a powerful stream of theological humility, stressing the limits of human understanding. For example, Judaism, dating back to the Torah itself, generally prohibits visual images of God, for we must never pretend that we can see God or imagine God's shape or form. Even the vocalization of the Tetragrammaton, the most sacred four-letter name of God, is prohibited, since we cannot know God's truest name. Maimonides is the best known proponent of the *"via negativa"* stream of Jewish philosophy, emphasizing that one can never state with any accuracy what we know about God, only what we cannot know.

The seventeenth-century Jewish philosopher Baruch Spinoza vividly describes the subjectivity of any one person or group's understandings of the Divine:

> Let us imagine ... a little worm, living in the blood ... This little worm would live in the blood, in the same way as we live in a part of the universe, and would consider each part of blood, not as a part, but as a whole. ... I believe that if a triangle could speak, it would say, in like manner, that God is eminently triangular, while a circle would say that the divine nature is eminently circular. Thus each would ascribe to God its own attributes, would assume itself to be like God, and look on everything else as ill-shaped.[11]

147

These few examples illustrate a well-developed tendency within Jewish tradition to be suspicious of false (i.e., humanly impossible) theological certainty. As the proverbial Hasidic master told his student, "If I could understand God, what kind of God would God be?" Given the mystery of human relationship with God, how could one claim that one's own understanding of Truth should be adopted by others?

Implications for conversion   The Jewish experience thus underscores the reality that the human grasp of the Ultimate can at best be partial. Particularly in our troubled world, an attitude of theological superiority, supersessionism, or presumption of absolute truth is offensive and inappropriate. On a more subtle level, those engaging in conversionary activity must exercise rigorous self-awareness, constantly exploring their own deeply held beliefs and judgments about the worth of religions different from their own. Without such rigorous self-monitoring, it may be impossible to arrest the movement from sharing to disrespect to contempt and then to violence.

Delight in the multiplicity of views: "controversy for the sake of heaven"

As is well known, virtually every page of the Talmud's 63 volumes includes a record of multiple views of any matter at hand. This unique aspect of Talmudic literature suggests that active exploration of differences of opinion actually serves the ever-evolving seeking after divine truth. Classical Jewish texts develop this view only in relation to views within the world of Jewish religious scholarship, and this view most assuredly did not prevent one school of Jews from condemning those Jews holding different views. Nonetheless, there is a well-established concept in Jewish sources that the development of multiple views of any matter (theological, ritual, or literary) serves the sacred quest for ultimate truth. In fact, the rabbis regularly reflect on the importance of studying minority views in the sacred literature, as today's rejected opinions may at some future time reveal a dimension of the Truth not previously understood.

These notions coalesce in a remarkable rabbinic concept, *"mahloket leshem shamayim,"* or "controversy for the sake of heaven." As articulated in the Mishnah,[12]

148

> A controversy for the sake of heaven will have lasting value, while a controversy not for the sake of heaven will not endure. What is an example of a controversy for the sake of heaven? The debates of Hillel and Shammai. What is an example of a controversy not for the sake of heaven? The rebellion of Korach and his associates. (Mishnah Avot 5:20)[13]

A controversy for the sake of heaven, like the many debates of rabbinic giants Hillel and Shammai (first century BCE) and their students, were arguments that served the divine, the search for truth, and the common good. Thus, these were debates worth developing through the generations. By contrast, an argument not "for the sake of heaven," but motivated by quest for personal power or in the service of selfish or trivial needs (as in the biblical rebellion of Korach and his band against the authority of Moses), has no lasting value. It is not a sacred debate.

Strikingly, then, exploring difference of opinion, even conflict (within the presumably safe and respectful confines of the house of study), is itself a sacred practice. Discussing the relative strengths and weaknesses of various perspectives is seen as life-enhancing, serving the collective search for understanding.

The sources go one step further, as in the following beloved text:

> One may say to oneself, "Since the House of Shammai says 'impure' and the House of Hillel says 'pure,' one prohibits and one permits, why should I continue to learn Torah?" Therefore the Torah says, "These are the words" (Deuteronomy 1:1): All the words were given by a single Shepherd, one God created them, one Provider gave them, the Blessed Ruler of all creation spoke them. Therefore make your heart into a many-chambered room, and bring into it both the words of the House of Shammai and the words of the House of Hillel, both the words of those who forbid and the words of those who permit. (*Tosefta Sotah* 7:12)

This beautiful text imagines a student in the academy expressing frustration with the endless debates over the meanings of Jewish texts, yearning for the certainty of univocal truth, of indisputable "right answers." In response, the Torah offers the words, "These are the words" (the first words of the book of Deuteronomy), to emphasize that the sacred word is not singular but plural. There are many sacred truths, many different perspectives, all of which have their source in the Divine. We are to conduct our inner lives so that we actively cultivate a "many-chambered heart,"[14] the capacity to hold

149

within us multiple truths, each of which can describe only a part of the fullness of reality. Only the One can perceive the whole Truth.

Implications for conversion   This rich tradition of honoring intellectual and philosophical debate suggests a worldview in which difference is not a problem to be eradicated but a tool for ongoing discernment of Truth. How would conversionary activity change if the practitioner practiced the rabbinic exhortation to make of the heart a many-chambered room? Such a person would hold the religion, culture, and self-understanding of the religious other in his or her heart. The relationship between the two would be seen as a vehicle for both to learn and grow, rather than a mandate for one to persuade the other to repudiate his or her beliefs. No single school of thought, religion, or society would seek to impose its own truth on others.

The value of diversity

Rabbi Jonathan Sacks's elegant phrase, "the dignity of difference,"[15] captures the notion that diversity is a purposeful and beautiful aspect of divine creation. The seemingly infinite variety of creatures, each with its own unique nature, and a world of difference in the ways in which human beings think, live, and believe, is an aspect of the wonder of creation, and evidence of the grandeur of God, as in the following beloved text:

> The human race was created from one person, to show the greatness of the Holy One, Blessed be God, for if a person strikes many coins from one mold, they all resemble one another, but the King of Kings, the Holy One, Blessed be God, made each person in the image of Adam, and yet not one of them resembles the other. Therefore every single person is obligated to say, "The world was created for my sake." (*Mishnah Sanhedrin* 4:5)[16]

The early modern Jewish philosopher Moses Mendelssohn (eighteenth century) intended something similar when he wrote:

> Dear Brothers, you are well-meaning. But do not let yourselves be deceived. To belong to this omnipresent shepherd, it is not necessary for the entire flock to graze on one pasture or to enter and leave the master's house through just one door. It would be neither in accordance with the shepherd's wishes nor conducive to the growth of the flock.[17]

The contemporary Orthodox Jewish theologian, Rabbi Irving Greenberg, also embraces this tradition of pluralism:

> Pluralism means more than accepting or even affirming the other. It entails recognizing the blessings in the other's existence, because it balances one's own position and brings all of us closer to the ultimate goal. Even when we are right in our own position, the other who contradicts our position may be our corrective or our check against going to excess ... Pluralism is not relativism, for we hold onto our absolutes; however, we make room for others' as well.[18]

Implications for conversion   The work of mission can only be appropriate in today's world if it refrains from delegitimizing or demeaning the worldviews, religious practice, and spiritual identity of adherents of other religions. This obviously rules out treating religious others with outward hostility and violence. But to seek to convert based on one's apparent concern for the soul of "the other" is itself supremacist. Rather, to be a person of faith in today's world demands deep respect for and curiosity about views different from our own. The religious impulse to share one's own beloved faith must allow for the possibility that the other's truth is also valid, and that all parties to interfaith conversation have much to learn from one another. It would be insulting to suggest to religionists of another faith that the world would be better off if they all adopted one's own beliefs. In fact, the faith of all people would be impoverished if the richness of religious diversity were to be eliminated from the world.

Human dignity

Jewish sources have their own particular expressions of the universally held value of the infinite worth and dignity of the human person. This belief is grounded in the foundational proclamation of Genesis 1: "And God said, 'Let Us make humankind in Our image, after Our likeness ...' So God created the being 'Adam' in God's own image; in the image of God was humanity created; God created them male and female" (Genesis 1:26–27).

In rabbinic literature, human dignity is called *"k'vod hab'riyot"* or "honor of created beings," emphasizing that God is the source of the dignity of the human person. The religious imperative to guard the dignity of every human being is foundational and unconditional.

A classic rabbinic text describes two pre-eminent scholars of the second century CE debating the question of which is the most essential principle in the Torah. Rabbi Akiva believed that the central teaching of the Torah was contained in the verse, "You shall love your neighbor as yourself" (Leviticus 19:18). Ben Azzai, for his part, replied that the fundamental principle was the following: "This is the record of Adam's line. When God created humankind, it was made in the likeness of God ..." (Genesis 5:1).[19] Ben Azzai was apparently concerned that the principle of love of other based on love of self was a precarious basis for ethics and human relationship, because those with weak self-regard would have an inadequate impetus to treat others ethically and empathically. Thus, Ben Azzai asserted that the Torah's most central teaching is that the true foundation for human dignity is the fundamental fact of the human person being created by God.

From this fundamental assertion follows a core principle of Jewish law, that human dignity takes precedence over a wide range of religious precepts:

> A Rabbinic prohibition is always and everywhere superseded for the sake of human dignity. And even though we are explicitly enjoined in the Torah not to depart from the Sages' teachings either to the right or to the left, this negative precept itself is set aside in the interests of human dignity.[20]

> Human dignity is very highly prized; there is no principle that is more highly prized. The rabbis laid down a cardinal rule: "Great is human dignity, which overrides any negative, rabbinic commandment, permitting its violation even by an active measure."[21]

The principle of human dignity has continued to be central in Jewish law and life, applied in contemporary Jewish jurisprudence to issues as wide-ranging as treatment of gays and lesbians and the US government use of torture. It is applied in ordinary human interaction, as in the well-known Talmudic teaching that shaming another person in public is akin to murder.[22] Notably, a variation of this teaching is codified in Jewish law, in that one who embarrasses another loses his or her (otherwise assured) place in the world to come.[23]

Implications for conversion While each religion expresses this conviction in its own unique language, all religions agree on the principle of human dignity as a fundamental value. Thus, conversionary activity that delegitimizes the religion, culture, or full humanity of others is a violation of a foundational religious imperative.

Empathy

As we have seen, the great second-century sage Rabbi Akiva named the biblical commandment to love one's neighbor as oneself (Leviticus 19:18) as the central teaching of the Torah, or, in Hillel's more concrete formulation, "That which is hateful to you, do not do to others."[24] In Jewish life and law, great care is taken to ensure that this principle suffuses every arena of personal and communal life. Thus, the principle of empathy infuses the teachings of Jewish law on everything from ethics of speech to care for the ill, the grieving and the poor, the conduct of business, and compassionate treatment of animals, to name just a few.

One striking example is a common explanation of the Torah's prohibition of mixing milk and meat, derived from the thrice-repeated biblical verse, "Do not seethe a kid in its mother's milk."[25] This is frequently understood to mean that one must imagine the pain a mother goat would feel if she knew that her offspring had been killed and was being seasoned with her own milk. Thus the observant Jew is reminded at every meal of the need to actively cultivate compassion for other created beings, especially for other persons.

Similarly, the Torah forbids the gathering of chicks or eggs in the presence of the mother bird. Rather, one is adjured to first send the mother bird away, so that she does not witness the taking of her young (Deuteronomy 22:6–7). Strikingly, the Torah promises long life – the ultimate reward – for observing this commandment. Thus, one is to cultivate empathy even for an animal's inner feelings, even in the course of exercising one's presumably legitimate rights.

As has often been observed, the commandment most often repeated in the Torah (36 times) is one or another variant of the command to guard rigorously the rights and dignity of the "stranger" in the midst of the community, as in the texts, "You shall not oppress a stranger, for you know the soul of the stranger, for you were strangers in the land of Egypt" (Exodus 23:9) and "When strangers reside with you in your land, you shall not wrong them. … You shall love each one as yourself, for you were strangers in the land of Egypt: I am Adonai your God" (Leviticus 19:33–34).[26]

This central religious imperative relates specifically to the treatment of a foreigner, a migrant, or one considered "other" in the midst of an otherwise homogenous community, based on the Jewish people's collective memory of having been oppressed foreigners in Egypt and, of course, in many other places through history. This primary command bases itself on the cultivation of empathy. You know what it is to be marginalized and oppressed, so you must never fail to respond to the pain of others suffering the same fate. In short, this command, so fundamental to Jewish religious consciousness, is based on the practice of attending to the sensitivities of the other.

Implications for conversion We know that the offer of a new religion can be experienced as the gift of new life, as a path to liberation. Yet mission is deeply disrespectful when it fails to consider empathically whether conversion may be experienced as an assault on the other's spiritual or cultural identity and integrity.

Enlightenment values: personal privacy

For many secular contemporary Jews, the teachings of Jewish tradition are no longer central for their lives. Yet they still find mission deeply objectionable, based both on Jewish historical memory and on liberal, Enlightenment principles, according to which religious beliefs are a matter of individual conscience. Thus, the phenomenon of mission may be viewed as a violation of personal privacy, and therefore offensive.

Conclusion

Religious mission is a complex matter weighted with deep religious and ideological convictions and historical memories for communities on both sides of the question. As we have seen, both the lessons of Jewish history and the teachings of Jewish tradition contribute a resounding note of concern and caution to the unfolding international conversation on the ethics of conversion. Jewish tradition, treasuring humility, diversity of views, human dignity, and empathy as primary values, highlights the problematics of conversionary activity. So, too, the historical experience of the

Jewish people offers a powerful cautionary tale about the harm that large-scale conversion can cause in the world.

At this moment in history, when religiously fueled conflict causes so much trauma in the world, those engaged in conversionary activity must take account of the ways in which attacks on another people's religious or cultural legitimacy can form wounds in that people's national narrative. Such assaults often leave a residue of fear, anger, suspicion, and distrust toward other peoples, from which hate and violence may flow.

At the same time, each nation or community is responsible for attending to the development of its own collective narrative, working to cleanse the narrative of destructive elements. As such, Jews, who have long been victims of religious hatred, must grow to realize that the proclamation of religious faith is a primary religious practice for some traditions, and a protected right in a world of religious plurality. To the extent that Jews are still traumatized by the historical consequences of religious supersessionism, it is our duty to attend to our own collective healing, so that we may see the challenges of today's world with more clarity of mind and heart, not only through the dark lens of a painful past.

One would hope that the current international dialogue on the ethics of conversion will give rise to deepened understanding on both sides of the question. May those whose communities have not been threatened by conversion hear deeply the voice of peoples hurt by mission in the past and present. And may those victimized by mission reach a measure of healing, so that they may honor the religious motivations of other religious communities, helping to create a world in which all peoples can live in peace and dignity.

Notes

1   I am grateful to Dr. Deborah Weissman, president of the International Council of Christians and Jews, for her special role in the genesis of this article. I deeply appreciate her generosity in inviting me to join the Thinking Together group, which has been a profound learning opportunity for me. She has also provided careful reading and wise counsel as I prepared these thoughts. Any flaws, however, are mine alone.

2   *Encyclopedia Judaica*, 2nd edition (Jerusalem: Thomson Gale and Keter Publishing, 2007), vol. 16, p. 590.

3   *Encyclopedia Judaica*, vol. 21, pp. 428–429. My thanks to my colleague Dr. Rabia Harris for alerting me to this incident.

4   Vayikra Rabbah is a collection of homiletical *midrashim*/expositions on issues in the biblical book of Leviticus, compiled in approximately the fifth century CE, including older materials.

5   The Babylonian Talmud, edited circa 500 CE, is the first great compendium of Jewish law and lore, including 63 volumes of the *Mishnah* (collected circa 200 CE) and voluminous commentary in the *Gemara*. The work includes law, homily, tales of ancient rabbis, and commentary on biblical verses.

6   See Rita Gross's description of "ethno-religions" in this volume.

7   The *Tosefta*, compiled early third-century CE, is a compilation of laws and commentary, parallel to the *Mishnah* (compiled circa 200 CE), belonging to the Tannaitic period, the earliest stage of Rabbinic Judaism.

8   Rabbi Joshua in *Tosefta Sanhedrin* 13:2.

9   *Selected Essays of Ahad Ha-Am*, translated from the Hebrew, edited and with an introduction by Leon Simon (Philadelphia: Jewish Publication Society, 1912), pp. 230–231.

10   *Israel: The Ever-Dying People and other Essays by Simon Rawidowicz*, ed. Benjamin C. I. Ravid (Madison, NJ: Fairleigh Dickinson University Press, 1986).

11   Baruch Spinoza, cited in Raphael Jospe, "Pluralism out of the Sources of Judaism: Religious Pluralism without Relativism," *Studies in Christian-Jewish Relations* 2.21 (2007), 107.

12   A 63-volume compilation of Jewish law, the Mishnah reflects the first stage of Jewish teaching, commentary, and legislation of the Rabbinic – that is, post-biblical – period. Compiled circa 200 CE.

13   Popularly known as *"Pirkei Avot"* ("Chapters of the Fathers" or "Ethics of the Fathers"), this is a tractate of the Mishnah (200 CE) that comprises brief ethical teachings and sayings of rabbinic scholars from the first century BCE to the second century, CE.

14   David Hartman's book, *A Heart of Many Rooms: Celebrating the Many Voices Within Judaism* (Woodstock, VT: Jewish Lights Publishing, 1999), uses this phrase as its central metaphor.

15   Rabbi Jonathan Sacks, *The Dignity of Difference: How to Avoid the Clash of Civilizations* (London: Continuum Books, 2002).

16   Dr. Deborah Weissman quotes from Aleksandr Solzhenitsyn's undelivered Nobel Prize lecture in 1970: "Nationalities are the wealth of humanity, they are its crystallized personalities; even the smallest among them has its own special colors, hides within itself a particular facet of God's design." She continues, "Indeed, for many, the cultural diversity of humankind is one of the main things that make our world interesting.

The contemporary environmental movement has heightened our awareness of endangered species of flora and fauna. We are (justifiably) supposed to be concerned with the preservation of every kind of insect, for example, not to mention the whales and many other creatures. Some would argue that this sensitivity should extend as well to human cultures, languages and tribes on the verge of extinction." ("What We Are and Who We Are: Educating for the Universal-Particular Dialectic in Jewish Life," in Jonathan Cohen (editor), *Studies in Jewish Education* XI (2005/06), 88.)

17 Mendelssohn, cited in Jospe, "Pluralism out of the Sources of Judaism," p. 108.

18 Rabbi Irving Greenberg, *For the Sake of Heaven and Earth* (Philadelphia: Jewish Publication Society, 2004), p. 196.

19 Translation from *The Contemporary Torah: A Gender-Sensitive Adaptation of the JPS Translation* (Philadelphia: Jewish Publication Society, 2006). Rabbinic passage found in Jerusalem Talmud, *Nedarim* 9:4.

20 Maimonides, Mishneh Torah, *Kila'im* 10:29.

21 Commentary of Rabbi Menachem HaMeiri (1249–1315, Provence), *Beit Habehirah on Berachot* 19b.

22 Babylonian Talmud, *Bava Metsi'a* 58b.

23 Maimonides, Mishneh Torah, *Hilchot Chovel Umazik* 3:7.

24 Babylonian Talmud, *Shabbat* 31a.

25 Exodus 23:19 and 34:26; Deuteronomy 14:21.

26 Translation from *The Contemporary Torah*, as above.

Further Reading

Books

Holtz, Barry. *Finding Our Way: Jewish Texts and the Lives We Live Today.* New York: Schocken Books, 1990.

Klein-HaLevi, Yossi. *At the Entrance to the Garden of Eden: A Jew's Search for God with Christians and Muslims in the Holy Land.* New York: William Morrow, 2001.

Sacks, Jonathan. *The Dignity of Difference: Avoiding the Clash of Civilizations.* London and New York: Continuum, 2002.

DVD

Menachem Daum and Oren Rudavsky (directors). *Hiding and Seeking: Faith and Tolerance after the Holocaust.* Documentary (85 mins).

Part III

Conversion and Human Rights

10

Conversion and Religious Freedom

S. Wesley Ariarajah

The issues related to religious freedom are as old as religion itself. Human history is marked by many conflicts based on tribal, ethnic, and religious differences. It also shows that different nations and cultural groups adopted a variety of traditional customs to protect the rights of individuals and communities. Recent centuries, however, have seen much violence based on religious intolerance. In response, the international community, especially in the post-World War II period, worked toward generating agreements among nations that would protect the basic human rights, including the rights related to religious beliefs. The Conventions, Covenants, and Declarations drawn up by the international community seek to safeguard different dimensions of individual and community rights through commonly held agreements. The earliest among them was the Universal Declaration of Human Rights of 1948, which says:

> Everyone has the right to freedom of thought, conscience and religion; this right includes freedom to change his [sic] religion or belief, and freedom, either alone or in community with others and in public or private, to manifest his religion or belief in teaching, practice, worship and observance.

Religious Conversion: Religion Scholars Thinking Together, First Edition.
Edited by Shanta Premawardhana.
© 2015 World Council of Churches Publications. Published 2015 by John Wiley & Sons, Ltd.

Explication and expansion of this provision, especially in relation to religious freedom, was made in Article 18 of the UN International Covenant on Civil and Political Rights, drawn up in 1966:

> Everyone shall have the right to freedom of thought, conscience and religion. This right shall include freedom to have or adopt a religion or belief of his choice, and freedom, either individually or in community with others and in public or private, to manifest his religion or belief in worship, observance, practice, and learning.

The articles from 1966 also had an additional provision that says: "No one shall be subject to coercion, which would impair his freedom to have or to adopt a religion or belief of his choice."

In some of the national constitutions, as in the case of India, for example, the right includes the word "propagate": "the right to believe, practice, and propagate one's religion."

Internal and External Manifestations of Religious Beliefs

Commentators on the religious rights enshrined in these articles point out that these provisions speak about both the "freedom of thought and conscience" and the "freedom of religion." This formulation is based on the reality that there are two dimensions to religious belief: internal and external. The "freedom of thought and conscience" relates to convictions and beliefs that one holds both on religious and other matters that may or may not find external expression, and the "freedom of religion" points to the external expression of those beliefs. Thus, on the matter of religion, the conventions attempt to protect not only the right of persons to hold any belief but also their right to "manifest" it in public through worship, observances, practices, and learning, both individually and collectively. The attempt here is to insist that it is not sufficient to allow people to "believe what they want to" or to reduce religion into "a private affair" or "a matter of the heart." Religious freedom includes the right to manifest what one believes, also in public.

Religious Freedom and Tolerance

In this respect one needs to pay attention to the distinction between "religious freedom" and "religious tolerance." In several countries where one or other religion is a predominant majority, the word "tolerance" is often used to indicate the status of other religious traditions. In some countries, like Saudi Arabia, the religious tradition of the majority is declared the religion of the state; while people of other religious traditions are tolerated, in the sense that they may live in the country and practice their faith in private, they cannot seek citizenship and no other religion is officially recognized. In Sri Lanka, while all religions are recognized and allowed to practice their faith in public, Buddhism as the religion of the majority is given a special place and is under the protection of the state. In England, while there is full and equal recognition of all religious traditions in practice, the Church of England maintains a special status and place in relation to the state. The predominantly Hindu India, despite the creation of the Islamic nation of Pakistan (East and West) at the time of its independence, chose to remain a "secular" state, in the sense of giving constitutional guarantee of equality to all religious traditions within its borders. Indonesia, the largest Islamic country in the world, despite its overwhelmingly Islamic population, officially recognizes five of the religious traditions prevalent in the nation for equal treatment within *panchaseela*, a fivefold principle of peaceful coexistence. In some Islamic countries, like Malaysia, while all religions are allowed to manifest themselves in public, it is permissible for a person to convert from one of the minority religions to the religion of the majority, but it is illegal to convert from the religion of the majority to that of a minority. Thus, the status of religions within the nations varies enormously. "Tolerance" is the word commonly used to indicate the levels of freedom that other religions enjoy in relation to the religion of the majority.

Tolerance is conducive to but does not constitute religious freedom. The Conventions move away from the word "tolerance" and place religious rights within universal human rights. Even as basic human rights are universal, cannot be overly qualified, or set to degrees of observance, religious rights must also be seen as equal rights shared by all citizens of a nation. In this view, privileging any one religion over others or granting only limited rights to minority religious communities would amount to violation of religious freedom.

The State and Religious Freedom

This brings us to the very important issue of the relationship between the state and the concept of religious freedom. At the superficial level, the state is important in so far as it is often responsible for the enactment of laws and practices that determine the levels of freedom offered to different religious communities within a nation. Often, it also enacts laws and provisions that limit the activities of religious communities, their participation in the welfare of the people, their place within the state, their relationship to believers in other parts of the world, and the flow and use of financial resources etc. Especially in countries where one religion is a predominant majority it is not uncommon for the state to limit the activities and external relationships of other religious communities.

However, there is also a deeper dimension to the relationship between state and religious freedom that has to do with the understanding of the nature and purpose of the state itself in the different religious traditions of the world. In a study on the relationship between religious liberty and the state, Ninan Koshy speaks of four models:

- theocracy, where the state is under the control of religious leaders or institutions for religious purposes;
- Erastianism, where the church (or religion) is under the control of the state (the term comes from the sixteenth-century Swiss German theologian Thomas Erastes);
- separation of religion and state, where there is a friendly separation of religious and political institutions that are not hostile to each other;
- separation of religion and state that is unfriendly, where the separated religious and political institutions are antagonistic to each other.[1]

Koshy also records a 1986 study where Elizabeth Odio Benito, the Special Rapporteur of the UN Commission on Human Rights, listed eight arrangements between religion and state, in order to distinguish some of the more subtle distinctions in the way the relationships are conceived and expressed:

- state religions;
- established churches (religion officially recognized by state laws);
- neutral or secular as regards religion;
- no official religion;
- separation of religion and state;
- special arrangements with a particular religious tradition;
- protection (only) of legally recognized religious groups;
- millet system, where a number of religious communities are officially recognized.[2]

The United Kingdom is a good example of the ambiguities that mark the state–religion relationship. It does not have a written constitution and its approach to issues of religious freedom evolved over the centuries. Although it does not have any statutes that prescribe freedom of all religious beliefs and practices, it is a signatory of all international conventions on human rights and those that protect civil and religious rights; all religions in its territory are free to exercise their religious beliefs in public. And yet, the Church of England is the established religion of the UK. Peter Cumper says that the Church of England's established status means that it enjoys certain privileges denied to other faiths. The Church is uniquely entitled to organize national events such as coronations and war remembrance services. Twenty-six senior Anglican bishops sit in the House of Lords (Parliament's upper chamber) and participate in decision-making processes.[3] The relationship between religion and state in the United Kingdom is an example of a nation that holds on to its ancient tradition, and yet does not use it to deny the equality of all citizens and their legitimate right to practice their religions in public.

In much of Europe Christianity had been the official religion of the state and constitutional steps had to be taken in countries like France, Germany, Sweden, to officially separate the two, even though centuries of Christian influence still dominate the ethos of the state.

Traditionally, Islam does not make a separation between religious, social, and political life and Islamic nations did not have the custom of drawing up a constitution to regulate the affairs of the nation. Donna Arzt says that in the postcolonial era all Islamic countries, with the exception of Saudi Arabia and Oman, have promulgated written constitutions. Today 34 states with majority Muslim populations have written constitutions. Of these, 23, in addition to Saudi Arabia and Oman, have officially proclaimed Islam as the state religion and Shari'a as the principal source of law. Arzt notes that there is diversity even within this reality. A few, such as Turkey, the Gambia, and Senegal, are avowedly secular; Iran is explicitly Islamic, and all others attempt to fuse the Shari'a and other perspectives, some of them limiting the application of the Shari'a only to family law.[4]

The level of religious freedom that should be offered to non-Muslim religious minorities within an Islamic state is an unsettled question within Islamic states. The Universal Islamic Declaration of Human Rights, adopted by the Islamic Council in 1981, Arzt points out, does contain references to the discourse found in international law. Article X, titled "Rights of Minorities," states: "The Quranic principle that 'there is no compulsion in Religion' shall govern the religious rights of non-Muslim countries. In a Muslim country, religious minorities shall have the choice to be governed by Islamic Law or by their own laws." Article XIII provides every person with the right to freedom of conscience and worship in accordance with one's religious beliefs, while Article XII (e) forbids "ridiculing, holding in contempt, or inciting hostility against the religious beliefs of others."[5] There have been other declarations, like the Cairo Declaration on Human Rights in Islam (1990), that also seek to hold a balance between affirmation of the Shari'a and the need to deal with religious plurality, with varying degrees of success.

It is important to recognize that some of the religious traditions have a theological / philosophical understanding of life in community that holds religion, culture, the state, and the legal system in a continuum; they do not see them as aspects that must be separated or seen in isolation from one another. A full discussion of the different models of this reality, the history of the ways in which it plays out in our day, and its implications in pluralistic situations is beyond the scope of this discussion. It is important, however, to emphasize that a discussion on religious freedom should pay attention to this reality. Historically, different religious traditions have moved through many phases of this reality and can shed light on the discussion from their varied experiences. Globalization, population movements, and the evolution of religiously and culturally pluralistic societies call for a fresh discussion of this issue.

In many ways, the state has become the main actor on issues of religious freedom in the modern period, and throughout history both the state and religious traditions have used and abused each other with regard to exercise of power and influence in society.

Religions and Religious Freedom

On the basis of the above, we should also pay particular attention to the role that religions themselves play in the question of religious freedom. As noted above, throughout history many religious traditions have used their alliances with political power to deny the religious freedom of others. But the problem goes even deeper. Many religious traditions have also developed religious self-understandings and theological assumptions about other religious traditions that militate against religious freedom of those different from them. Exclusive claims to truth or special revelation, claims to divine authority, claims to land based on Divine promise, militant and aggressive understandings of mission, denigration of other religious traditions as pagan, heathen, superstitious and so on have often justified callous disregard of the religious rights of others. Most religious traditions are yet to develop sufficient theological and pastoral practices that would give equal respect and authenticity to a plurality of religious traditions.

Conversion and Religious Freedom

The word "conversion" has many meanings, and is discussed in greater detail in a separate chapter of this volume. At the basic level it can point to a transformation or change of heart and mind on the part of a person on the basis of new experiences or convictions or beliefs. Conversion can also have external manifestations like one changing one's religious affiliation publicly or moving from one community to another. Involved in the issue are one's right "to convert others" into one's faith or engage in activities that seek "to gain converts" to one's religious tradition. Also involved in the issue is the right of a person "to become a convert" and join a new religious community.

It is clear that the intention of the covenants and declarations on religious freedom is that each individual has the right to his or her religion by birth or by choice, and the right to practice it privately or with others. Most nation-states and religious communities appear to accept this right in principle. However, as mentioned earlier, in many countries – especially where there is a special relationship between religion and state or where the state is theocratic – the tendency has been not to deny but to limit the exercise of religious life in public and in community. This also includes limiting any attempt to propagate one's faith. The extent and degree to which these limitations are placed overtly or covertly vary from nation to nation.

The more relevant aspect of the covenants and declarations, especially in relation to the debate on conversion, has to do with the provisions in the agreements "to change to" or "to adopt" a religion of one's choice. This was understood as a right that needs to be protected both to uphold one's freedom of conscience, and as a matter of basic human rights. Some of the religious traditions and states, however, challenge this right and have instituted provisions within the state or religious laws to prohibit the option "to change" or "to adopt" a religion of one's choice, and to punish where this takes place. In some countries, like Pakistan and Egypt, there have been highly publicized cases of persons put on trial for choosing to change their religious identity.

The main argument for this course of action has to do, as mentioned earlier, with different understandings of the location of the religious rights. While some see religious rites as belonging to the individual, others see religious rights as those which the community holds, and as the identity marker of the community. In this context an individual "adopting" a new religion as a matter of conscience is seen as betraying the community of which she or he is a part. There are a number of unresolved issues here on the nature of the rights as they relate to individuals and community. It would appear that the provision in the conventions of the right "to have" a religion or "to remain" in one's religious tradition was intended not only to protect one's religious rights but also to curtail any attempts by the state or non-state actors to force, induce, or in other ways pressure individuals and communities to move from one community to another.

Within Islam itself there are other significant issues of religious rights, especially in relation to religious dissent, movements of reform, apostasy, blasphemy, and the role of women in religious leadership, that are at different stages of discussion in different Islamic countries. Clement John documents several concrete cases where blasphemy laws are abused in Pakistan to act against minorities or to punish a Muslim who has changed his or her religious allegiance.[6]

Missions and Religious Freedom

This brings us to the heart of the conversion debate, which has to do with "missions" to propagate one's faith among other believers. The conventions and constitutions argue for the right "to manifest," "to teach," and in some instances "to propagate" one's religious tradition. Most religious traditions, with the exception of traditional religions like those of Native Americans and those of African tribal groups, have, to different extents and in different periods of time, propagated their faiths. However, some of the major world religions, like Christianity, Islam, and Buddhism have missionary mandates as part of their belief systems. Here one can broadly identify five different positions that have relevance to the discussion of religious freedom:

- those religious traditions that do not engage in propagation of their faith and are opposed to missions aimed at them;
- those who propagate their faith but are intolerant toward missions aimed at their own community;
- those who propagate their faith and are also open to others to propagate their faith, also aimed at their own community, thus claiming that propagation of one's faith as a basic right;
- those who accept the rights of all communities to propagate their faith but insist on ethical and non-coercive methods of propagation;
- those who support the rights of all individuals to adopt, remain in, and change their religious affiliation as a personal right but are opposed to organized missionary activity to gain converts.

169

Four basic issues that arise from the above need special consideration:

1. *Reciprocity.* The first relates to reciprocity. As religious traditions begin to relate closely with one another, the position that holds that a particular community has the right to convert others but would not allow conversion of their own believers has come under increasing pressure. This has been a matter of tension especially between some of the Islamic countries and Western nations with Christian majorities. Many Christians in the USA and in some of the European countries, for instance, are troubled by the fact that while there are heavily funded Islamic missions from Saudi Arabia in Western countries, there is no possibility for Christian minorities living in Saudi Arabia to build a church even for their own worship in community.

2. *The right to remain in one's faith.* The second is the much more complex issue of the rights of individuals and their relationships to the rights of the community as a whole. This issue relates to missionary methods, political or economic pressures, and demographic realities that overtly or covertly violate a person's religious right to "remain" in his or her religious tradition. This is also related to current discussions on cultural imperialism, the use of mass media, economic disparities and so on as they relate to conversion. Some religious communities hold that many of the international conventions on human and religious rights arise out of the Western humanistic tradition and put all the emphases on the rights of individuals. They claim that these conventions do not take sufficient note of the large sections of human community where the primary focus is on the interest of the community within which the rights of the individuals are enshrined. In some of these traditions, it is claimed, of necessity the rights of the community take precedence over the rights of the individual in order to protect the integrity, identity, coherence, and unity of the community. It is argued that even though it is important to protect the rights of the individuals from the possible oppressive dimensions of community pressures, there is reason to look more carefully at the balance between these two rights especially where religion is understood primarily as a manifestation of life in community. In other words, today some argue that the "right to remain" in one's faith is in need of greater protection than the "right to adopt" or "change" one's

faith, or that the "right to remain" must be seen as a more fundamental right than "to change."

Others, coming from other experiences, disagree and say that there are inalienable rights of the individual that need to be protected, precisely because of the ways in which basic rights of individuals have been and are being denied or violated in the name of the community, tradition, or religious teachings. This matter needs greater exploration; perhaps the religious communities with different views on this subject should engage in developing new guidelines that define the borders of individual and community rights and the ways in which they can be held in tension so that one is not used to exploit the other.

This is also important because of the increasing numbers of violations of basic human and religious rights, including the right to life, which is defended in the name of community rights. While some of the accusations in the Western mass media of violation of human and religious rights in Islamic countries are, in fact, based on cultural insensitivity and the expectation that everyone must agree with the definition of rights framed by the West, there is increasing unease within all religious communities when some of the basic rights of women, children, immigrants, minority communities and others are denied and defended on the basis of religious, cultural, and community rights. Here again it is not easy for any community to determine when religious beliefs are abused in another community. We need to find ways to engage in dialogue on this question to find commonly agreed criteria to evaluate specific cases.

3. *Alliance between religion and state.* Third, one of the intentions of the conventions is to free individuals and religious communities from the oppressive control of the state, and to prevent religious communities using the state as an instrument to suppress the religious rights of other communities. Historically, the abuses in this area have been so massive that many insist that the only way to overcome this danger is through the separation of religion and state. However, as seen earlier, there are religions that see personal, family, social, economic, and political dimensions of life in a continuum and see the benefit of maintaining it. Further, they claim it as part of their religious self-understanding. Others are quick to point to the difficulties such an understanding presents to the rights of religious minorities on matters of religious

practice, and to their civic right to be equal citizens of a nation-state. We have shown that there are many different ways in which religion and state relationship can be fashioned and that it is indeed possible to build models that can overcome possible abuse. This is another area that needs careful consideration and common agreements.

4. *The right to propagate one's faith and unethical missionary practices.* The last question has to do with the complex issues related to the right of individuals to share their faith, the right of persons to remain in their faith, the right to adopt a new faith, and the accusations of unethical methods of winning converts. This has been a difficult problem to resolve mainly because of the ambiguities involved in making judgments about people's intentions and motives; competing claims are made about the motives and ultimate goals of missionary activities and of those who choose to adopt a new religion. There are communities that engage in unethical missionary practices by using coercive methods, by misrepresenting the faiths of others, or by the use of inducements. Some have also rightly been accused of exploiting the poverty of other people to increase the growth of their own faith community. There is no doubt that some of the Christian missionary activities in the "third world," emanating especially from the USA, are conducted in a culturally insensitive manner for the purpose of simply increasing the numbers of their religious community. There are also good reasons to believe that, often, material inducements are used to gain converts. These certainly need to be condemned and one should plainly maintain that shutting them down would not involve a violation of the religious freedom to share one's faith.

However, genuine desire to share one's faith with others, humanitarian assistance programs to those in desperate need, and attempts to help people liberate themselves from oppressive situations have also been prevented under the guise of rejecting unethical means of conversion. This is a pressing problem today in counties like India and Sri Lanka and has been the cause of active violence against one community by another. In India, there are many clear instances of unethical missions from Western countries like the USA conducted by those who come from outside or by their agents within the country. In responding to these unethical missions some of the regional

Indian states have promulgated laws banning conversion under certain circumstances, which unfortunately are open to a wide variety of interpretations. Since the application of these laws can easily become indiscriminate, the nation may be in breach of some of the provisions of religious freedom of its regular citizens, namely, to propagate one's faith and to adopt a faith of one's choice. For instance, many of the Christians who lost their lives, or homes, or had to flee their homes in the anti-Christian violence in Gujarat and Orissa, in India, were innocent victims of an indiscriminate response to Christian missionary activities, both ethical and unethical.

Recognizing the complex issues involved in this question, religious communities have come up with "Codes of Conduct" that are appropriate for sharing one's faith with others. The implementation of these codes will help to ease some of the tensions and conflicts that have risen over this issue.

Is Religious Freedom an Absolute Right?

One of the issues that need some consideration here is whether religious freedom is an absolute right. In drawing up its statement on religious liberty in the aftermath of World War II, the World Council of Churches, for instance, held that "the freedom of religion is fundamental to all other freedoms." The document of the Second Vatican Council dealing with this issue, *Dignitatis Humanae*, declared that "the right to religious freedom has its foundation in the very dignity of the human person, as this dignity is known through the Revealed Word of God, and by reason itself."[7] Yet, there is general recognition that, like all other rights, religious freedom also has its limits, and that a claim that it is absolute in all its dimensions would lead to the abuse of these rights. At the same time, there is also concern that religious rights could be suppressed under the pretext of "law and order" or "well-being of the community" or "national interest" and so forth.

Already in 1948, the Amsterdam Assembly of the World Council of Churches felt the need to address this issue. It affirmed parts of the right as inalienable and others as subjected to limits:

a. The liberty of conscience or right to determine one's belief is practically subject to no legal limitation at all.

b. The liberty of religious expression is subject to such limitations prescribed by law as are necessary to protect order and welfare, morals and the rights and freedoms of others.
c. The liberty of religious association is subject to the same limits imposed on all associations by non-discriminatory laws.
d. Similarly, the corporate religious freedom is limited by the provisions of non-discriminatory laws passed in the interest of public order and well-being.[8]

What the Amsterdam Assembly sought to do was to reiterate that all rights are, of necessity, limited by other equally important concerns of society. But at the same time, it insisted that there are elements within religious freedom, as the freedom of conscience and belief, which are absolute and non-negotiable. One should also note that the Assembly is careful to maintain that the limitations on the rights, when necessary, have to be "non-discriminatory" so that the limiting clauses are not used to deny the rights of only sections of the population. Unfortunately the limitation clauses intended for extraordinary situations are often abused, and states use the pretext of national security, public order, and so on to interfere with the legitimate exercise of religious freedom. One of the accusations against the United States is the way it used the Homeland Security Act in the post 9/11 period. Because of possible abuses, today there are calls to declare more dimensions of religious freedom as absolute rights. An accompanying essay on religious freedom in this volume takes concrete instances of how judges and jurors in South Africa, for instance, attempt to deal with the ambiguities involved in applying the convictions about religious freedom in relation to other legitimate social interests and rights.

Spirituality and Religious Freedom

The discussion above shows that, in the final analysis, religious freedom is not just a legal issue but also a spiritual one. Religious communities need to find ways in which explication of their beliefs, their understandings of sharing their faiths, the methods used to do so, and their approach to other religious traditions respect the dignity and humanity of all their neighbors. Love, respect, compassion, justice, and peace are affirmed by all traditions. There is a universal belief that one should not do to others what one would not want others to do to oneself. The way a religious tradition looks at the rights of others is a sign of its own spiritual maturity. Religious traditions also need to engage in in-depth dialogue about the issues mentioned above, and should together stand up against violations of religious freedom, wherever it comes from, and whoever is affected by it. The drawing up of "Codes of Conduct" is one of the steps, but what needs to happen also is the elimination of the need for such codes. No religious community will be able to address this question to the satisfaction of all. This is one issue that cries out for interfaith dialogue, mutual understanding, and collaboration in the interests of the whole human community. This volume is a witness that it is indeed possible to have a multi-faith approach to this complex issue. The final chapter offers a glimpse into what can come out of such a multi-faith approach.

Notes

1 Ninan Koshy, *Religious Freedom in a Changing World* (Geneva: WCC Publications, 1992), p. 36.
2 Koshy, *Religious Freedom*, p. 37.
3 Peter Cumper, "Religious Human Rights in the United Kingdom," *Emory International Law Review* 10.1 (1996), 115–126.
4 Donna E. Arzt, "Religious Human Rights in Muslim States of the Middle East and North Africa," *Emory International Law Review* 10.1 (1996), 140.
5 Arzt, "Religious Human Rights in Muslim States," p. 142.
6 Clement John, *Religion, State and Intolerance* (Geneva: WCC, 2009), pp. 42–59.
7 The Vatican II document *Dignitatis Humanae* can be found in Walter H. Abbot, *The Documents of Vatican II* (Piscataway, NJ: New Century Publishers, 1966).
8 Quoted in Koshy, *Religious Freedom*, p. 42.

Further Reading

Kim, Sebastian C.H. *In search of Identity: Debates on Religious Conversion in India*. Oxford: Oxford University Press, 2005.
Lamb, Christopher. *Religious Freedom: Contemporary Practices and Controversies*. London: Continuum, 1999.

S. *Wesley Ariarajah*

Thames, H. Knox, Chris Seiple, and Amy Rowe. *International Religious Freedom Advocacy: A Guide to Organizations, Law and NGOs*. Waco, TX: Baylor University Press, 2009.

Mustafa, Faizan. *Conversion: Constitutional and Legal Implications*. New Delhi: Kanishka Publishing House, 2003.

Taylor, Paul M. *Freedom of Religion: UN and European Human Rights Law and Practice*. Cambridge: Cambridge University Press, 2006.

176

11

The Right to Religious Freedom and Proselytism
A Legal Perspective

Ravin Ramdass

Introduction

Freedom of conscience and religion is said to be one of the *oldest* of the internationally recognized freedoms.[1] The importance of this right is emphasized in the opinion of the Constitutional Court of South Africa, one of the *youngest* democracies of the world: "The constitutional right to practice one's religion is of fundamental importance in an open and democratic society. It is one of the hallmarks of a free society."[2] Religious freedom is the first right listed in the Bill of Rights, and thus is often referred to as the "First Freedom" in the American Constitution.[3] Religious freedom is deemed to be integral to our dignity, growth, and self-worth and is one of the pillars of a free society. Notwithstanding its importance – and, one may surmise, because of its importance – the protection of this right remains an important challenge.

Religious freedom is widely considered a human right.[4] Whether it is also a legal right[5] can be somewhat contentious, particularly when the legal right is in conflict with the human right. In this chapter, religious freedom is seen from the perspective of being a human right that is upheld by the legal system whilst being mindful of the danger of the relationship between the state and religion undermining the human right by legal means, as was the case

Religious Conversion: Religion Scholars Thinking Together, First Edition.
Edited by Shanta Premawardhana.
© 2015 World Council of Churches Publications. Published 2015 by John Wiley & Sons, Ltd.

in apartheid South Africa. The discussion focuses on the issue of conversion and proselytization and the tension created by the alternative, and sometimes exclusive, claims that religious freedom is a human and not a legal right and vice versa.

Religious freedom is a complex right with a plethora of interpretations, from the inviolability of truth claims of the major communities of a state on the one hand, to the protection of minorities and their beliefs on the other, with many shades of gray in between. This chapter considers religious freedom as a legal right and addresses the content of this legal right, the issue of proselytization and the right to religious freedom, the upholding of the right and, finally, in a broad manner, some legal implications with regard to the issue of conversion.

Religious Freedom as a Legal Right

The legal basis for the right

> For centuries, the relationship between church and state and between religion and law dominated politics in large parts of the world. The history of this relationship is complex, but, for present purposes, it suffices to say that in the western world the alliance between church and state proved to be an unholy one, and it was in reaction to religious persecution by the state that the idea of human rights first developed. The earliest advocates of religious freedom therefore combined calls for religious tolerance with calls for a secular state which did not favour one religion over others. Today, the interpretation of the right still reflects its historical origins in that it turns first on the extent to which the state may recognise or "establish" a religion, and, second on the freedom to exercise a religious belief.[6]

The recognition of this right to religious freedom finds its expression in many constitutions of countries of the world and in several conventions to which a vast majority of countries are signatories. The right to religious freedom is protected in the International Bill of Rights that consists of three documents: the Universal Declaration of Human Rights, the International Covenant on Civil and Political Rights (ICCPR), and the International Covenant on Economic, Social, and Cultural Rights (ICESCR). The ICCPR and ICESCR are treaties that elaborate the rights specified in the Universal Declaration and, as of June 2004, the ICCPR had 152 state parties and the ICESCR had 149 state parties.

In various countries of the world, the right to religious freedom has been entrenched in their constitutions and is often in line with the Universal Declaration of Human Rights. In the United States, religious freedom is the first human right to enjoy constitutional protection in the form of the Virginia Statute for Religious Freedom. Written in 1779 by Thomas Jefferson, it proclaimed:

> No man shall be compelled to frequent or support any religious worship, place, or ministry whatsoever, nor shall be enforced, restrained, molested, or burthened [*sic*] in his body or goods, nor shall otherwise suffer, on account of his religious opinions or belief; but that all men shall be free to profess, and by argument to maintain, their opinions in matters of religion, and that the same shall in no wise diminish, enlarge, or affect their civil capacities.[7]

South Africa, one of the youngest democracies in the world, protects the right to religious freedom in section 15 of its Constitution:

15.1 Everyone has the right to freedom of conscience, religion, thought, belief and opinion

15.2 Religious observances may be conducted at state or state-aided institutions provided that:
   a. those observances follow rules made by appropriate public authorities;
   b. they are conducted on an equitable basis
   c. attendance to them is free and voluntary.

15.3 a. This section does not prevent legislation recognising
      i.   marriages concluded under any tradition, or a system of religious, personal or family law; or
      ii. systems of personal and family law under any tradition, or adhered to by any persons professing a particular religion.
   b. recognition in terms of paragraph (a) must be consistent with this section and the other provisions of the Constitution.[8]

Having outlined the legal protection of the right to religious freedom, it is necessary to consider the right more closely especially with regard to what the content of the right to religious freedom encompasses.

In considering any human or legal right, it is important to consider the content[9] of the right.

The content of the right

In assessing the content of the right to religious freedom, it is important to consider the scope of the right as well as the application of the right.

The scope of the right has both a core and a penumbra.[10] Here penumbra refers to the application or infringement of the right beyond the clear bounds of the core of the right of religious freedom. Both will be discussed in turn.

The core of the right to religious freedom   The right to religious freedom encompasses:

- the right to adopt a religion or belief of one's choice;
- the freedom to manifest in public or private one's *religious teachings* either individually or in community with others;
- the freedom to manifest in public or private one's *religious observances* either individually or in community with others;
- the freedom to manifest in public or private one's *religious practices* either individually or in community with others;
- the freedom to manifest in public or private the *worship of one's religion* either individually or in community with others.

The essence of the concept of freedom of religion, according to the Canadian courts as opined in *S v. Lawrence*, is "the right to entertain such religious beliefs as a person chooses, the right to declare religious beliefs openly and without fear of hindrance or reprisal, and the right to manifest religious belief by worship and practice or by teaching or dissemination."[11]

Freedom of religion includes both a right to have a belief and the right to express such belief in practice. In *Prince*,[12] the Constitutional Court of South Africa confirmed that the South African Constitution protects religious belief and the practice of manifestation of belief and prohibits coercion or restraint of religious belief or practice. The Court has on two occasions, both in the Solberg[13] and in the Christian Education South Africa[14] cases, considered the content of the right to freedom of religion. On each occasion it accepted that the right "at least comprehends (a) the right to entertain the religious beliefs that one chooses to entertain; (b) the right to announce one's religious belief publicly and without fear of reprisal; and (c) the right to manifest such beliefs by worship and practice, teaching and dissemination."[15]

A more comprehensive list of the kinds of religious practices or manifestations of a religious belief that would be protected is detailed in Article 6 of the United Nations Declaration on the Elimination of All Forms of Intolerance and Discrimination Based on Religion or Belief, passed by the United Nations General Assembly in November 1991. These include the freedom to:

- worship or assemble in connection religion or belief, and to maintain such places for these purposes;
- establish and maintain appropriate charitable or humanitarian institutions;
- make, acquire, and use to an adequate extent the necessary articles and materials related to the rights or customs of a religion or belief;
- teach religion or belief in places suitable for these purposes;
- write, issue, and disseminate relevant publications in these areas;
- solicit and receive voluntary financial and other contributions from individuals and institutions;
- train, appoint, elect, or designate by succession appropriate leaders called for by the requirements and standards of any religion or belief;
- observe days of rest and to celebrate holidays and ceremonies in accordance with the precept of one's own religion or belief;
- establish and maintain communication with individuals and communities in matters of religion and belief at the national and international level.[16]

Implicit in the right is the absence of coercion or restraint. The coercion referred to is both direct or indirect (where the effect of legislation or action is not directly coercive but has the effect of being coercive). An example of direct coercion would be where a law bans a particular church or religious group or prohibits a particular religious practice. Indirect coercion would be, for example, when the state compels one to take a religious oath as a condition of public employment or eligibility for an elected position although one does not subscribe to those religious views, or where the state forces a person who is not a member of a church to pay taxes that are, in turn used to fund the church or where a person is compelled to observe a holy day of a particular religion. A more common form of indirect coercion occurs when states enact facially neutral laws – laws that do not engage expressly with or refer to religious practice (or belief) – that apply to religious organizations and adherents, since laws enacted apply to everyone. "While such 'neutral' interference would apparently be more benign (and ostensibly much less likely to be motivated by religious preferences or bigotry), it could have a severe impact on religious organisations or communities. A religious group's way of life or its rites of worship could effectively be prohibited. Believers could be coerced into acting in ways inimical to their faith."[17]

On the other hand, in the face of competing rights, one may argue that the state may curb the right to religious freedom. In South African case law one may cite the example of the Christian Education case,[18] wherein Christian Education South Africa, a forum of Christian organizations, challenged the prohibition of corporal punishment as an infringement of their right to religious freedom. The crux of the argument was that the Christian organizations sanctioned the use of corporal punishment as a means of "biblical correction" and the prohibition of corporal punishment by law is an infringement of their religious rights to bring up their children according to Christian principles. The Constitutional Court agreed that this was an infringement but also ruled that a limitation of this freedom was justified and legally sound, as corporal punishment was a cruel and inhumane manner in which to treat children. In a further case, Prince,[19] a member of the Rastafarian religion, argued that making the use of cannabis illegal infringed his right to religious freedom as the smoking of cannabis was allowed in the Rastafarian religion. Again, the Court ruled that there was infringement of his rights but the infringement was legal as the use of a habit-forming drug that was detrimental to physical and mental health could not be justified even in the face of compromising the right to religious freedom.

It is therefore clear that there is a well-circumscribed core to the religious freedom right. However, the right also has a penumbra wherein the right is not clear cut and the right is nonetheless in more subtle and obscure ways infringed.

The penumbra of the right to religious freedom   In the penumbra of the right to religious freedom, the cardinal feature is subtle non-quantifiable coercion.

The protection against subtle non-quantifiable coercion

The right to religious freedom has often been infringed, particularly in the case of minorities by governments that align themselves with a particular religion, often the religion of the majority. Despite conventions and constitutions of individual states entrenching the right to religious freedom, the entanglement of state and religion that often leads to the infringement of religious freedom is not explicitly dealt with – the protection of religious freedom from state interference has to be inferred or at best is only implied. This highlights the issue of subtle non-quantifiable coercion of adherents of religious groups not "entangled" with the state.

In the United States there are specific anti-establishment clauses which prevent the state from specifically supporting a particular religion to the disadvantage of other religions. The Establishment Clause mandates a separation between church and state. The ICCPR, however, does not contain such an establishment clause. Neither does the South African Constitution.

Whether it is proper for the state to give its imprimatur of approval to a particular religion arose for consideration by the Constitutional Court of South Africa in three cases including the Solberg[20] case in which it was contended that the Liquor Act 27 of 1989 that prohibited the sale of liquor on Sundays evinced a religious purpose. It was "alleged that 'in due submission to a sectarian Christian conception of the proper observance of the Christian Sabbath and Christian holidays or, perhaps, to compel the observance of the Christian Sabbath and Christian holidays and that such a sectarian aim constituted an infringement of the right to freedom of religion."[21] However, the Court found in this particular case that the appellants could not prove that the sale of liquor on the days mentioned infringed on their religious freedom: there was a kind of artificiality in the argument that it did infringe their right to religious freedom. In a similar case, the Canadian Supreme Court ruled that the appellants did not adduce any evidence to support their allegation that their religious freedom was infringed and therefore their appeal was dismissed. What these cases seem to underline is that it is very difficult to assess the subtle non-quantifiable coercion and then to prove that it imposed a significant burden on the victims of such coercion. Herein lies the importance of distinguishing between religious freedom as a human right and religious freedom as a legal right. It is the enactment of legislation that creates the legal right and often legislation is unable to protect – or in fact infringes – the right to religious freedom.

More importantly, however, it was clear from the Solberg case that the Constitution precluded the state from showing a special affinity with Christianity. The appellants failed not because the Constitution allowed a special affinity for Christianity but because they could not discharge the onus on them to prove their case. In the United States, the Establishment Clause clearly follows the same approach that the state could not show an affinity for any religion. Similarly, in many countries around the world, states cannot show affinity for any religious tradition to the detriment of others. The problem, however, still remains that often seemingly innocuous and neutral legislation has the effect of subtle non-quantifiable coercion: a phenomenon difficult to prove or to determine the effect of. Practically, therefore, this means that the religious freedom of certain groups may be infringed, but to obtain legal relief is often difficult given the present legislation.

Subtle non-quantifiable coercion is particularly pronounced in the school environment and in prisons and becomes more subtle as one moves away from these captive environments. The fact that the coercion is more subtle does not detract from its oppressive nature and makes it imperative that, for the protection of the freedom of religion, the endorsement of any religion that results in indirect coercion should be prohibited. This argument is supported by several courts including the US Supreme Court.

While it is clear that endorsement of any religion by the state should be prohibited, what has not been decided by the courts is what the extent of state involvement should be. Would any government action with a religious purpose necessarily be precluded on the basis of being "subtly coercive"? Would such a strict separation between state and religion actually advance religious freedom? The answer to both the questions is no.

There is no reason why state involvement with religion, or government actions that have a religious purpose or effect, would necessarily be coercive (even indirectly or subtly) and thus be inconsistent with the penumbra of the right to religious freedom. There is furthermore no simple correlation between separation of church and state and total religious freedom. While complete identification of church and state clearly undermines religious freedom, a rigorous policy of state non-identification with religion would likely be violative of freedom of religion.[22]

A good example of the subtle non-quantifiable coercion is seen in pre-apartheid and post-apartheid South Africa. It is accepted that Christianity was the preferred religion in pre-apartheid South Africa. Christianity was also the religion of the privileged white race. This privileged race was able to impose its religious teachings on other race groups and this was supported by the state. The union between the state and the Christian religion was mutually comple-mentary – the Church was able to justify the superiority of the white (mainly Christian) race while the apartheid state supported the evangelical and proselytization agenda of the Church. The judiciary was also compromised by this association and that further impinged on the religious freedoms of other traditions who happened to belong to the so-called inferior race. In post-apartheid South Africa it is therefore imperative that there is a healthy separation of state and church – not to the extent that there is a complete separation but to the extent that the state can be involved in the restitution of the victimized religions and in the prevention of such abuse again.

The relationship of state and religion varies from absolute theoc-racies on the one hand and legal orders characterized by hostility and overt persecution of religious orders and adherents on the other. Following the one extreme of absolute theocracies, one may have countries with an established church: an established church is com-patible either with a system in which there is a virtual monopoly in religious affairs, or one in which there is substantial toleration of other beliefs. Third, there are countries with an endorsed church – wherein the church is accorded special acknowledgment and maybe treatment, although is not formally affirmed as the official church of the nation. Fourth, there are co-cooperationist regimes where no special status is granted to dominant churches, although the state cooperates with the church in a number of ways, for example collecting taxes for the church or in arranging religious education. Fifth, there are accommodationist regimes wherein there is cooperation between state and church but not direct financial subsidies to the religious group or to religious education. Under these regimes the state is able to accommodate religion and the religious wishes of its citizens by, for example, acknowledging the importance of religion as part of the national or local culture, allowing religious symbols in public settings, and permitting tax, dietary, holiday, Sabbath, and other kinds of exemptions. Sixth, there are separationist regimes that are less accepting of state involvement with religious activities. Seventh, there are political arrangements marked by inadvertent insensitivity to religion; and, finally, there are the legal orders that are hostile and overtly persecute religious orders.

This detailed exposition is important in that it is the kind of relationship between state and church that by its very nature alone can have significant ramifications for religious freedom. Furthermore, the type of relationship between the state and the church has important implications for the issue of religious conversion. It would certainly appear that the middle four models would be most conducive to religious freedom and probably the most persuasive case can be made for an accommodationist approach. This approach appears to be preferable to a separationist stance because it would permit a government in certain circumstances to enact laws that have the primary or incidental purpose of benefiting a particular religion without the shackles of endorsement and it allows for the worship or expressions of faith to have a public as well as a private dimension. Prohibiting religious observances or other expressions or manifestations of faith in public can constitute an infringement of the religious faith of certain adherents. "Stated differently, a policy banning all worship or religious instruction from state institutions is not neutral vis-à-vis different religions (or even all adherents of one religion), or between religious adherents, atheists and agnostics. This proposition has been acknowledged and affirmed by the German Constitutional Court."[23]

Religious equality In protecting against the "subtle coercion," it is important to explore whether the protection implies a guarantee of equality of all religions. The Constitution of South Africa undeniably manifests a concern for equality and a respect for diversity. "Nevertheless, it would not seem to be textually required, or conceptually coherent for the right to freedom of religion, belief or opinion to be read to require equal treatment."[24] Canadian jurisprudence also does not see this as the essence of the concept of freedom of religion. The Canadian courts are more concerned in respect of religious freedom not to equality of religions but to coercion as an infringement of religious freedom. It is clear that equal treatment of all religions may in itself lead to infringements of religious freedom particularly with respect to minority religions. A government which remains passive when the free exercise of minority religions is suppressed by dominant forces in society is implicated in the violation of the freedom of religion. However, these claims rest in other areas of the Constitution, notably the equality clauses. The infringements are therefore considered within the ambit of the equality clauses of various constitutions of countries of the world rather than in the ambit of the religious freedom clauses.

The limitation of the right of religious freedom

"In democratic societies, several religions often coexist. It may at times be necessary to limit the right to religious freedom of one religion in the interest of the upholding other fundamental human rights like dignity, equality and freedom."[25]

In democratic societies, in which several religions coexist within one and the same population, it may be necessary to place restrictions on freedom to manifest one's religion or belief in order to reconcile the interests of the various groups and ensure that one's beliefs are respected.[26]

The right to religious freedom may be limited in the following instances:

- if such limitations are prescribed by law; and
- if they are necessary to protect public safety, order, health, or morals;
- or the fundamental rights and freedoms of others.

Important emphasis here is given the fact that to limit the right to religious freedom, the limiter of the right must be able to prove that such limitation is prescribed by law *and* such limitation was necessary to protect public safety, order and health and/or the fundamental rights and freedoms of others.

187

The South African Constitution, like several other constitutions, also allows the limitation of the right to religious freedom where – like in other freedoms – such limitation would be justified in a democratic society based on human dignity and equality. This allows for some individual case-by-case consideration of the limitation of the right to religious freedom.

How would one, therefore, determine if the right to religious freedom has been infringed?

The stages of the freedom of religion enquiry   The first enquiry would be whether there was clear intent to infringe the religious freedom of adherents. This would be, for example, where the government of a state would intentionally pass a law that legally sanctions the infringement of the religious freedom rights. It this is so, then the next consideration would be to consider whether such infringement was justified in a democratic society based on human dignity and equality, as in the case of corporal punishment in the Christian Education case discussed above. If the limitation is justifiable, then for it to withstand a constitutional challenge it must be applicable generally to the whole population and not to a select group of people only.

The more contentious and difficult area is where governments pass ostensibly neutral laws that are then challenged as infringing on the religious freedom rights. The first issue that the courts will now consider is the sincerity of the believer in the belief. The court cannot simply accept without any enquiry that a religious belief has been affected by legislation or any act. The court, in remaining sensitive to the varieties of beliefs and the constitutional commitment to diversity, will only in exceptional cases conclude that a religious belief is not sincerely held. An exceptional case would be where a belief has been trumped up in an attempt to obtain an exemption to cater for personal predilections. The religious beliefs in question do not have to be objectively reasonable or sophisticated or coherent, or universally accepted by adherents of the particular religion. In fact the South African courts have not held thus far that a belief has not been sincerely held. At this stage of the enquiry, the courts have to be convinced that the particular infringement relates to a religious belief, as non-religious beliefs do not have the same protection as religious beliefs in international human rights documents. An opinion, for example, will not be afforded the same protection as a sincerely held religious belief.

The next stage of the enquiry is to consider the nature of the burden that has to be imposed on a religion in order for there to be violation of the right to freedom of religion and belief. The claimant has to satisfy the court that a substantial burden on the exercise of the freedom of religion is imposed by the offending legislation or act. The court has to be satisfied that the prohibited practice is a central tenet of the religion. In the case of religious conversion the court has to be satisfied that proselytization is a central tenet of the religion for the religion to escape legal prohibition.

The offending practice may also be prohibited on the basis of other provisions of the Bill of Rights – for example on the basis of infringement of the right to equality, or on the invasion of privacy. When there are other protections offered, these protections will be invoked first. In the case of corporal punishment, which was pro- hibited in schools and then challenged by the Christian Education forum, the court ruled not in terms of the infringement of religious freedom but rather on the basis of the violation of the right to human dignity and the protection against cruel, inhuman, and degrading treatment or punishment. In the case of religious conversion, where such attempts at conversion amount to hate speech, the court will invoke the protection against hate speech clauses.

Essentially, no matter which theoretical approach is followed, the substantive questions remain the same. The first question to ask is whether the different degrees of protection must be afforded to different beliefs depending on their content. If so, religions that promote key constitutional values, such as dignity, equality, and freedom, must be afforded greater protection than those that seek to undermine them. However, if content differentiation is rejected, one must try to identify a content-neutral principle to differentiate between legitimate and illegitimate types of limiting the freedom of religion. Denise Meyerson has presented the powerful argument that the most important principle is harm: religious practices may only be limited if they cause harm.[27]

As there can be no such thing as a wrong belief or idea, and as beliefs as such cannot cause harm, there is no justification for thought control. A distinction must be made between the holding of a belief and the public expression of a belief. As with other forms of expression, there may be legitimate reasons for limiting proselytizing – for example, on the basis of the harm it may cause or in the interests of public order. The state may, and indeed must, prohibit practices that cause physical or emotional harm to persons. The legitimacy of such prohibitions is widely recognized not only in South African but in many other countries as well.

Finally, it is important to emphasize that the right to religious freedom has a vertical application between the state and the citizens, and a horizontal application between citizen and citizen. To achieve the goal of religious freedom, there must be protection in both these areas – between state and citizen and between citizen and citizen.

Proselytization and the Right to Religious Freedom

In considering the issue of proselytization, one may subject it to the same enquiry outlined above. The enquiry can be conducted in the case where the proselytized alleges that her religious rights have been infringed, or in the case of the proselytizer who alleges that a prohibition on proselytization infringes his right to religious freedom.

In the case of the proselytized, the enquiry will firstly entail whether there is intentional state legislation that allows for the infringement of her right. If this is so, the enquiry ends and the court will then have to decide if such legislation meets the requirement of being acceptable in a free and fair society based on equality and human dignity: if yes, the legislation will be ruled to be constitutionally acceptable. If, however, the offending act or legislation is such that it is neutral, then the enquiry will be whether there is a particular belief that the proselytized sincerely holds. If so, the next stage of the inquiry is whether the proselytizing act creates a substantial burden. If it does, the act is an infringement of the religious freedom of the victim of such proselytizing acts.

A closer analysis in the case of conversion is necessary. In the horizontal application of the right to religious freedom, one will most probably be confronted with the allegation by the proselytized that her rights to religious freedom have been infringed. If she believes with sincerity (and not merely for some other reason) that she should not be subjected to the proselytizing action, she would have satisfied the first stage of the enquiry. If, however, she cannot prove, and most probably she would not be able to, that the proselytizing action goes against a central tenet of her religion, she would fail. How does a Hindu, for example, prove that proselytization goes against a central tenet of her religion?

In the case of the proselytizer, he or she can easily resort to legislation and international law that guarantees him the freedom to share his religion with another – this is a guaranteed freedom even in the ICCPR. In countries with anti-conversion laws, of course, his rights will be determined in terms of that legislation and he may then challenge the constitutionality of those laws. In the absence of such legislation, he will probably be legally entitled to share his religion within the scope of his religious freedom. If the court has reason to consider the matter further, he will have no difficulty satisfying the next part of the enquiry that his belief is sincere and that it is a central tenet of his religion. In these circumstances, it is clear that conversion will be allowed and the proselytizer would be, at least substantively, performing a legally sanctioned act. This analysis, however, makes no provision for the consequences of such an act, and such an act may only be limited if it is a threat to public order or infringes the religious freedoms of another – to prove that the religious freedoms of the proselytized are being infringed is near impossible given the analysis carried out above. This model therefore, is not helpful as it may allow any form of proselytization provided that such proselytization is not illegal on some other account, for example, violence or hate speech. Hence, there is a wide area of freedom granted to the proselytizer with significant potential for discrimination against the proselytized.

However, a further and preferred model is the one that considers the harm that the proselytizing act causes to the proselytized. This harm goes beyond the physical harm and includes emotional harm. The argument therefore is that it appears that conventions and constitutions in the name of freedom of religion accept that proselytization is substantively correct. This matter, I believe, needs further interrogation as many of the conventions and constitutions of countries are influenced by Christian thinking. It is acceptable, and even legitimate, for proselytizing religions to claim the right to proselytize in the name of religious freedom, and yet, the mere act of proselytizing may be an impairment of the dignity of the proselytized. The anomaly here is that the conventions and constitutions are there to protect the right of human beings to dignity and yet sanction the impairment of the dignity of the proselytized. So, is it that proselytizing is substantively correct? If one takes the "harm" approach, then if one can prove that one suffers harm either because one is prevented from proselytizing or being converted, then one may argue that an infringement of the religious rights of the respective person has occurred. This approach seems to be the easier approach by which the proselytized may succeed in a claim, and it certainly will be more difficult for the proselytizer to succeed in his claim to proselytize if the proselytized can easily prove that he suffers harm.

With regard to an infringement, I would like to suggest that for an act to be legally correct, it must be both substantively and procedurally correct. In the case of proselytization, it would appear that the present legal position is that it is substantively correct, although there is need that this be interrogated more vigorously. Can we say that conversion is substantively correct if we consider the following observations?

> The Christian missionary mind set is generally depicted as that of simple religious folk with a pure desire to peacefully spread their gospel and message of love. In reality, their methods of propagation are often anything but peaceful and usually leave behind a native population stripped of their culture and often decimated ... In the words of one resident of Thailand, "They [Christian missionaries] seemed that they did not show any interest for our culture. Why? They are just eager to build big churches in every village. It seems that they are having two faces; under the title of help to suppress us. To the world, they gained their reputations as benefactors of disappearing tribes. They built their reputations on us for many years. The way they behaved with us seemed as if we did not know about god before they arrived here. Why do missionaries think they are the only ones who can perceive God?"[28]

It is clear that one cannot even remotely aver that such action is substantively correct.

The methods (procedurally) used to proselytize are varied, from overt methods to more subtle but pervasive methods, from legal to illegal methods, from ethical to unethical methods and from peaceful to violent methods. In a Vatican co-sponsored meeting, the nature of proselytization was discussed in 2005. It was clear from this meeting that some religious groups abuse liberties by proselytizing, or by evangelizing in aggressive and deceptive ways.

A point in question is Iraq, which has become an open field for foreigners looking for fresh converts. Some Catholic Church leaders and aid organizations have expressed concern about new Christian groups coming in and luring Iraqis to their churches with offers of cash, clothing, food or jobs. Reports of aggressive proselytism and reportedly forced conversions in mostly Hindu India have fueled religious tensions and violence there and have prompted some regional governments to pass laws banning proselytism or religious conversion. Sadhvi Vrndva Chaitanya, a Hindu monk from southern India, told the Catholic News Service that India's poor and uneducated are especially vulnerable to coercive or deceptive methods of evangelization. "Aid work must not hide any ulterior motives and avoid exploiting vulnerable people like children and the disabled, she said."[29]

One cannot forget the hidden face of the proselytizer – the huge funding for proselytization, the propaganda in the Western media, the infiltration of education systems, the mediums that become the messages in proselytization (as, for example, in South Africa, where the religion of the white man had to be superior to the religion of the inferior black). All in all, we have, therefore, very sophisticated and subtle methods of proselytization on the one hand, and the more visible and mundane methods on the other.

From a legal perspective, one has to say that where fraud, deceit, and violence are used then one may resort to appropriate legal remedies. However, concerning the more legal but unethical methods, one has to consider the harm that proselytization causes in determining the legality; maybe it is time for our jurisprudence to evolve in that direction.

Furthermore, where it can be proved that proselytization threatens the public order – as in Nagaland, for example, where "Christianity has wiped out a whole way of life, erasing centuries of tradition, customs and wisdom. It has caused people to hold their own religion in contempt and look westwards to an alien culture,"[30] or in Africa where Muslim and Christian evangelization has disrupted several communities and has led to violence – there is adequate legal reason to limit the freedom of religion.

Religious Freedom as a Human Right

It is clear from the above discussion that there are huge lacunae in accepting that religious freedom is merely a legal right. If one avers that that is all it is, then one is hamstrung by the ideological limitations of this view. Seeing it as a legal right is reducing the status of this right and limits one then to the view that religious freedom as a right has to be enforced and implemented legally. Clearly, from the above discussion, the protection of this right legally is very limited and grossly inadequate. The evolution of the right to religious freedom has come from its origins, in which its vertical application was considered, to more contemporary consideration where its horizontal application is evolving. However, for this evolution to bear the desirable fruit, it is important that the ideological shift is made from it being a legal right to one in which it is considered a human right. This ideological shift will ensure that it is elevated beyond the realm of the courts to the realm of public discourse. It will further ensure that the discussion evolves beyond the enforcement of rights to one in which the broader and richer concepts of humanity and the respect of the rights of others rather than the mere enforcement of any one becomes central to the consideration of the right. In African culture, the spirit of *ubuntu*[31] – or the concept of *sarvodharma*[32] in Hinduism – speaks to this same issue: that more important to the enforcement of my rights are the upholding of the rights of others. It is in this realm of religious freedom as a human right that we can enjoy the great richness of this right. It is here that religious communities can make their most significant contribution: to transform their communities into activists for the rights of others rather than bigots preserving their own.

Conclusion

The right to religious freedom is a fundamental and inviolable right that should be jealously and vigorously protected. The protection of this right should not rest in the hands of the judiciary alone, and religious communities need to break the shackles of bigotry and fundamentalism in the hope that they become custodians of these fundamental rights. While it would appear that the vertical application of the religious freedom right appears a lot easier to achieve, it is in the area of the horizontal application that religious communities have to come to the fore – and, critically, in the area of proselytism. It is with regard to the horizontal application of the right to religious freedom that it is imperative that religious freedom is seen as a human right. Religious communities being involved in the business of enhancing human dignity cannot be the perpetrators of infringements of the right to human dignity, and most certainly not in the area of religious freedom. As champions of human rights, religious communities cannot escape the compelling persuasion that it is only when religious freedom is perceived to be and practiced as a human right that the true humaneness of their traditions is informed by the divinity of their beliefs.

Notes

1 S. Woolman, T. Roux, and M. Bishop (eds.), *Constitutional Law of South Africa* (Cape Town: Juta, 2009), 41.11.
2 *Prince v. President of Cape Law Society;* 2002(s) SA 794 (CC). 2002(3) BCLR 231(CC).
3 United States Department of Justice. www.FirstFreedom.gov.
4 A right is a *human* right if the rationale for establishing and protecting the right is, in part, that conduct that violates the right violates the imperative to "act towards all human beings in a spirit of brotherhood." Michael J. Perry, "Freedom of Conscience as Religious and Moral Freedom," *Journal of Law and Religion* (2014), 2.
5 A legal right is a right that accrues to a person (or juristic person) by law.
6 J. De Waal, I. Currie, and G. Erasmus, *The Bill of Rights Handbook*, 4th edition (Cape Town: Juta, 2001), p. 288.
7 Thomas Jefferson, Virginia Statute for Religious Freedom, 1779.
8 The Constitution of the Republic of South Africa.
9 The content of a right may be defined as what a right entitles one to and what obligations one is subject to in terms of the right.
10 "Penumbra" as defined by the Oxford Dictionary is an area of obscurity or uncertainty.
11 *S v. Lawrence* 1997(4) SA 1176(CC).
12 *Prince v. President of the Law Society,* Cape of Good Hope 1998(8) BCLR 976 (CE).
13 *S v. Solberg* 1997(4) SA 1176 (CC), 1997 (10) BCLR 1348(CC).
14 *Christian Education South Africa v. Minister of Education* 2000(4) SA 757.
15 Woolman *et al., Constitutional Law of South Africa,* 41.18.
16 Woolman *et al., Constitutional Law of South Africa,* 41.18–19.
17 Woolman *et al., Constitutional Law of South Africa,* 41.21.
18 *Christian Education South Africa v. Minister of Education* 2000(4) SA 757.
19 *Prince v. President of the Law Society,* Cape of Good Hope 1998(8) BCLR 976 (CE).
20 *S v. Solberg* 1997(4) SA 1176 (CC), 1997 (10) BCLR 1348(CC).

21 Woolman *et al.*, *Constitutional Law of South Africa*, 41.25.
22 Woolman *et al.*, *Constitutional Law of South Africa*, 41.25.
23 Woolman *et al.*, *Constitutional Law of South Africa*, 41.27.
24 Woolman *et al.*, *Constitutional Law of South Africa*, 41.29.
25 De Waal *et al.*, *Bill of Rights Handbook*, p. 295.
26 A. Labi, "European Court Upholds Turkeys Ban on Student Headscarves," *Chronicles of Higher Education*, July 16, 2004, A34.
27 De Waal *et al.*, *Bill of Rights Handbook*, p. 295.
28 See "Controversy and Christian missionaries": http://en.wikipedia.org/wiki/Mission_(Christianity)#Controversy_and_Christian_missionaries
29 C. Glatz, "Legislating Conversions: Weighing the Message versus the Person," Catholic News Service. http://www.catholicnews.com/data/stories/cns/0602925.htm (accessed January 2015).
30 Akhil Baratiya Vanavasi Kalyan Ashram, 50 Golden Years; A Shree Multimedia Presentation. http://www.hindudharmaforums.com/showthread.php?t=2458.
31 *Ubuntu* is a rich concept in which the central tenet is, "I am because you are."
32 In *sarvodharma*, the importance of the common good is emphasized rather than the individual good alone.

Part IV
Looking to the Future

Epilogue

To Learn and to Encourage
Insights from the Thinking Together Group

Shanta Premawardhana

We have been engaged in serious interreligious discussion about the problems and issues related to religious conversion, using the approach that we discussed in Chapter 1. In our conversation **we have learned** many things, building on the perspectives of our separate traditions and on the work described in the chapters "Defining Religious Conversion" and "Models of Religious Belonging." In the process of learning, **we have also come to encourage** one another into building newer and healthier communities of interreligious peace and harmony. Here are some of those, stated in very brief form, beginning with what we have learned.

What We Have Learned

We have learned that there are many types of religious conversion and many opinions about conversion in the different religious traditions. These attitudes toward the legitimacy of, and need for,

Religious Conversion: Religion Scholars Thinking Together, First Edition.
Edited by Shanta Premawardhana.
© 2015 World Council of Churches Publications. Published 2015 by John Wiley & Sons, Ltd.

conversion have some correlation with the different models of religious belonging. Contrary to a common presupposition, not all religions want to gather converts to their fold or regard their beliefs and customs as relevant to or necessary for all people. Other religions understand it to be a religious obligation to make their beliefs and customs available to all. Missionary activity on the part of such religions and the ways in which it is done have caused difficulties for many communities.

Sharing of faith

We have learned that we have a right to share our religious tradition, and to invite others to consider or embrace our faith. In exercising this right we need to guard against becoming obsessed with converting others. The right to share our traditions includes the obligation to be sensitive to the life and culture of those receiving the sharing.

We have learned that a callous approach to others is one of the most destructive behaviors found in some forms of sharing. Our invitation should not be exercised by violating others' rights or religious sensibilities, but with utmost respect for the other.

We have learned that there is a great deal of difference between neighborly sharing of faith and large-scale, organized missionary programs. Such programs often use methods that are of great concern to us. Often such efforts lack respect for other traditions, do not observe the religious rights of individuals and communities, and are not based on accurate knowledge of other religious traditions. They are prone to engage in manipulative practices to gain converts.

We have learned the importance of remembering that the persons with whom we are speaking have authentic religious experiences and beliefs that we, as outsiders, can never fully understand. We need to consider ways for the sharing of our traditions to be done in mutuality, not as full pitcher to empty vessel, but as persons of one faith to persons of another.

We have learned the importance of a basic rule in efforts seeking to influence the religious beliefs of others: approaches that are distasteful to us ought not to be used on members of other faiths. No one appreciates manipulative or forceful attempts to convince him or her to abandon his or her own religion in favor of the religion that is being presented.

We have learned that the sharing of our religious traditions usually leads to deeper understanding of our own tradition, because, in our sharing, we are encouraged to wrestle with questions that we wouldn't ask without engagement with others.

We have learned that sharing faith meaningfully occurs only in the context of a relationship of trust and mutual respect. Sharing is an expression of friendship. The character of our lives is the most eloquent sharing of our faith.

Human rights

We have learned that there are three basic human rights that must be recognized when discussing religious conversion, based on universal values of human dignity, freedom, and equality. These are (i) the right to remain in one's religion, (ii) the right to change one's religion, (iii) and the right to share one's religion. These rights are not absolute, but can be limited and come with obligations.

We have learned that the right to remain in one's religion must be highlighted and guarded. This is essential to the other two rights. The obligations of those who remain in their religious tradition include, among others, maintaining respect for those who choose to leave the tradition, and taking responsibility to learn about other religious traditions. At the same time, we understand that anyone in any religious community globally should be able to change their religious affiliation without fear of any kind of reprisal, whether economic, physical, social, or emotional. The obligations of those who change their religious affiliation include learning to speak with sensitivity about the religious tradition and people they have left.

When individuals or groups leave a tradition, there will be understandable, and sometimes marked, emotional and communal responses. However, we are particularly aware of the disruption to a community that can come when large numbers of people convert out of one community and into another.

Because of such communal disruption, **we have learned** that large-scale missionary initiatives must be critically and carefully examined. At the same time, we also see that oppressive forms of community may need to be challenged, and that this may be done through the sharing of other religious perspectives. Therefore, we also recommend that, if traditions experience a large number of conversions or mass conversions out of their religions, they look self-critically at their tradition to ascertain if it is failing large numbers of its members, rather than simply condemning conversion.

Regarding both the right to remain in a tradition and the right to change one's tradition, **we have learned** that many religions are inconsistent, welcoming converts in but persecuting converts out of the tradition. This double standard must be questioned.

Religious freedom

We have learned that religious faith is meaningful only when freely chosen. No religion is served if converts are gained through unethical methods of coercion, through threats, through the promise of economic or political rewards, or through the misrepresentation of oneself or others. No tradition should exploit vulnerability in times of material and emotional distress for the purpose of gaining converts.

We also see that no tradition is served when it uses temporal power to impose its beliefs on those whom it controls. While we understand that religious communities often turn to the state for protection, we also see that the state can and often does violate the religious rights of individuals and groups. **We have learned** that vigilance needs to be exercised regarding state coercion and the state favoring the dominant religious tradition over others.

We have learned that we as religious people must concern ourselves with "freedom of religion," which is a complex combination of legal and human rights. We aspire to uphold human rights voluntarily, but also see the need for legal remedies, which stem from failure in our relationships. We also see the need for continuing attention to the laws affecting religious rights, and for appealing to human rights to transform legal systems.

Humanitarian work

While deeply appreciating humanitarian work by religious communities, **we have learned** that it should be conducted without ulterior motives. In offering humanitarian service, especially in times of distress, working together across religious boundaries can offer a hope and effectiveness that is too often missed in a rush to respond as separate communities.

We have learned that what we can do together we should never do separately. In fact, we note the strength and possibility in working together to address human needs and issues as peoples of diverse religious traditions. While all religious communities have many activities that are and should be done separately, in working on social needs and issues of justice, we applaud religious traditions working together.

Internal and external diversity

When we speak within our own communities about these matters, **we have learned** that we need to use the language, sources, and means of communication best suited to each community. We realize that there is disagreement and tension in our communities in relation to the issues of sharing our faiths and interfaith relationships. Discussion in each of our communities about these matters will require respectful intra-communal exploration and discussion.

We have learned that every religion is internally diverse in many ways, which means that we must be careful when making generalizations about religious traditions.

We have learned that some generic terms, such as "community," may point to very different realities in the different religious traditions. For example, the Buddhist *sangha*, the Christian church, and the Muslim *umma* are all "community" in their respective traditions, but they are not the same thing. We need to guard against the confusions that could result if we do not recognize the different connotations of these generic terms.

What We Would Encourage

In the process of "thinking together," we not only learned several valuable lessons regarding the question of religious conversion, we also gained a level of confidence in one another that has emboldened us to pool our hopes for better interreligious relations, especially in the area of religious conversion. We present a set of encouragements that will help us and all religious communities toward building and maintaining healthy interreligious relations.

We encourage anyone engaging in any kind of interfaith interactions, including the sharing or promoting of his or her own faith, to do so on the basis of accurate and empathetic knowledge about other faiths. Based on such knowledge, in our sharing we should be willing to change our views both about our own religion and our neighbors' religions. It is unreasonable to expect of others what we are unwilling to undertake ourselves – the possibility of change.

It is important to recognize that each religion has a complex tradition of textual interpretation and many contested texts. **We encourage** each tradition to recognize the inevitability of different interpretations of key texts, each of which is dependent on context. These differing interpretations will affect how individuals share their religious tradition.

Because of the inevitability of continuing religious diversity in the pluralistic world in which we all live, **we encourage** each tradition to develop theologies of religious diversity that recognize the dignity and preciousness of the various traditions while also protecting each religion's sense of its own value and relevance.

Many, but not all, of the religious traditions of our world share the conviction that their teachings and practices are potentially beneficial to all human beings. This conviction is at the heart of the desire and willingness to share these teachings with others. **We encourage** those who wish to share their faith to do so only at the neighbor's own invitation.

Our experience has taught us the importance of being open to the possibility that we may learn as much about the Ultimate from those with whom we share as we hope they may learn from us. Part of humility in our sharing is practicing utter transparency, and therefore **we encourage** a sharing of both the brighter and darker sides of our own religious tradition.

The sharing of faith claims must be done in humility and not with arrogant disregard for the claims of others. Therefore **we encourage** all who share their religious traditions to seek to hear, understand, and honor the beliefs and cultures of the persons with whom they are sharing.

We encourage active cultivation of humility, remembering that no one can express the whole truth in words and symbols. Truth transcends our understanding, language, and symbols. Truth is more that we can ever comprehend.

In conclusion, we wish that "gentleness and reverence" prevail at all times – gentleness in our approach to each other and reverence toward one another's religious traditions.

A Study Guide

Deborah Weissman

The Thinking Together group has not by any means exhausted all that we need to learn about the issue of religious conversion. The following Study Guide is offered as a way to continue the conversation and to think together more deeply in relation to our own contexts. The study is organized into several sessions so that only a portion of the book is to be read each time in preparation for group discussion. Most of the essays in the book have a list of books for further reading; those may also be used for preparatory reading. The sessions are organized in such a way that the composition of the study group may be either of one religious tradition or of several traditions.

Session I: Opening Session

Aim: The aim of this session is to help the group to come to know one another better in relation to the issue of conversion.

Preparatory Reading: None.

Religious Conversion: Religion Scholars Thinking Together, First Edition.
Edited by Shanta Premawardhana.
© 2015 World Council of Churches Publications. Published 2015 by John Wiley & Sons, Ltd.

Questions for Discussion:

1. When you hear the word "conversion," what are your initial thoughts? What persons, programs, events, concepts, or ideas do you associate with that word? Record the various definitions of conversion that emerge from this discussion to be used during the next session.
2. What are your own experiences of the process and the event of conversion? If you are a convert, share your experience in your small group. If you are not, have you witnessed, read about, or observed conversions? Share your stories with the group.
3. Is your tradition one that seeks to convert others or is it one that does not? How do you feel about that?
4. Have you worked with others or alone in a program that attempts to convert people to your own religion? What are your observations, agreements, and disagreements with that process? (If the group consists only of those who belong to religions that do not seek converts, this question may be irrelevant and may therefore be left out.)

Session II: Multiple Meanings of Conversion

Aim: To recognize the multiple meanings of religious conversion and locate one's own definition within it.

Preparatory Reading: Chapter 2 – Defining Religious Conversion, by M. Thomas Thangaraj.

Questions for Discussion:

1. Recall the definitions of conversion that the group had recorded in the last session. Do any of them bring nuances or newer dimensions to the four meanings offered by Thangaraj?
2. Does your own religious tradition view conversion in any of these ways? Is the word welcomed and used frequently? Or does your tradition consider conversion as a word foreign to your tradition that therefore should be shunned?
3. Which are the meanings of conversion that are proper for understanding the process of conversion?

Session III: Models of Religious Belonging

Aim: To understand how various models of religious belonging impact the way we view the phenomenon of religious conversion.

Preparatory Reading: Chapter 3 – Models of Religious Belonging, by Rita Gross.

Questions for Discussion:

1. Under what conditions might an ethno-religion might become a universalizing religion? Also under what conditions might a branch of a universalizing religion take on some or even many characteristics of an ethno-religion?
2. Discuss the pros and cons of each model of religious belonging – the ethno-religious perspective, multiple religious belonging, internal and external diversity and pluralism, and exclusive truth claims.
3. Could interreligious hostility be reduced if all religious people gave up exclusive truth claims for their religion? Is that possible?

Session IV: Buddhist Perspectives

Aim: To familiarize us with the history of Buddhist non-violent expansion and its perspectives on religious conversion.

Preparatory Reading: Chapter 5 – Buddhists on Religious Conversion, by Mahinda Deegalle.

Questions for Discussion:

1. What would "religious conversion" mean in a Buddhist context? How is it different from the definitions you have discussed so far?
2. How do the Buddha's teachings about freedom of thought impact your understanding of religious faith as revealed?
3. If the notion of "mission" can be applied to the Buddhist context, how is it different from the way other religious traditions use the term? In what ways is Buddhism a "missionary" religion? In what ways is it not?

Session V: Christian Perspectives

Aim: To understand Christian viewpoints with regard to religious conversion and activities linked to conversion efforts.

Preparatory Reading: Chapter 6 – A Christian Perspective on Conversion, by Jay Rock.

Questions for Discussion:

1. In what ways do you agree or disagree with the idea that Christianity's identity as a "community of converts" gives Christians a particular character, and a particular need to be aware of how this experience affects their sharing of faith?
2. How and where have you seen the understanding and practice of Christian evangelization change? Are there forms of evangelism that you have encountered that are disrespectful, manipulative, or harmful?
3. In what ways do you see interreligious engagement as capable of clarifying, or changing, the understanding of your own faith community?

Session VI: Hindu Perspectives

Aim: To understand Hinduism's non-proselytizing character and appreciate the lessons one may learn from such a stance.

Preparatory Reading: Chapter 7 – Conversion from a Hindu Perspective, by Anantanand Rambachan.

Questions for Discussion:

1. How may we promote relationships among persons of different faiths that are non-proselytizing in nature?
2. What is the proper role of the state, if any, in addressing tensions and concerns relating to conversion?
3. How may persons of different faiths cooperate in the alleviation of human suffering without the anxiety that such aid is an inducement to conversion?

Session VII: Islamic Perspectives

Aim: To see the differences between Islamic and Christian views of mission and thus gain a deeper understanding of Islamic perspectives on conversion.

Preparatory Reading: Chapter 8 – Islamic Perspectives on Conversion, by A. Rashied Omar and Rabia Terri Harris.

Questions for Discussion:

1. What sort of picture of the world justifies aid evangelism? How might that world picture take shape in a person? In a society? What influences might alter such a world picture?
2. What sort of picture of the world underlies criminal prosecution for apostasy? How might that world picture take shape in a person? In a society? What influences might alter such a world picture?
3. The authors propose that "The ongoing challenge for Muslims and Christians is to find an ethical consensus on what Woodberry usefully describes as 'mutual respectful witness.'" What might be some productive steps toward establishing such a consensus?

Session VIII: Jewish Perspectives

Aim: To understand the Jewish perspectives and see their usefulness in enhancing your own tradition's viewpoints.

Preparatory Reading: Chapter 9 – Jewish Perspectives on Conversion, by Amy Eilberg.

Questions for Discussion:

1. How can painful memories be used for good purposes? Can this happen under all circumstances?
2. What motivates a person to convert to another religion? What motivates someone to seek converts to his or her religion? What motivates a person to deter converts?

3. Rabbi Eilberg has listed a number of Jewish teachings that could form the basis for an approach to religious tolerance. Are these teachings relevant to your own beliefs and traditions? Why or why not? Can you find other insights within your own religious culture?

Session IX: Conversion and Human Rights

Aim: To recognize the complexities of appealing to human rights and religious freedom in matters concerning religious conversion.

Preparatory Reading: Chapter 10 – Conversion and Religious Freedom, by S. Wesley Ariarajah; and Chapter 11 – The Right to Religious Freedom and Proselytism, by Ravin Ramdass.

Questions for Discussion:

1. How does one deal with the claim that preaching with the intention to convert and to call others to cross over to one's community is part of one's faith? What is the place of such conviction in a multi-faith society?
2. "Religious freedom is not an absolute right." Is there any truth to this claim? If so, what are the circumstances under which religious freedom should be compromised?
3. "Since it is very difficult to determine or establish the true intentions and motivations of those who preach and those who convert, this matter is one that cannot be resolved through legislation." Is there any truth to this statement? Discuss the benefits and limitations of a legal approach to the issue of conversion.

Session X: Concluding Reflections

Aim: To integrate what is learned in the previous sessions into a meaningful whole and be enabled to articulate one's own position on religious conversion.

Preparatory Reading: Epilogue; and Chapter 4 – Conversion Sought and Feared, by Hans Ucko.

Questions for Discussion:

1. What are the new insights you have received during this pro-
    cess of thinking together on religious conversion? In what ways
    do those insights owe their emergence to the process of *thinking
    together* itself?
2. Is it possible for a person who believes and practices *one* religion
    to accept some notion of *plural truths*? If so, how? In what ways
    may one accept multiple views without sinking into an
    "anything goes" kind of relativism?
3. Do you see the sharing of your faith with others as something
    that can promote interreligious friendship? If not, why not? If
    so, what are some of the concrete steps you or your religious
    tradition may take to promote healthy sharing of one's faith
    with others?

Index

Religious Conversion: Religion Scholars Thinking Together, First Edition.
Edited by Shanta Premawardhana.
© 2015 World Council of Churches Publications. Published 2015 by John Wiley & Sons, Ltd.